AF846478

AFRICAN HERDERS

African Archaeology Series

Series Editor
Joseph O. Vogel

The **African Archaeology Series** is a series of volumes intended to present comprehensive and up-to-date summaries of current research on the African cultural past. The authors, who range from paleoanthropologists to historical archeologists, all are presently active in their disciplines, work in Africa, and detail the results of their ongoing research interests. Though the essential subject matter of each volume is drawn from archaeology, each is equally dependent upon investigation of the historical and anthropological records as well. The authors understand the diversity and depth of African culture and history, and they endeavor to explore the many sources of the African experience and the place of the African past and lifeways in the broader world. At the same time, while intending to reach an audience beyond specialist confines, the series permits Africanist scholars the opportunity to extend authoritative information beyond the narrow limits of the monographic site report, in order to transform their field results into more general syntheses, giving context and meaning to a bare bones archeological record, exploring and utilizing new techniques for explaining as well as comprehending the past.

Books in the Series:

I. Chapurukha M. Kusimba, *The Rise and Fall of Swahili States* (1999)
II. Michael Bisson, S. Terry Childs, Philip de Barros, and Augustin F. C. Holl, *Ancient African Metallurgy: The Socio-Cultural Context* (2000)
III. Innocent Pikirayi, *The Zimbabwe Culture: Origins and Decline of Southern Zambezian States* (2001)
IV. Sibel Barut Kusimba, *African Foragers: Environment, Technology, Interactions* (2002)
V. Augustin F. C. Holl, *Saharan Rock Art: Archaeology of Tassilian Pastoralist Iconography* (2004)
VI. J. David Lewis-Williams and D. G. Pearce, *San Spirituality: Roots, Expression, and Social Consequences* (2004)
VII. Peter Mitchell, *African Connections: The Archaeology of Africa's External Interactions* (2005)
VIII. Andrew B. Smith, *African Herders: Emergence of Pastoral Traditions* (2005)

Submission Guidelines:
Prospective authors of single-author or coauthored books and editors of anthologies should submit a letter of introduction, the manuscript or a four- to ten-page proposal, a book outline, and a curriculum vitae. Please send your book manuscript or proposal packet to:

African Archaeology Series
AltaMira Press
1630 North Main Street, #367
Walnut Creek, CA 94596

AFRICAN HERDERS

Emergence of Pastoral Traditions

Andrew B. Smith

ALTAMIRA PRESS

A Division of Rowman & Littlefield Publishers, Inc.
Walnut Creek • Lanham • New York • Toronto • Oxford

ALTAMIRA PRESS
A Division of Rowman & Littlefield Publishers, Inc.
1630 North Main Street, #367
Walnut Creek, CA 94596
http://www.altamirapress.com

Rowman & Littlefield Publishers, Inc.
A Member of the Rowman & Littlefield Publishing Group
4501 Forbes Blvd, Suite 200
Lanham, MD 20706

PO Box 317
Oxford
OX2 9RU, United Kingdom

Copyright © 2005 by AltaMira Press

All photographs are from the author's originals unless otherwise noted.

All rights reserved. No part of this publication may be reproduced, stored in a retrieval system, or transmitted in any form or by any means, electronic, mechanical, photocopying, recording, or otherwise, without the prior permission of the publisher.

British Library Cataloguing in Publication Information Available

Library of Congress Cataloging-in-Publication Data

Smith, Andrew B. (Andrew Brown), 1941–
African herders : emergence of pastoral traditions / Andrew B. Smith.
p. cm. — (African archaeology series)
Includes bibliographical references and index.
ISBN: 978-0-7591-0747-2
1. Pastoral systems—Africa. 2. Herders—Africa—Social conditions.
3. Africa—Social conditions. 4. Africa—Economic conditions.
5. Africa—Politics and government.
I. Title. II. Series.
GN645.S568 2005
636.08'45'096—dc22
2004017588

Printed in the United States of America

∞™ The paper used in this publication meets the minimum requirements of American National Standard for Information Sciences—Permanence of Paper for Printed Library Materials, ANSI/NISO Z39.48–1992.

Contents

To John Desmond Clark, Mentor Extraordinaire,
with Affection and Thanks

List of Illustrations

Figures

Tables

Foreword

Transhumant herdsmen were once common throughout the Old World. But they seem admirably suited to African environments. Yet, of the three basic indigenous economic patterns on the African continent, pastoralism is probably the least understood by the general public, and it is very underinvestigated by archaeology. At the same time, the idea of the nomadic herdsmen once seemed a romantic one, perhaps fostered by the youthful adventures of Duveyrier living among the Tuareg, or Halèvy among the Bedouin, in the mid-nineteenth century. Nowadays, African herdsmen usually come to mind only as victims of drought conditions in the Sahel or in touristy presentations of the Maasai.

Though there are classic anthropological studies of herder societies, the archaeology, though well founded, is more sparing in the literature and more difficult to accomplish in the field than some other kinds of Africanist field research. While farming settlements leave a palpable impress on the landscape in the form of soils disturbed by the action of iron hoes and the remnants of *daga* structures, and while even the recurrent camps of foragers leave an impression as stone scatters in rockshelters or beside lakes and rivers, herder camps are ephemeral. Granted this is a simplification, but as Andrew Smith mentions, the camps of herdsmen are not only as transient as those of foraging hunters, but also, though they are larger, their material remains tend to be of light-weight tools and perishable materials leaving little more than the palimpsest of the frequently visited locale. Here and there are places where herder-artists left pictorial evidence of their passage, but even these are often read as art rather than as documentary history—a testament to the worldview or aspirations of the herdsmen.

Deeply embedded in that worldview is the relationship of individual herdsmen to their livestock, a bond as strong as that which binds people into a society. It is fair to say that all societies have a central core of belief and ritual that acts to give meaning to life, justifying one's place in the universe. So profound is the bond between the herd and its human guardians that to an alien observer it would be difficult to determine who is the master. The herdsmen labor to preserve the integrity of the herd from weather, shifting rainfall patterns, depleted forage, and depredations by wild animals or raiding humans. At the same time, the herd supplies access to sustenance and, importantly, bestows on its owner prestige, political and social status, and the medium for investing in the borrowing and lending of stock that both disperses one's assets and forges crucial social links with other cattle owners.

Further essential social and economic linkages evolve from advantageous marriages, obtained through the medium of cattle transfers, whether through a daughter's bride-price or from a prominent family as the outlay for obtaining a bride and an alliance with new kin. Among the cattle-owning agriculturist Tonga in southern Zambia, who I am familiar with, cattle were apparently kept as much as social pawns than as economic ones. In theory, none of their cattle were slaughtered for their meat, although at ritual occasions—weddings, funerals, and the like—meat was served; the donor, usually the village head, added to his prestige by the gift. Herein lies one of the many paradoxes of the herders' attitude toward their animals, that they are both a potential food source and a social asset that must be preserved at all costs, to be butchered only under a social pretence. This lifeway, then, is a complex set of attitudes and relationships where people create the usual trinity of social alliances through birth, marriage, and initiation, in addition to their relationship to their herds.

That the herds required constant attention goes without saying. African climates are everywhere dominated by monsoonal patterns of alternating rainy and dry seasons requiring the movement of cattle away from seasonally desiccating areas toward the richer, recently rain-watered pasturage. Life on the cattle drive is one of tedious day-to-day pedestrian passage across well-known landscapes, relieved by the nightly pitching of camps and early decamping in order to move on toward potable water or green pastures. The myriad sounds and smells and the choking dust of the driven cattle marching at slow pace are the heart of the herder's experience. At the same time, the need to be vigilant against the loss of animals to straying or predators bestows a sense of urgency to the enterprise. Youths guarding the herd become familiar with each animal, ensuring its presence and its safety. Meanwhile, females and mature men engage in a variety of culturally prescribed domestic chores. And so it goes, a cycle of movement from dry-season camps to wet-season ones and back, within a cycle of the life stretching from birth to death spent in the company of one's fellows and one's herd. That this is a viable strategy for supplying one's material needs in the climatic regimens of Africa is no surprise. It is ecologically logical and time-tested.

This is the world that Andrew Smith introduces us into and describes for us, not only in its present guise, but also as a developing system begun early in the Holocene as the climatic regimens of the preceding Pleistocene subsided and hunter-foragers initiated a series of experiments managing the more docile of their former prey. Understanding the ways of these animals, achieved from long experience, made the practice of animal management congenial to their lifeway and led, eventually, to the genetic manipulations inherent in domestication. In presenting archaeological evidence of the earliest pastoralist societies in Africa, Smith deals with thorny questions of their genesis and their relationship to similar strategies developing in the Near East, on the slopes of the Zagros Mountains and elsewhere. By implication, the material correlates of the herder lifeway discovered by archaeology suggest the development of the unique aspects of the herdsmen's worldview and the ritual use of cattle to substantiate that view.

Accepting the fact that animal domestication in Africa was strongly influenced by events in the Levant, and that African pastoralism developed in the north of the continent, Smith meticulously traces the extension of herding regimens into regions far to the south while tackling such questions as the transmission of cattle to the Khoesan-speaking peoples, the entrance of agriculturists (some with, and others without, livestock) into territories pioneered by herders, and factors such as environment and disease that limit the keeping of stock. Present-day herdsmen are certainly limited in the pursuit of their traditional patterns of movement and social interaction by the nation-states and the frontiers that have grown up around them. Though their future may now be threatened, their long and vital history on the continent attests to the adaptability of this lifeway and the genius of human societies. This is the story that Andrew Smith brings to us now.

By summarizing nearly 10,000 years of herder history in Africa and the Near East, Andrew Smith offers us an excellent perspective on the archaeological investigation of the origins of food-producing economies, as well as the essential role that herding societies had in their genesis. Even more than a study of herding's beginnings and subsequent development, this book offers the reader valuable insight into the workings of herdsmen societies, the place of such groups in African history, the role of livestock in shaping their worldview, and the manner that they spread, adapting to African landscapes.

Joseph O. Vogel

Preface

As I write this manuscript, there is a session at the 2004 Society for American Archaeology meetings in Montreal being organized on the prehistory of nomads, to be followed by a workshop on this topic at the University of California at Los Angeles later in the year. The number of people from all over the world who have shown interest in the Montreal session highlights its currency and the challenge of finding some of the most archaeologically elusive societies. Topics for discussion include defining nomadism and how to recognize nomads in archaeology, material culture of nomads, ecological modeling of mobility patterns, and archaeological examples. Small-scale, mobile groups may leave little in the archaeological record, and only intensive and accumulative study of small scatters may produce a coherent picture. Although I am specifically concerned with pastoral nomads, I am aware that hunting societies may leave similarly limited residues, as may refugees fleeing wars and famines.

My perspective is that Africa has never been isolated from the rest of the world, and while I argue that, as far as domestication of animals is concerned, the Near East had great influence on North Africa, there is no reason to assume that it was just a one-way affair. This is particularly the case with ceramics, which seem to have appeared in the Sahara much earlier than in the Near East. I am concerned that the importation of the name "Neolithic" assumes that Africa went through the same sequence that was experienced in the Near East and Europe (Sadr 2003). The term is loaded with historical baggage even in its area of origin, where ground stone and pottery were seen as integral to its definition, and so entails assumptions that cannot always be sustained, such as naming early food-producing societies in the Levant "Pre-Pottery Neolithic."

The ideas in this book are the product of almost 40 years of work in various countries of Africa. They began with graduate seminars in Berkeley under the supervision of Professors Desmond Clark and Glynn Isaac and were formally devised as a Ph.D. topic while I assisted Desmond excavating at Adrar Bous, Niger, as part of the British Aïr Mountain Expedition in 1970. This constituted the fieldwork for the first half of my thesis. The work for the second part was conducted in Mali at Karkarichinkat in 1972. Prof. Raymond Mauny was instrumental in offering help and advice in working on this site, which he had reported at the 2nd Pan-African Congress of Prehistory in Algiers in 1952. While in the field, I was visited by Dr. and Mrs. Jean Gaussen, who had driven across the Sahara in their tiny Citroen "meharie." They were extremely kind hosts when I visited them in France at their home in Neuvic after my fieldwork. This gave me the opportunity to examine the collection from Mali they had amassed over the years.

It was during my stay in Mali that I made Tuareg friends who were always willing to answer my questions. Many of them had to abandon the Tilemsi Valley temporarily as a result of the cumulated drought of the early 1970s, and I visited them in the refugee camp in Niamey, Niger, in 1974. Since then, the destructive war in eastern Mali of the 1990s has made contact very difficult.

My interest in the prehistory of southern African herders allowed me to build on my experience in North Africa when I took up the teaching position at the University of Cape Town in 1977. The antiquity of herding society at the Cape had just been confirmed by radiocarbon dating of the upper deposits at Die Kelders, and this gave new impetus to creating models for pastoral archaeology.

African pastoralist societies have held a fascination for many people who have immersed themselves in their nomadic existence. In his autobiography, *The Life of My Choice*, Wilfred Thesiger (1987) describes his dealings with the Afars and Danakil of Ethiopia in the 1930s. He was the first European traveler to cross the Rub al-Khali (the Empty Quarter of Arabia) with Bedouin guides, and his later life became a celebration of his respect and admiration for African herders, as he chose to spend parts of his year with Boran cattle keepers in northern Kenya rather than live in the United Kingdom. It was a great privilege for Jeremy Swift and me to meet Thesiger in Francis Edwards's bookshop in London after A. J. Arkell's library came up for sale and to talk about our common interest in herders. Similarly, Theodore Monod, the grand old man of the Sahara, traveled by camel through much of the French Sudan before the Second World War. On his camel in 1966, he met the delegates to the Dakar Panafrican Congress on their field excursion to the Mauretanian desert. He was such an erudite scholar, and had his finger on most of Saharan studies, that when I visited his office in 1972 he was able instantly to identify a crab claw I had unearthed at Karkarichinkat in Mali. Henri Lhote also dedicated much of his life to Sahara studies, and the two editions of *Les Tuaregs du Hoggar* (Lhote 1944; 1955) remain important basic ethnographic texts. He was very gracious and allowed me access to the faunal material he had collected at Arlit in Niger when I was in Paris. Unfortunately, his name has been somewhat sullied by recent revisionist writings questioning some of the ways in which data on Tassili rock art were gathered (Keenan 2002) and by accusations of forgery.

In many ways, I was fortunate to study in an anthropology department in the United States under Desmond Clark, as his vision of things "archaeological" meant that ethnography was never very far from the surface in any archaeological study in Africa. It is in memory of that vision that I dedicate this book to John Desmond Clark.

The reader will see that modern African pastoralists hold many of the keys to understanding the past and certainly put a human face on the cultural discards of the past 8,000 years. While we know a great deal about the prehistory of pastoralism in Africa, there are still many gaps. I have tried to offer an up-to-date picture of current knowledge, as well as a few ideas that might bridge some of the gaps.

1

African Herders: An Introduction

The noisy cow gives no sour milk

—Zulu proverb (from M. Poland et al., *The Abundant Herds*)

The animals mill around the well at Tin-Aoukert (fig. 1.1). As each skin bucket is pulled up by a rope attached to a camel and the water tipped into the trough alongside, the thirsty animals jostle to get their heads in. The herder shoves others aside when they finish. The continuous activity goes on all day, with new herds arriving as the others leave. Camels, cattle, goats, sheep, and donkeys are all accommodated. This is the Tilemsi Valley in the West African Sahel, some 80 km north of Gao on the Niger River, eastern Mali. Similarly, 700 km to the east, at Tegidda n'Tesemt, northwest of Agadez in Niger (fig. 1.2), skin *guerbas*, or water bags, containing more than 15 liters are slung below the belly of a donkey (fig. 1.3) to be carried back to camp for both human and very young animal needs. Camps are rarely less than five kilometers from the wells, since the area around the watering point is invariably denuded of vegetation for quite a radius, eaten by the animals brought in over a long time. It all looks chaotic, but there is a coherent system, and each herder negotiates his turn to get access to the simple wooden pulley–wheel that aids in drawing the water, 60 m below the surface.

Traditional pastoral systems in Africa are now thousands of years old, but the basic needs of the animals are just the same today as they were in the past: pasture and water. It is from the basic Latin root *nomas*, meaning "one who moves from place to place to find pasture," that the word *nomad* comes. The pulley–wheel and deep well notwithstanding, tapping underground water to satisfy a herd takes modern herders just as long today as it would have taken those we recognize in the archaeological record.

Figure 1.1. Tuareg drawing water from the well at Tin Aoukert, Tilemsi Valley, Mali.

Figure 1.2. Animals being watered by Tuareg men at Tegidda n'Tesemt, Niger, while women carry a guerba *for household use.*

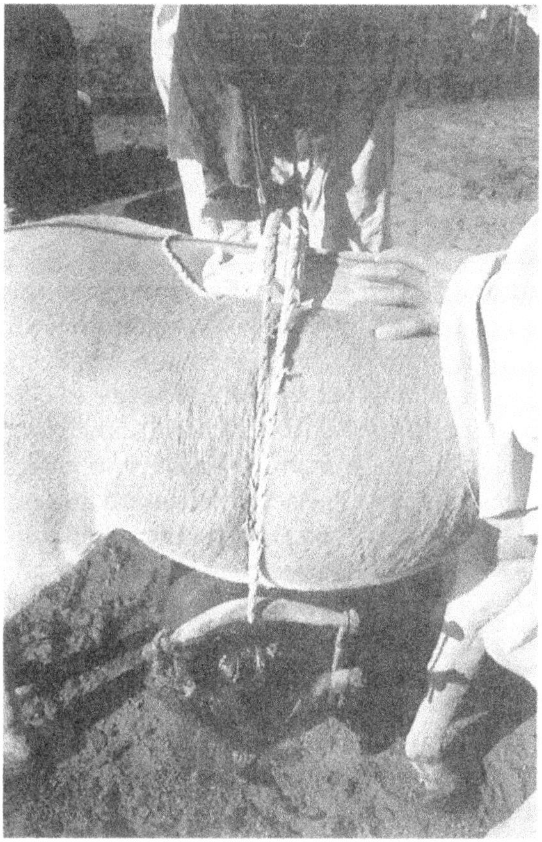

Figure 1.3. Guerba *slung beneath the belly of a donkey to be carried back to camp.*

To most of the Western world, herders are known only in a very "Orientalist" fashion (Said 1995), that is, in "the projection, on people other than oneself, of one's idea of what they are" (Gordimer 2003). It is not surprising that a number of early anthropologists were colonial officers, since learning about "native" people was a way of controlling them for the imperial machine. Popular films, such as the new version of *The Four Feathers*, depicting Sudanese warriors, or *Lawrence of Arabia*, serve to enhance the perception of "the native" not only as different, but also for the most part backward and primitive. By way of contrast, the film *Gabeh*, made by an Iranian, is a sensitive and colorful depiction of nomadic life in Iran. European visitors to East Africa or the Sahara invariably meet local people, and their visits would be incomplete without being photographed with Maasai or Tuareg herdsmen. The casual visitor inevitably has little idea how these people really live, especially when times are hard and both people and animals are starving, nor is aware that in spite of hardship their lifeways are rational systems whose beliefs and the philosophies that underlie them may go back many millennia.

The history of contact between Europeans and traditional pastoral people has created myths around the latter and, sometimes, even respect for their ability to live in remote places and their fierce defense of their territories and animals. British expeditionary forces in the nineteenth century had just as much difficulty dealing with the "wily Pathan" of the Northwest Frontier of what later became Pakistan as U.S. troops have had in modern Afghanistan after the Taliban expulsion in the twenty-first century. Similarly, the Nuer in the Sudan were able to organize themselves against British troops wishing to stamp their imperial authority, so that "it was not until 1928 that the intractable Nuer were finally pacified" (Holt 1961: 116).

With a shrinking world where it is difficult to get away from Western goods and technology, where the satellite phone and global positioning systems reduce any traveling risk, perhaps the herdsman is due respect for his capabilities of handling the vagaries of African environmental conditions. The traveler can always leave and go home. To the pastoralist, the herd is forever.

Herding Societies

Although many groups of people keep domestic stock, all herding societies are not the same. There is a continuum that ranges from transhumant pastoralism to sedentary stock owners, which Cribb (1991: fig. 2.1) sees as the interaction between mobility and subsistence. Rosen (1988: 504) separates the evolution of agricultural systems in the Near East from pastoral nomads. He says, "The evolution of domesticates is also to be distinguished from that of domestication economies, and even within domestication economies there is significant variation that is worthy of investigation." In his view, specialized village herding is not the same as nomadic pastoralism.

At the pastoral nomad end of the continuum are people who are constrained, not only by the needs of their animals but also by an environment that requires them to move in search of pasture. In Africa, these are the grassland areas where annual rainfall is below the minimum required for dry agriculture. These groups need to be on the move constantly, and all material culture has to be portable.

At the other end of the continuum are sedentary villagers whose wealth is tied up in large stock units (camels or cattle), but whose diet mostly comes from the plants grown in fields around the village. In southern Africa, such villages in the nineteenth century became whole towns, such as Dithakong and Kaditshwene (Booyens 2000) or Molokwane, where the huts and kraal areas can be seen in aerial photographs (fig. 1.4). At K2 next to Mapungubwe at the Shashi/Limpopo confluence, there was a huge cattle kraal where six meters of deposit were accumulated within a period of around

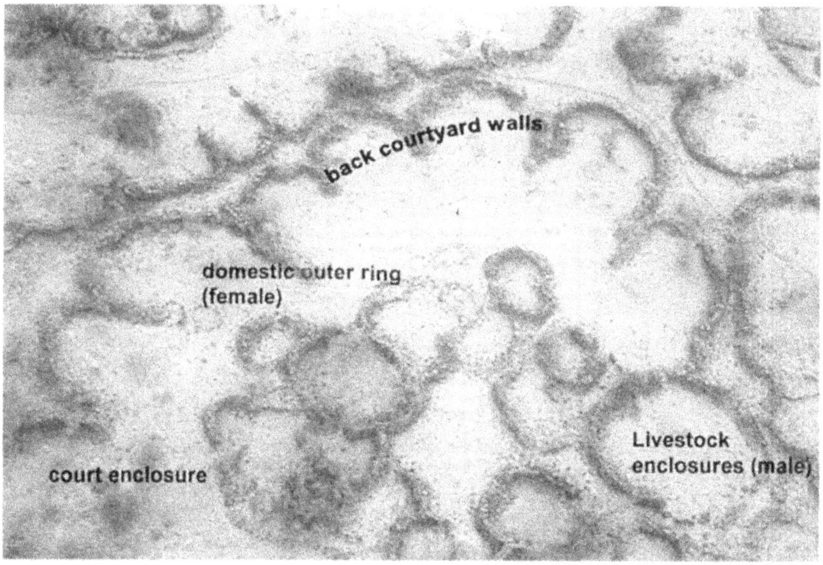

Figure 1.4. Aerial photograph of settlement at Molokwane, near Rustenberg, South Africa, showing domestic space and kraals (photo: *Archaeology Archive, University of the Witwatersrand).*

300 years (Voigt 1983). This is an indication of the importance of cattle as wealth and power. The intensity of occupation presumably meant that the cattle would have to have been taken to pasture each day or to temporary camps set up away from the town. There is good historical information on the movement of Tswana capitals over time (Huffman 1986). This was probably due to both political and environmental concerns, such as the needs of the animals requiring fresh pasturage as an area became overgrazed, although the need for firewood for fuel and iron smelting would have been a contributing factor as well.

Between these two extremes are those owners of stock who cultivate gardens, but part of whose group may spend long periods away from the homesteads looking after the herds. Dyson-Hudson (1966: 38) says the Karimojong activities and values are predominantly pastoral, but they are involved in cultivation, which provides the bulk of the food for the women and children. For the Nuer (Evans-Pritchard 1940: 83), the seasonal movement is between the homesteads and fishing camps along the White Nile. Young people go with the animals to the stock camps, and they might leave the elderly (or less mobile) in the permanent villages with a *milch* herd for their needs (a *milch* herd is one that provides the family with access to milk).

African Pastoralism

African pastoralism conjures up images of the dusty herd moving across the landscape, and of the herder with his stick across his shoulder or standing on one leg leaning on his spear, gazing into the distance. Nomadic pastoralism is an adaptation that allows the herd's needs, primarily water and pasture, to be met and that requires residential mobility on the part of the herders, because the herd can quickly overgraze an area if it stays too long. The family, thus, is transhumant: literally, "moves across ground," that is, seasonally moves the livestock to new pastures. In many parts of Africa, this is an adaptation to the grasslands, such as the Serengeti, that often sustain a high biomass of ungulates. Usually, transhumance is not a random movement, but a pattern that is repeated annually. During these annual cycles, herdsmen will be using seasonal pastures that are reasonably (but not entirely) dependable. The grassland areas of Africa are usually found in rainfall regimes of less than 400-mm, that is, below the basic minimum for successful rain-fed agriculture. As a result, transhumant pastoralism is an adaptive strategy utilizing grasslands as an ecological niche where the domestic herds maximize productivity.

An attempt has been made by Cribb (1991) to tease apart the concepts of "nomadism," "pastoralism," and "transhumance." While the terms may be loosely used by various authors, Cribb's survey of the literature (18–19) only shows that there is a great deal of variability and flexibility in how pastoralists organize their lives, which is more a reflection of their pragmatic and opportunistic lifestyle than of an ecological imperative imposed by the practice of stock keeping. However, his models are all from the Near East, where residential mobility might be less of a factor than pasture territory ownership and the fact that herders and agriculturalists may live side by side in the same village. The situation may be different from place to place throughout Africa.

Is African pastoralism different from that found in the Near East? As we shall see, without doubt the history of the development of pastoralism in the two areas has different trajectories. In the Near East, grain agriculture preceded animal domestication, and domestic grains were central to the nomadic diet, even if the focus was on the herd, such that semi-permanent structures were built where a family might spend a good part of the year.

In Africa, there seem to have been adequate amounts of wild grains of various types (cf. Gast 1968; Tubiana and Tubiana 1977; Smith, S. E., 1980) to satisfy the needs of the nomads. Thus herding societies existed in North Africa for at least 3,000 years before agricultural systems developed (Marshall and Hildebrand 2002). The focus on land and territory in the Near East was bound to be different from that in Africa, although Arabian pastoralism has strong similarities to that of the Horn of Africa and the Sahara.

Fratkin et al. (1994) have shown how variable African pastoralist societies can be. They are aware, as is Hodgson (2000), that colonial influences have heavily impacted how any given society might look today, and even groups within reasonable proximity to each other, such as the Turkana and Rendille, show different herding practices (Fratkin et al. 1994: 6).

Pasture Territories and Resources

In general terms, the area used by nomadic pastoralists has to meet the annual needs of the herd. From a short-term perspective, the annual round seems "fixed" in the cultural memory, to be repeated each year with minor variations, depending on rainfall and pasture availability (fig. 1.5). Stenning (1957), however, has shown that the areas used by herders might change over time.

Using the example of the pastoral Fulani, Stenning describes three different types of movement:

> *Transhumance:* a north/south movement attuned with seasonal variation in pasture and pressure from trypanosome-bearing tsetse flies;
>
> *Migratory drift:* the gradual movement away from different pasture zones that were used in the past, perhaps for family reasons, and may happen within one generation, but usually over two or more;
>
> *Migration:* movement to a completely new area, often as a result of warfare or political pressures.

Nomadic life has built into it a degree of flexibility that allows the herders the freedom to opportunistically take advantage of new pasture conditions. As an example of migration, the Chamanamas Tuareg, today found in the lower Tilemsi Valley north of Gao, were met by one of the first Europeans to visit the area, Heinrich Barth, in 1854, 300 km further west, near Tombouctou (Barth 1859: III, 420).

Herders jealously guard their pasture territories against outsiders, although within a group there is no individual ownership; but if population density of the animals is high, some form of negotiation has to take place to avoid conflict. Boundaries exist between the territories of different groups, and the higher the density of human and animal populations, or pressure from the vagaries of climate, the more rigid the boundaries become. If droughts are

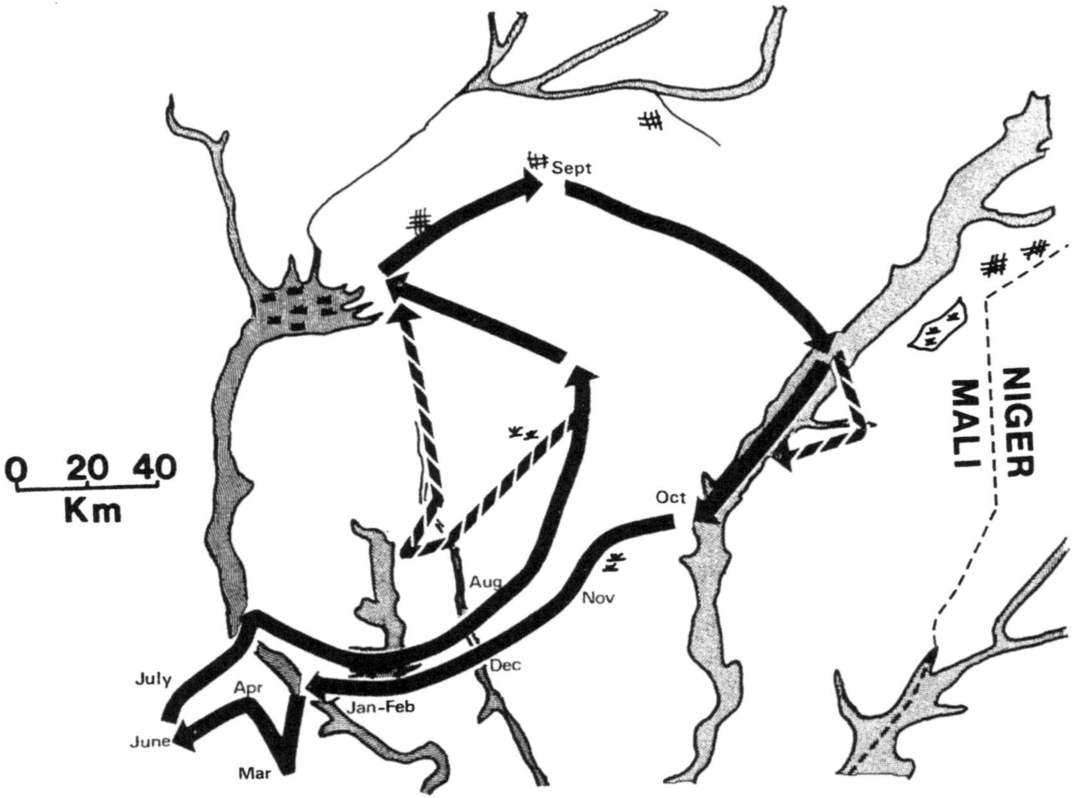

Figure 1.5. Annual transhumance of Kel Telataye Tuareg of Mali. Solid arrows show monthly movement of main camp; hatched arrows show side trips of lower caste Iklan to harvest wild grains (after Smith, S. E., 1980).

a common problem or rainfall varies from place to place each year, such event-driven systems require the institution of protocols that will allow access by different groups over time. If the protocols are followed, access will seldom be denied, as the pasture may be good in your area this year, but next year you might have to go someplace else, so they become a technique for risk avoidance. Herd owners also might loan part of their herd to a bond friend who gets access to the milk yield. This is an insurance policy whereby the herd gets distributed across space, evening out the chances that in the worst drought conditions some of the herd might survive.

Another way to avoid tensions is to have a serial use of pasture territories, with herds moving in and out of a region, to be followed by others (Barth 1959–1960). This is a model practiced by some herders in Iran that may include movement between high-altitude summer pastures, which become snow covered in winter, and lower-altitude winter areas.

Pasture is only one-half of the pastoral equation. Access to water is just as important, as cattle, even those well adapted to dry conditions, need to be watered every other day, and young animals or sheep should be watered every day. During and after the rains, surface water in pools or pans makes life easy. All too often, these are temporary, and the water evaporates after the rainy season. During the dry season, herders will have to make do with subsurface water, either from deep wells tapping an aquifer or in river beds. In either case, digging is necessary, and ownership of the water is in the hands of the person who keeps the water point open. Access can be gained by others only through payment of a gift. Where permanent rivers exist, there may be a retreat to the riparian pastures.

Another pastoral resource is access to trace elements, often in the form of salt licks, soil, or mineralized water, which the animals ingest. In the Sahel of West Africa, the herds are taken on this "cure salée" during part of the annual round, over a period of one or two days (Bernus 1979). This way, any trace element deficiencies in the diet of the animals are minimized.

The dry season is the lowest common denominator, and herding strategies must be capable of dealing with this time of year. Distance between water and pasture increases to such an extent at this time that weaker animals will be put under great pressure, and if the rains are delayed or fail, many may not survive.

Raiding among African Pastoralists

Fukui and Turton (1979) would like to make a distinction between raiding and warfare, which among East African pastoralists is not that easy to do. If we define warfare as a strategic activity for overcoming an enemy, with the view to completely defeat them, then on the whole most of the aggression among herders in Africa should be called "raiding," whose end is mostly to steal animals. Raiding can escalate to a point where the size of a party is huge enough to be called an army that is out to annihilate its enemies, but this is the extreme end of the continuum. Even among the Boran of the border between Kenya and Ethiopia, who had tactical success in using horses for raids, the individual "was a raider on horseback, not a cavalryman in the European sense of the term" (Fukui and Turton 1979: 7).

By assuming that among African pastoralists most aggressive intergroup action is raiding, and that this is a common occurrence, we must ask ourselves what adaptive advantage it offers the herders. In general, raiding is not about killing your neighbor, but about stealing his livestock (and possibly women, although this may be an aberration). In doing so, a young man could acquire enough livestock to pay bridewealth, and "big men," who achieve social rank through stock ownership and their relations with other stock owners, could enhance their status by having more cattle to loan out. This may be the critical reason for cattle raiding, since even given the general polygynous nature of pastoralist societies, the natural increase in herd size may be insufficient to meet the needs for the cattle expended as bridewealth (Fukui and Turton 1979: 9).

But is that all there is to raiding among pastoralists? It would seem not. At the personal level, a successful raider gains an enhanced social status, both as warrior and as stock owner. This social standing and the wealth attained allow him to acquire more wives and, potentially, father more progeny, which would not only have a

Darwinian effect, but also supply the male children needed to care for the stock and females to be utilized as bargaining chips in the acquisition of further animals through the negotiation of their bridewealth. At the same time, since these are small-scale societies, we may detect a need to defuse the inherent tension between age grades, where the elders have power over younger "warriors," since they control the animals to be given for bridewealth. A successful raider, however, is able to establish his own herd, family, and reputation. Besides the size of one's herd or the extent of one's household, prestige can also be displayed through the medium of decorative scarification, as is practiced by the Bodi of Ethiopia, for example (Fukui 1979).

As a further result, raiding may not only relieve inherent social tensions within the group, but it may also produce a useful redistribution of herds over space and among groups. It gives individuals prestige and fine tunes the capabilities of the warrior age sets. Thus, from an elder perspective, raiding may confer the greater advantage of "maintaining internal order [as opposed to] . . . mobilizing for external aggression" (Fukui and Turton 1979: 11).

Unlike agriculturalists, the raids usually have little to do with territorial conquest. Even when there are grains ready for harvest, they may still be left behind when the cattle are driven off. In the larger scheme of things, however, a group might gradually push another aside over a period of time, particularly if control over water holes offers a strategic advantage. Stenning (1957) has shown how Fulani herders may move to new pastures if the political situation becomes untenable.

We must, of course, recognize that the scale of escalation of aggression might be exacerbated by the addition of firearms into the equation. Gray et al. (2003) argue that the introduction of the AK-47 into East African pastoralist life, in conjunction with severe ecological pressures, is tearing traditional Karamojong pastoralist society apart. They show that homicide levels among men between 30 and 60 years of age have reached epidemic proportions (37 to 44 percent of males in this age group who died did so violently). Such extremes impact directly on females and children, since the loss of mates and fathers means less food support and, compounded by drought and disease, results in high deaths among the more vulnerable part of the group. Whether, indeed, this is a positive feedback mechanism that will ultimately lead to social dissolution is an interesting question. Pastoralists are imminently adaptable, so perhaps the AK-47 is just a new and more vibrant selective mechanism that, given time, will even itself out among the warlords, as in Somalia, until a new dispensation is in place.

Cattle Identification

Virtually every African pastoralist society has a detailed classification system that makes for ease of identity of individual animals, communication with peers, and knowledge of the herd's status. Certain animals have personal value; the Nuer (Evans-Pritchard 1940: 46–47) will decorate and sing praise songs to their name oxen. Among herders as widespread geographically as the Tuareg (Nicolaisen 1963: 96–98), Toubou (Baroin 1985: 37–38), Nuer (Evans-Pritchard 1940: 42–43), and Zulu (Krige 1977: 187), the animals are known intimately, and each coat color has a special name. Cranstone (1969: 251) says that Lapps have over 50 names to describe their reindeer, as combinations of coat color and antler shape. Galaty (1989: 219) notes that

> In addition to patterns of identification built up through experience, livestock identification also occurs through systems of symbolic classification of a cultural order, in particular through ear marks and brands which signify the owners' family and descent group, livestock names, and descriptives. In the case of names, the Maasai endow all cattle in a particular "lineage" with a single appellation, proper not to the apical bull but to the bovine "matriarch."

The Maasai use five different attribute types to describe their cattle: status (sex, maturity, whether castrated or not), elementary colors, elementary patterns (e.g., spotted, striped, streaked), horns (presence or absence, shape), and other distinctive characters (e.g., blindness or lameness). Each attribute can be simple or combined to make more complex descriptions. The more detailed the description, the easier to identify individual animals among very large herds. In fact, even though herdsmen may be innumerate, they know how many animals they have, and should one go missing, it is recognized by the space it leaves in the herd. By having such complex descriptions, the herder is able to scan his herd as it returns to the kraal in the evening using a series of mental steps. Some animals are identifiable by their behavior or their place in the herd, such as always grazing to one side or grazing apart, and these animals may be looked for first. The "lineages" of the cattle are also taken into consideration, as another way to "count" them. The herder will also go to sleep thinking about his herd and may "see" any missing animal in his dreams (Galaty 1989: 226–28).

The colors of Zulu cattle have names that refer to birds, wild animals, reptiles, insects, plants, or other things in the environment, such as stones, ash, shadows, and clouds. These cattle names and imagery become metaphors for human actions and descriptions and are used in praise poems. Chief Galenja Biyela was described as "Pawer of the earth, Galenja breaks out the anthill, the bull that breaks out the anthill" (Poland et al. 2003: 93). This is a reference to the display of power and resolve of a bull pawing the soil and rubbing his horns on an anthill. Warriors carried shields made from ox hide, with each regiment having its own color.

Among the Bodi of southern Ethiopia, cattle identity and symbolism take on an even greater dimension that affects a man's psychological well-being. The Bodi have descriptive techniques that are equally as detailed as the Zulus', and each clan has a specific color pattern symbol, which means that an elder who dies is buried in the skin of an animal with the clan pattern. A man will identify himself very closely with an animal of a special color pattern that becomes his *morare*: "He decorates it with a special bell and with other ornaments and, while herding it in the grazing areas, he is particularly careful to observe its behaviour, assessing, for example, its health and intelligence. If he decides to make it his favorite animal he will, after several months, make four slits in its right ear. If it is a cow neither he, his father, his father's brothers, his mother nor his mother's brothers must drink its milk. Nor must they drink the blood of any animal with which he has identified himself. Favorite animals are usually oxen but occasionally a cow . . . is chosen. It is no exaggeration that a man regards his life without his *morare* as hardly worth living" (Fukui 1979: 170). This event is so intense that, when such an animal dies, the man may go out to kill a member of a neighboring group. The man does not go alone, because such killings need to be witnessed. Special scars are cut into his arm to demonstrate the killing has occurred. So special is this relationship between the Bodi and their *morare* that they believe cattle do not belong to the animal world, but to that of men, and a man will sacrifice another animal to aid a sick *morare*'s recovery, "as though he wished himself to recover from an illness" (Fukui 1979: 175–76).

This extreme example of the relationship between a man and his name animal illustrates that the animals and their place in the society infiltrate everything that the herder does or thinks about. The complex ties are extremely personal, being both symbolic and emotional, and they color attitudes that have major implications for herd production and management (Galaty 1989: 217). The fact that individual animals are given personal attention means that the traditional herding is labor intensive, and every member of the family is usually involved at some level.

Gender in African Pastoralist Societies

Within African pastoralist societies, there is a basic gender dichotomy: men look after the animals, while women tend to the domestic sphere. In Fulani society, this has a spatial dimension, where the calf rope separates the two domains. The calf rope is where young calves are tied while they are in the camp. The herd is kept to one side of the rope and the family huts on the other. The calf rope has an important symbolic role to play, and it is to be found in calabash decorations (Le Quellec 2002).

There has been a tendency in the ethnographic literature to elaborate on the role of the herd, that is, the men's domain. Certainly, the more public, and therefore visible, part of pastoralism revolves around the herd's needs and around young men singing to their oxen or riding camels with all their finery, making more noise than their female counterparts. Most of the heavy work, such as watering the animals, is done by men, and in ritual the men are usually the ones to slaughter the sacrificial animal. Men, owners of stock, sit in formal public discussions and engage in political and economic decision making. At the same time, deriving authority from their status as owners of livestock sanctions men's power over women. Acts such as wife beating seem to be acceptable (at least to the men). Although this is seen as a means to keep a fractious wife in line, it is usually mediated by a strong social condemnation whenever there is excessive harm to the woman. Since the role of men and the politics of stock ownership have a dynamic quality that attracts immediate attention, the place of women in these societies has been greatly underreported.

Women's work in the domestic domain tends to be much less alluring (at least to some investigators), as it involves the commonplace chores of collecting water from the well for cooking and washing, bringing in firewood, and looking after the day-to-day needs of the family by making sure the domestic herd gets milked and everyone fed (fig. 1.6). As a consequence of the research interests

*Figure 1.6. Tuareg (Iklan) woman winnowing threshed wild cram-cram (*Cenchrus biflorus*) in the Tilemsi Valley, Mali.*

of many researchers, the true role of women in African pastoralist societies has tended to be underresearched, underestimated, and downplayed. However, as in many instances of exploiting the ethnographic present to explain the past, a further delving into the record discovers a richer texture, and a quite different situation, in the past. A Khoekhoe woman's identity with the domestic space is situated in her ash heap. She will clean out the hearth in her hut every day and deposit the ash on the ash heap, usually located several meters from her hut. Even if she moves away, no other woman would dream of using the ash heap in her absence (Archer 1994). Ultimately, it is the past state of affairs that will interest us. However, we should first establish how the more recent state of affairs of women in pastoralist societies came about.

Hodgson (2000: 1–2) reviewed and then critiqued the "orthodox" view of pastoral societies as being patrilineal and patriarchal. The view that women were totally subordinate to men, and that women's role in the society was constrained to the domestic sphere and thus negligible, compared with the political and economic power wielded by men has been repeated by many authors (e.g., Spencer 1965; Evans-Pritchard 1951; Galaty 1979). Hodgson suggests that this is an androcentric position that in many ways is the result of the number of male researchers who have worked on pastoralist societies in the past. By taking a historical perspective, she has been able to suggest that the current position of women in Maasai society, for example, has been conditioned by attitudes engendered during the colonial period. Contrary to women's rather demeaning place at the beginning of the twenty-first century, in the past women were much more independent of men. They were active as traders, bringing much needed agricultural foods into the homestead, especially during the dry season. Women were also very active in ritual matters and thus had social and political power.

In Hodgson's analysis, the devastating effects of cattle disease and smallpox epidemics among humans in the late nineteenth century were followed by colonial attempts to put more and more power into the hands of the elders. This was a classic European colonial pattern, the imposition of "indirect rule." The colonists needed to be able to negotiate with "native" people, so they subverted the leadership roles by giving power and authority to individuals where previously chiefs were *"primus inter pares"* (first among equals) (Schapera 1930: 227). Baroin (1985: 75–76), describing the Toubou of Niger and Chad, says that the French colonial administration, in establishing its authority, needed to find "chiefs" among the local population who would serve as spokespersons and intermediaries of the groups they wished to control. As they failed to find a stable chieftainship they could deal with, they created almost all the pieces of the system that exists today. This pattern of designated authority had an established precedence, having been instituted when the Dutch gave staffs of office to Khoekhoe "captains" in the eighteenth century at the Cape and, in Britain, after Culloden in 1745, when Scottish chiefs who had opposed the Pretender, Charles Stuart, had greater authority pressed upon them by the English than had existed before the Jacobite uprising.

In addition, once the British took possession of German East Africa (Tanganyika) after the First World War, they began a process of commodification of livestock and introduced a cash system so that people could pay taxes. This resulted in changed social values, as men learned to sell animals in the marketplace, while women were gradually disenfranchised from the shared rights in cattle they had once held. Men became the taxpayers, not women. Something similar was suggested by Jacobsohn (1995; pers. comm.), who describes how Himba men in northern Namibia became negotiators with the outside world. They took jobs, marketed animals, learned to speak other languages, and dressed in Western clothes. Women, by contrast, were more and more constrained to the domestic sphere, did not come into contact with other people, and continued to wear traditional dress. As a consequence, they were seen as "backward" (as described by the state president, Sam Nujoma). Himba women, feeling a sense of isolation and wishing to replace some of their self-worth, turned to trance dancing in order to fill the social void created by their altered status in their traditional societies.

Sullivan (2000: 145) says that the community game guard system given over to male hands further undermined women's place in Damara society in Namibia. Although the system was set up to prevent poaching and to preserve wildlife for the tourist industry, the local people saw elephants as either a threat to their women's gardens or as game to be hunted and eaten. However, there were provisions for women to have a say in how the conservancies work, and as a result their families derive benefits without the intervention of elder males.

In a variety of instances, women retain punitive rights affecting moral behavior in their group. In Spencer's view (1988), women become the moral arbiters. Although women are individually constrained by men among the Maasai, Spencer (1988: 205–206) describes women's rituals of rebellion, as well as what he calls "mobbing" by women. The former are fertility ceremonies, but they can lead to the latter when women get angry and organize themselves to counteract what they collectively see as immoral behavior, such as incest or even miscarriage or stillbirth, "which are assumed to have been caused by wanton intercourse during the tabooed pregnancy period." The anger becomes violent, and the miscreants are soundly beaten. In one case, an elder had his earrings torn off, ripping his ear lobes, his genitals stamped upon, and his favorite ox slaughtered when he was accused of raping a "daughter."

In a number of societies, such as Khoekhoe, women can inherit stock, and they can disburse it to whomsoever they wish. A husband will look after his wife's animals, but he may not get rid of them without her permission (Smith and Webley 2000). In Toubou society, at marriage a wife brings animals with her from her relatives; she may give some to her husband to look after or she may opt to give them to relatives to take care of. Men usually decide about their dispersal, although if the herd remains intact, her sons will inherit (Baroin 1987).

Regardless of ownership, women need to have a small herd around the homestead or camp for family use. Her children tend these animals. The cows can be allowed to free range away from the camp, provided there are no predators in the area. Since the young calves are kept in the camp, their mothers will return in the evening to feed them (and provide humans with milk). Not all women are involved with animals, however. Bantu-speaking mixed agriculturists in southern Africa do not allow women near the herd. Men do all milking, and women's role is relegated to tending the gardens. Such is the division of labor between the sexes that among the Zulu, while an older man may have a small garden for tobacco, he will never plant food crops (Krige 1950: 190).

As women's status changes with age, they are able to operate independently, like a male elder. Little (1987) observes that among the Il Chamus a widow can even organize stock loans for herself, and Rasmussen (2000) has shown that among the Tuareg postmenopausal women can operate with much less constraint than younger women.

Pastoralist Children

Another aspect of pastoralism that tends to be ignored is the situation of children. They have even less status than women, but are always active in the background doing chores, watching, and listening (fig. 1.7). Both boys and girls are expected to look after the domestic herd, in order to learn the practice of tending the animals, preparing for the time when they will undergo initiation and passage into adulthood.

The education of a young man in Maasai society is well defined by Spencer (1988: 51): "A boy's upbringing is geared towards the unremitting care of stock. From the time he can barely walk, he may try his hand at herding, clutching an upraised stalk as he

Figure 1.7. Kel Telataye boys in camp, eastern Mali (photo: *Susan Gunn).*

stumbles towards the smallest stock as if to round them up.... His father or his older brothers teach him how to control the herd and to respond to any situation that may arise... and to make his own judgments during the day.... [T]his wider understanding grows out of the intimate knowledge of cattle, goats and sheep.... Their long hours give them encyclopedic knowledge of each herd in their neighborhood." They can therefore assist older members of the group with information about dispersal of indebted cattle used in marriage negotiations.

Pastoralist children emulate their elders by playing herding games, modeling miniature homesteads and kraals (fig. 1.8) and making clay figurines of cattle or camels. Among the Bodi of southern Ethiopia, young boys represent cattle with pebbles that they organize according to color within toy kraals. This way, they learn the complicated cattle color system that is the basis of their social organization. By the age of 12, when he will be expected to be able to herd cattle, a boy will be proficient in the cattle naming system based on coat color (Fukui 1979: 165–66). Young boys may be given full responsibility for looking after small stock. Childhood relieves no one of duties to the

Figure 1.8. Toy hut and kraal of Nama children in Richtersveld, South Africa.

general good. Children are expected to assume responsibility and to pull their weight within the labor-intensive herding regime from an early age. Tuareg boys as young as 10 years leave camp tending flocks of sheep by themselves for weeks at a time, subsisting entirely on the milk of the sheep and what plant foods (berries, gum) they might gather. As in any other society, young girls are expected to look after their siblings and to share in cooking, firewood collection, and other domestic chores.

Hunters and Herders, or the Domestication of People

The transhumant pastoralist life and the nomadic hunting one are remarkably similar. Both hunting and herding societies are mobile, and much of their lives are involved in dealing with animal behavior. The organization of cohorts imparts similar divisions of labor. In both economic groups, men deal with animals, and women the domestic sphere. The difference between them is said to lie in their methods of extracting meat "off the hoof." That is, hunters, for the most part, stalk wild game that can be said to be taking care of themselves, in contrast to herders, who have to look after domestic stock. In both cases, though, the lifeways of the human communities are tied not only to the animals they use as a food source, but also to the animals' dependence on favorable conditions of rainfall patterns, pasturage, and the distances traversed to find them.

Although both hunters and herdsmen have a great deal of freedom under normal circumstances, the ecological needs of the domestic stock place constraints on the pattern of the pastoralist regime. All this has serious social and processual implications, because, at some time in the past, not only were animals and plants becoming domesticated, but so too were humans, who now had responsibility for them. The animals and plants became valuable assets that needed to be nurtured and protected from predation, whether from wild animals, disease, or other humans. The discipline of herding requires that the needs of the herd are paramount. In this way, the animals become "family," and the bigger the herd the greater the responsibility.

The degree of constraint increased when domestic grains were included in the dietary repertoire. This meant the tending of gardens and protecting them from the herd and birds. Many nomads disdain agriculture, preferring to exchange the product of their herd for grains grown by others, or as tribute, as was the case in the Sahel before European intervention stopped raiding.

In many parts of the world, hunting and foraging continued down to the twentieth century. Although most hunting groups had contact with farmers or herders, and some even worked for them, they did not become food producers themselves. Even when they had access to animals that were so tractable that domestication would have been relatively easy, some hunting groups were quite content to let them take care of themselves. The eland, *Taurotragus oryx*, is a good example. The Bushmen of southern Africa revere this the largest of the African antelopes as an animal of great procreative power. It is considered the rain animal and as such is seen as a source of fertility, both of the landscape and of humans. When a young woman has her first menses, the group will perform the eland bull dance in her honor (Lewis-Williams and Dowson 1989: 119). To eat eland fat is to have sex, or as Biesele (1993: 197) puts it, after a successful hunt the hunter would lie next to his wife and be happy "because the meat had fat and was fat." Thus, "Eating, and sleeping with, are equated symbolically."

Thus the eland has enormous symbolic value. It is also very tractable, although attempts at domestication have been less than successful, but it can be milked, and it produces richer milk than cow's milk. The eland may have been controlled and led over the countryside in ritual to bring rain; to quote Lewis-Williams (1981: 107): "we must allow the possibility of these eland, not normally eaten, being captured, led and killed in rain-making rituals." It is not certain, however, even with depictions of animals apparently being led in the rock art, that this should be taken literally, since Bushman shamans were perceived to be capable of wondrous things in their altered states of consciousness, such as out-of-body travel to the land of the gods. As part of this belief, the act of painting was seen as instrumental in affecting a cause, such as bringing rain.

The eland may have been controlled, but it was never domesticated by the Bushmen. Since domestication implies ownership, this may be a clue to why the Bushmen preferred to let eland roam freely. No private ownership of meat is allowed in Bushman society, which requires equal sharing.

In a perceptive comparison between hunters and herders, Ingold (2000) sees these two economic groups as having a different worldview in regard to the animals they are in contact with, and this perception colors how they arrange their social relationships. A hunter does not "control" the animals. "The animals in the environment of the hunter do not simply go their own way, but are supposed to act with the hunter in mind. They are not just 'there' for the hunter to find and to take as he will, rather they present themselves to him" (71). Any coercion betrays the trust that both hunter and prey give to each other, and an animal will desert the hunter (i.e., the hunter will not be successful). Thus a hunter should not take more than he is "given." Ingold suggests this has implications in human relations among hunters: you can ask for what others have, but not demand more.

Domestication changes the relationship between people and animals, since the stock are "dominated," and therefore the idea of "trust" found between hunters and prey falls away. While Ingold's analysis (2000: 73) suggests that the instruments of herding, for example, whips or hobbles, are meant to control, among herders, anyone maltreating their animals is despised. "Control" taken to its logical conclusion may imply that animals and women need to be "tamed" by physical abuse. However, as suggested above in the section on gender, extreme practice of physical abuse may tend to be a recent idea, as men have, on the one hand, been given greater authority, but on the other, have been forced to conform to new outside pressures, for example, markets and taxation, which have often resulted in psychosocial imbalances and trauma in a more competitive environment. Extreme examples of this might be the ethnic conflicts in Rwanda in 1994 and Darfur, Sudan, in 2004, among societies that traditionally have had strong cattle-based economies where land and resources are becoming scarce.

It is obvious that, even when the necessary wild resources were available, they were not automatically domesticated. In fact, we must separate out concepts of "control" from actual "domestication." There is ample evidence for control of wild resources, such as plants

(Tubiana and Tubiana 1977), and given time and pressure from other people, perhaps the resources could be moved to new environments, with concomitant genetic changes taking place. An excellent example given by Flannery (1969) is of a selection for woolly sheep, rather than the more hairy forms. Unfortunately, for the woolly variety, the *Stipa* grass, which grows in the area of natural wild sheep progenitors, has a seed that bores into the skin below the wool, causing serious disabilities among the flock. The answer to meet the demands for wool production was to move the woolly animals to lower elevations, where *Stipa* did not grow.

Should we separate out milch pastoralism from carnivory, as among reindeer herders, as Ingold (1980: 25) suggests? Reindeer herders allow their domestic herds to breed freely with wild animals, thus there is no morphological change evident among the domestic animals. This creates a dilemma for the archaeozoologist. How would an archaeologist be able to recognize that domestic animals existed among reindeer herds? These animals are primarily used for meat, although skins are a needed by-product. Evidence for domestication might come from indications of a social nature, such as penning, but this could be confused with similar patterns seen in controlling wild animals for specific purposes, for example, ritual.

Domestication, then, is part of a process of control and manipulation of a species, but in archaeological terms, only when there are morphological changes that can be recognized in plant or animal remains can we be sure that domestication has taken place. Other criteria, such as movement to new environments, secondary products (such as fibers from animal coats), and figurines suggesting milking, can then be used to support the argument.

As we will see, evidence from sites in the Near East shows that people were experimenting with farming grains about 11,000 years ago. These included wheat, barley, lentils, and peas. It was a thousand years later before we see any significant morphological changes to animals as a result of domestication. Only then can the skeletons of domesticated animals be recognized in the archaeological record, but people may well have been controlling the movement of animals for a long time before that.

A simple definition of domestication for archaeological purposes is *an intentional manipulation of genetic material of select plant and animal species*. This implies that humans were choosing the traits that would benefit them, such as increased productivity, easier extraction or harvest, and easier control.

Domestication of Animals: How Did It Happen?

Not all animals that have close relationships with humans have been domesticated. We have mentioned the example of the eland above, but how do the animals that were domesticated differ from those that were not?

The key to understanding the process whereby some animals were domesticated and others not seems to lie in the herd behavior of individual species. Most animals, especially young antelope, can be tamed when they are young, but for food production the animals need to be bred under conditions where they will be readily accessible for human use. Wild game animals can be controlled by modern farming methods, using fences, and today farmers in South Africa have a market for springbok (*Antidorcas marsupialis*) and gemsbok (*Oryx gazella*), but there is little attempt to change these animals or to modify their behavior. The breeding habits of these antelope species are for dominant males to control a harem of females against other males. This makes the males virtually unmanageable during this period. As Joubert (1989: 155) says, "Because game are less manageable, but in particular because they are subject to specific social systems, it is impossible to harvest them in the same way as domestic stock." After the breeding season, the males separate, leaving females and young alone. Thus the social behavior is highly variable and seasonal.

By contrast, the African buffalo (*Syncerus caffer*) and the eland have much looser social systems. This means that "individuals in a herd are tolerant of one another and antagonistic interactions are rare. Such animals often form large herds and when they split up, subsections frequently join neighboring herds and there is an exchange of individuals among herds" (Joubert 1989: 152). One researcher into the behavior of the African buffalo (Mloszewski 1983) was able to move freely among the herds, as long as he was seen. Thus hunters, who know their prey species intimately, could use this herd behavior to their advantage to casually herd the animals. Over time, the animals would become used to the humans, and a symbiotic relationship would grow between them. We might suggest that the loose social behavior of buffalo could be analogous to that of wild cattle (*Bos primigenius*) or wild sheep (*Ovis orientalis*) or wild goats (*Capra aegagrus*), making these animals prime targets for domestication.

Two stages have been suggested in the process toward domestication:

1. capture and taming of young animals (controlling their movement)
2. intentional breeding (manipulating the genetic material)

It is only with the latter that the archaeozoologist can reasonably recognize differences between wild and domesticated forms, although semiwild animals could be moved out of their native habitat, providing a clue to their control by people.

The first phase of control over animals is what Bökönyi (1969: 219) would prefer to call "animal keeping": "the primitive form of animal breeding without purposeful selection or the control of feeding." This is basically what reindeer herders of Scandinavia practice today. The operative word is "breeding," but animals may have been controlled in their wild state, by herding them together for a specific or limited purpose, such as ritual. There is no intention of breeding, and the animals are still wild, so such a definition becomes fuzzy.

A variation on the usual domestication process has been offered by Schleidt and Shalter (2003), who see the skills of wolves using herd behavior to their advantage as a model for early herding. In fact, they go even further and suggest that "pastoralism" was well developed among wolves before modern humans were on the scene and that humans may have learned "pastoral" techniques from wolves. While interesting, this idea can only refer to the beginnings of reindeer and caribou "herding" in northern latitudes of Eurasia. Today, the Inuit use the behavior of wolves to recognize when there are caribou in the area, and they chase the caribou by pretending to be wolves (see films on the Netsilik Eskimo by Asen Balikci; Balikci 1970).

Domestication of Animals: Why Did It Happen?

An intuitively obvious reason why animals were domesticated was to have them close to hand for easy access, as either a meat or a milk source. But this does not explain why people should have taken on the responsibility for the animals, instead of just allowing them to free range and to cull when needed. Being responsible means you are tied down (just ask any dairy farmer who needs to milk his cows twice a day). Equally, you need to protect the animals (your investment) from theft or predation.

It is well known that domestic animals to traditional herdsmen are more than just a meat source. Animals are wealth and are given as bridewealth payments, so they are usually slaughtered only on special occasions, such as funerals and rituals (naming ceremonies, marriages, rainmaking, etc.). This leads to the conclusion that the animals are closely intertwined with human social needs: economic, aesthetic, and ritual.

If the animals play such important symbolic and ritual roles today, we might suggest that this may have been one important reason for their control and domestication in the past. Such an idea was alluded to by Smith (1969: 313), who saw the history of animal cults in Dynastic Egypt as coming out of a previous desert hunting/foraging use of wild animals. This suggestion might be applicable over a wide area, since cattle figurines are found very early on in the Neolithic, as are shrines with cattle horns, or bucrania, in the Near East.

Cattle and sheep have another advantage: they are rich in fat. This is in stark contrast to most game animals, such as gazelles, which tend to be very lean. Fat was one of the more difficult dietary needs for hunters to fill. Such scarcity among southern African hunters has resulted in fat being given the status of mystical potency, along with honey and the sweat of a healer in trance (Lewis-Williams 2002).

Nomadic herding societies today contain the experiences of the past. While historical influences, such as colonialism, may have affected how they are presently organized, the basic theme of mobility in search of pasture and water remains a given today as in the past. The gender separation and age roles in pastoralism mean that all members of the society have a crucial role to play in successful survival of the family and herd. Age grades in many of the herding societies are structural mechanisms to allow smooth passage of control of the herd from one generation to the next, while making sure seniority and experience are given precedence, just as raiding is a means to redistribute the herd and hone the skills of the warrior groups.

It is not easy to find these social formations in the archaeological record, but clues might be sought in differences in settlement type or spatial task differentiation, such as in the ownership of domestic space by women's ash heaps among the Khoekhoen or the decoration on pots or calabashes of East African herders. Variability in grave goods or ceremonial spaces often leave unique residues that indicate deep meaning within the beliefs of past people.

2

The Material Culture of Nomadic Pastoralists

Today they moved to distant camps
who before just a shout would bring

—Bedouin poem (from L. Abu-Lughod, *Veiled Sentiments*)

The material culture of a nomadic people, virtually by definition, needs to be light and portable. Thus most of the cultural material is made from skin, fiber, and wood. Inevitably, much of the material is that which is used in herding activities, such as hobbles and halters for restraining the animals, saddles and reins used in riding or draft, and milking vessels. Of course, this is by no means all. Pastoralists, like all people, have a penchant for looking good, so clothes and ornaments are important; so should be the equipment for their animals, such as blankets and saddlebags. I was told by one informant that a young Tuareg man will sing songs about his camel, his saddle, his sword, his clothes, and his lady friend, in that order (fig. 2.1). Nicolaisen (1963) recorded in detail the range of items used by the Kel Ayr and Kel Hoggar, two Tuareg groups in Niger and Algeria. The items depicted, of wood and skin, are both functional and aesthetic. There is a caste of artisans (*Inadan*) who make the artifacts. They also work metal, but even metal objects, such as cases for amulets, jewelry, knives, and swords, tend to be relatively small and light. Similarly, the beauty and care spent in making cultural material is evident in the everyday items in Fulani life, photographed by Carol Beckwith (Beckwith and van Offelen 1983).

Cribb (1991) attempted a typology of dwellings among pastoralists in the Near East. These range from simple tents to permanent houses. In Africa, a similar range can be found, depending on the mobility of the group. Stone-walled structures are very rare when compared with the Near East, but in both regions pastoralists can

Figure 2.1. Soulemane ag Kiyou of the Chamanamas Tuareg of the Tilemsi Valley, Mali.

have more than one dwelling type. A more permanent structure will be found where a site is repeatedly reoccupied. Some huts, such as the Maasai *manyatta*, may be occupied for a considerable period of time before the family sees the need to move to a new location.

Nomads have a range of shelters. These can be made of skin, woven mats, wool, or other cloth material, all of which are spread over a wooden frame. But they must all be able to be dismantled and

Figure 2.2. Drawing of Khoekhoe family moving camp (from Daniel 1804–1805).

rolled up, so they can be carried on the backs of camels or draft oxen (fig. 2.2). Temporary stock camps can also have various structures. Among the Nama of the Richtersveld of the Northern Cape, South Africa, if a man moves his stock by himself to a new grazing area away from the family, he may just build a simple brush windbreak for the night (fig. 2.3). More permanent structures might be built if his wife is in residence, but even this is not done immediately. When a couple moves their camp to a new location, if the structure is needed it is taken apart (fig. 2.4), and their belongings are piled up to be carried on the back of a pickup (the modern oxen) (fig. 2.5). When a woman arrives at her new camp, she raises a temporary shelter (fig. 2.6) and after a few days will organize the hut structure (fig. 2.7). If she is going to stay only a short time, the cladding will be burlap bags or plastic sheeting (fig. 2.8). In more permanent locations where the woman is in long-term residence, often because of proximity to schools, she will make formal reed mats for covering her hut (fig. 2.9), a pattern well documented in the nineteenth century (fig. 2.10). She may even have a cinder-block house with a corrugated iron roof in town and use her mat hut as a cooking area, since it is much cooler in summer.

Figure 2.3. Brush windbreak constructed by shepherd at Anniesfontein, Richtersveld, South Africa, with his goats and sheep in the background.

Figure 2.4. A Nama family in the Richtersveld dismantling their camp and preparing to load their belongings on a pickup.

Figure 2.5. A Nama family's belongings in a new camp after a move.

Figure 2.6. A Nama woman in her temporary camp set up after a move.

Figure 2.7. A temporarily abandoned Nama camp along the Orange River in the Richtersveld, showing the hut and cooking area. The structure is left in place in anticipation of reoccupation later in the year.

Figure 2.8. Doing ethnobotany among the Nama of the Richtersveld. The rough jute cladding indicates that the wife and children are only in the camp temporarily, as they will return to the village and to school.

Figure 2.9. A permanent mat hut at Norivier in Namaqualand.

The structure's poles have to be bent into shape by heat and water and pegged to dry (fig. 2.11), and when a hut is removed the postholes can clearly be seen for a short time (fig. 2.12). The layout of the camp shows the domestic space, with its own ash heap (fig. 2.13), which belongs to an individual woman, and the kraal for keeping the goats and sheep at night as protection against jackals (fig. 2.14).

Tuareg hospitality requires a guest to be served tea, and a woven mat windbreak might be erected around the fire while the social niceties are performed. This same mat could also be used around the skin tent to provide protection from the night winds (fig. 2.15).

Modern herders use metal pots and basins and, increasingly, plastic containers for liquids. These have replaced ceramic vessels, which were more common in the past. Both Lhote (1944: 280–81; 1947) and Nicolaisen (1963: 231, 257; plates 186, 187) noted that the Kel Ayr and the Kel Ahaggar Tuareg still used earthen pots during their period of fieldwork in the 1940s and 1950s. These vessels were not made by the pastoral Tuareg, but were obtained cheaply from sedentary people, such as the Harratin, in the desert oases.

Figure 2.10. A sketch by Charles Davison Bell of a Namaqua hut and family in the early nineteenth century.

Figure 2.11. Nama hut structure poles being bent after wetting and heating.

Figure 2.12. Postholes from Nama hut structure.

Finely made painted wares were used in the early twentieth century, and Nicolaisen (1963: 260) found broken pieces in stone houses at Iferouane in the central Aïr Mountains that were destroyed by the French during the 1917 revolt. By 1968, Gast noted in his detailed report on food and food preparation among the Kel Ahaggar that very few clay pots were to be found (Gast 1968: 336), as most cooking vessels were of metal (Gast 1968: plate 63) and easily obtained from traders who were moving into the desert towns from the north. Because of the light weight and strength of metal, it is understandable that ceramic would give way to metal. The friability of an earthenware vessel has meant that the sherds are some of the best indicators of human existence, certainly among prehistoric nomads. (Glynn Isaac used to say that pollution began with the invention of fired clay vessels.) Meat can be cooked directly on the coals, and milk or other dairy products can be stored in leather bags. But cooking pots are an advantage when preparing grains for porridge. The occurrence of durable, low-cost clay vessels probably has much to do with the unattended boiling of the water necessary to the preparation of ground cereals and vegetable foods. As such, they are a marker of the shift to

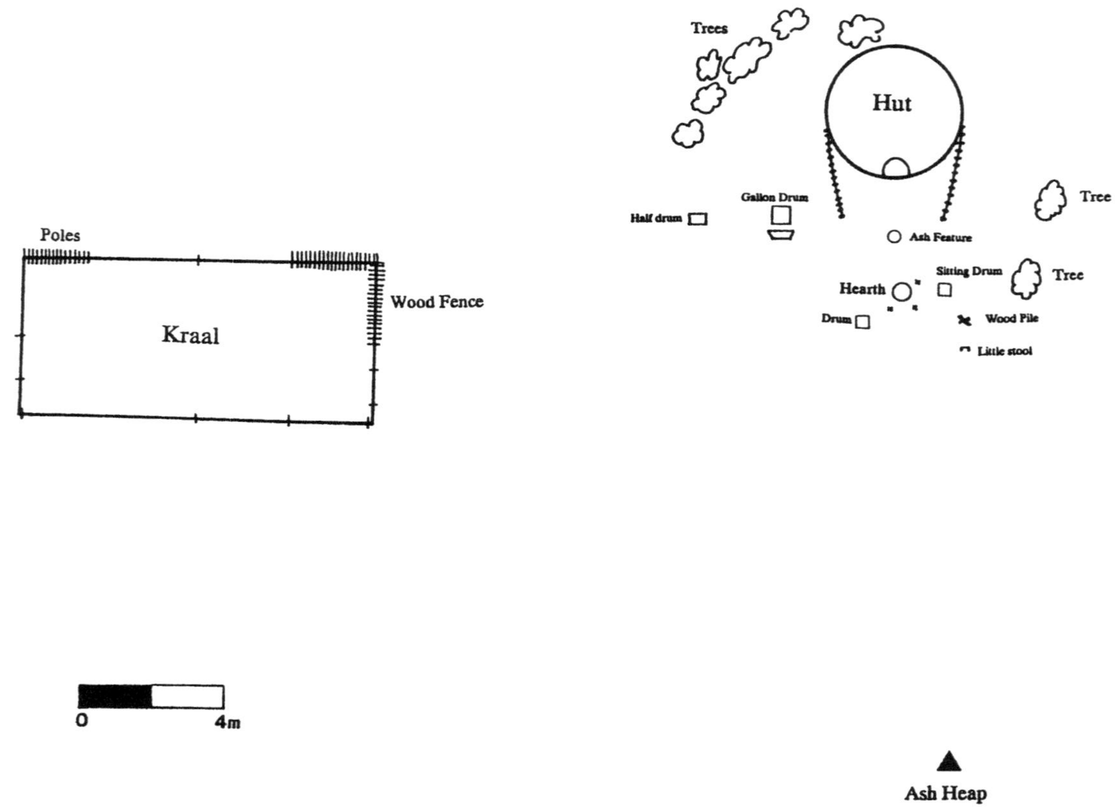

Figure 2.13. *Layout of Nama camp in Richtersveld (Mütti 1992; reprinted by permission).*

Figure 2.14. A Nama camp along the Orange River at the Richtersveld, showing the domestic unit and kraal for keeping small stock at night.

Figure 2.15. Tuareg skin tent with mat windbreak, Tilemsi Valley, Mali.

Figure 2.16. Himba milking basket from northern Namibia.

high caloric plant food diets and a good indicator of how important grains were in the lives of people in the past. Milking can be done directly into clay pots or wooden bowls, but basketry is also used and can be sealed by butterfat, making the vessel watertight (fig. 2.16).

Many pastoral groups use grinding equipment, primarily for processing grains (fig. 2.17), but other materials can also be ground, such as ochre for body decoration or for slip on pottery. Because large grindstones are heavy, they were probably left behind when the group moved on, with the assumption that they would be reused once the camps were reoccupied. Himba in northern Namibia leave a number of their material possessions behind (or did, before tourists started to steal them as souvenirs). Large grindstones take a long time to fashion, so are used until they get worn through. At Tin Aoukert in Mali, the shortage of large stones in the area has meant scavenging from archaeological sites for grave markers. As figure 2.18 shows, a prehistoric grindstone has been engraved as a tombstone by modern Tuareg herders.

Until recently, the stone artifacts used by herders included "flints" for use in fire making. The Tuareg of the Tilemsi know all

Figure 2.17. Dinka woman grinding maize, Gezira, Sudan.

the prehistoric sites because they are a source of *tifarrissen* (flint). Lhote (1944: 278) noted that the Kel Ahaggar were still using stone bracelets or arm rings as a means of warding off sword blows.

Skin bags are essential items for carrying food, water, or other accoutrements. These are often made from goat or other small ungulate skins, which are removed intact when the animal is butchered, so a minimum of sewing is required. Water stored in these bags oozes through the skin, evaporating on the outside to keep the water cold.

A great deal of effort goes into the headdress or covering. A young Tuareg man will have a fine turban (*litham*) of heavily impregnated indigo dye, which is worn only on special ceremonial occasions. The face is covered by the cloth. How much of the nose is exposed depends on the social situation: a person who is *honte* (literally "shamed" but really meaning showing respect to elders, or not being among his own kin) will show nothing but his eyes (Murphy 1964).

Other African herdsmen will spend hours helping each other with their hair, especially before dances where young women will be

Figure 2.18. Prehistoric grindstone inscribed in Arabic and used as modern Tuareg grave marker, Tilemsi Valley, Mali.

present. The finery and makeup used by young Fulani men is truly magnificent when they dress for the *geerewol* ceremony (Beckwith and van Offelen 1983). Similarly, a young Maasai *moran* will be well decked out for the *eunoto* festival (Amin et al. 1987).

Weapons are equally prized and often highly ornamented. A Tuareg sword has a beautiful painted leather scabbard, and the hilt is finely crafted metal work. Maasai spears are works of art, as was other African weaponry so eagerly collected by colonists and displayed by Pitt Rivers in the museum at Oxford or in various empire exhibitions in Britain in the nineteenth century (Coombes 1994). These weapons were frightening to the middle-class audience and seen as symbols of African "savagery."

"Invisibility" of Pastoral Societies in the Archaeological Record

Because of the need for light, portable goods made from organic materials, there is a tendency for pastoralists to be elusive in the archaeological record. The problem was stated very clearly by Robertshaw

Figure 2.19. Camp of Chamanamas Tuareg, Tilemsi Valley, Mali (the tent in the background belongs to a cousin: separation is an indication of kinship distance).

(1978: 29), who mapped an abandoned Nama kraal on the Orange River: "Though the site was occupied within the last twenty years, the position of the dwelling hut or huts could only be estimated from the small amount of wood and matting that remained. As this will undoubtedly perish within a few more years no trace of any huts will survive for future archaeologists to excavate" (See fig. 2.12).

For most of the year, nomadic Tuareg camps consist of several skin tents with close relatives living right next to each other, and more distant kin within shouting distance (fig. 2.19). The tent flap is kept open during the day to allow the breeze to penetrate (fig. 2.20). During the height of the dry season, however, a brush hut (*paillote*) may be used, as these allow the wind through, so are much cooler (fig. 2.21). Those camps that are occupied for only a few weeks leave a minimum of residue. Bone, plastic, and a possible metal fragment were all that remained from the camp of the Kel Bardag II faction of the Chamanamas in the Tilemsi Valley after the people had moved (fig. 2.22). Wind blowing over the sandy substrate quickly obscured hearths and the dung left by tethered small stock and calves. The few informal poles used to tie the edges of the tent flap down might last a few more weeks, but within two months it would be virtually impossible to say anything about the camping site, even if it could be located.

Figure 2.20. Skin tent of Souleymane ag Kiyou, with flap raised during the day.

The problem relates to both the organic nature of the remains and to the length of time a site is occupied. The more mobile the herders, the less likely they are to leave traces of their passing. Thus, pastoralist archaeology is highly dependent on sites that have been repeatedly reoccupied. S. E. Smith (1980) has suggested that the layout

Figure 2.21. Hot, dry season camp of Chamanamas Tuareg, Tilemsi Valley, Mali, using straw cover. The calves are tied under the tree to encourage their mothers to return in the evening.

Figure 2.22. Remains of Kel Bardag II fraction camp in Tilemsi Valley, Mali, after several days departure.

of camps may vary with the season. For example, Tuareg will have a much tighter camp layout during the rains, since they use dunes that allow water to run off in order to prevent flooding. During the dry season, households are more dispersed across the landscape, although close relatives will have their tents next to each other (Smith 1992: figs. 6.1, 6.2). Pastoralists therefore may rely on microenvironments that are capable of supporting mobile groups and that have resources attractive enough to encourage people to come back to the same place year after year. The result is that we have only a restricted window on the annual transhumant cycle, seeing them, perhaps, for a limited seasonal use of the landscape. Examples of seasonal usage are fishing camps, such as Karkarichinkat (Smith 1975), or sealing camps, such as Kasteelberg (Smith 1993a). Fortuitous siltation events on a flood plain, however, such as that at Bloeddrift 23, might preserve some materials in situ and offer archaeologists a different window on pastoralist occupation (Smith et al. 2001). Also, special rainfall conditions, such as those that allowed the reoccupation of Ngamuriak (Robertshaw 1990; Marshall 1990a), could mean the buildup of deposits throughout the year.

Even if Childe (1936: 81) was correct when he said that "Tents need not even leave deep postholes to mark where they once stood," it is often deep postholes that demarcate the extent of hut layout. This has been demonstrated in various parts of the world, as by the tents of Pleistocene hunters in Ukraine (Klein 1973: fig. 25). Among the Nama, deeper postholes in a regular pattern may show where a hut once stood (fig. 2.12). Since this pattern is repeated on many sites, it can be used as a predictive model, at least for more recent camps. The Burchell (1822) drawing of a Khoesan camp (fig. 2.23) shows how, historically, camps were laid out, before present-day nuclear family camps became common.

Not all pastoralist equipment is organic. In the past, there have been cases where stone was used to form the base of organic structures and remained visible once the canopy disappeared, as in the Namib (Kinahan 1991); but in Africa, unlike the Near East, this is the exception rather than the rule. Similarly, ceramics and flaked stone tools have been widely used throughout Africa by herders. These can offer clues to the passing of herders, but in areas such as the Southwestern Cape of South Africa, where the plough may have been used subsequently, even these get obscured.

Archaeological "visibility" always creates problems for the prehistorian. In the case of pastoralist archaeology, we might say the situation is heightened and may lead to the question: "Is absence of evidence evidence of absence?" Is it possible that we could detect the former presence of pastoralists by the effect they had on other people in the environment, even though we cannot see the nomads themselves? This is a bit like detecting black holes by the effect they have on other stars. An example of this is the large ostrich eggshell beads showing up on later hunting sites in the coastal forelands of the Cape. The hunters of the Cape generally made beads with an outside diameter less than five millimeters, while beads on herder sites were greater than five millimeters (Smith et al 1991). Within the past 500 years, however, large beads started to show up alongside the smaller beads on hunter sites. In one case, the site of Voelvlei, of 81 ostrich eggshell beads found, only one measured less than five millimeters. Along with these were formally retouched stone tool hunting equipment and some colonial artifacts (radiocarbon dated at 400 years ago). An interpretation of this is that the hunters were

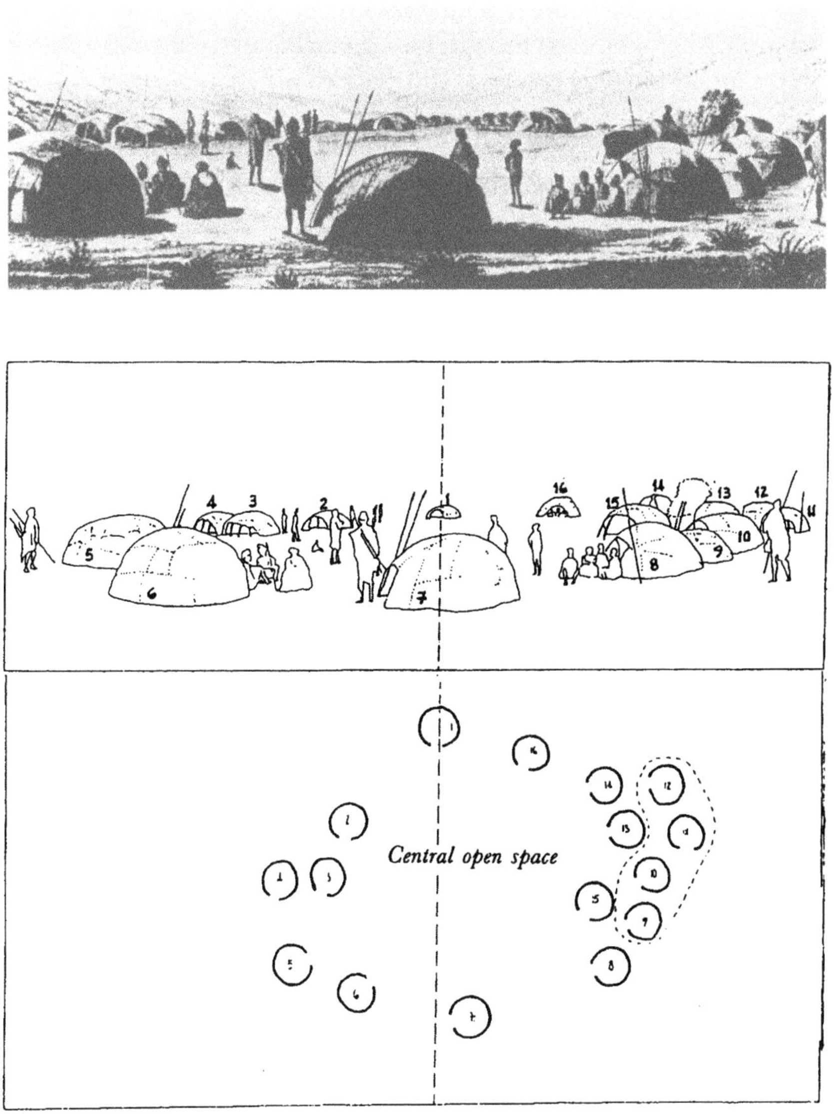

Figure 2.23. *Burchell's 1822 drawing of a Khoekhoe camp and an attempt to show it in plan form (Parkington and Mills 1991; reprinted by permission).*

using some of the cultural material of other people in their vicinity, including herders, even though we are unable to see the pastoralists in the archaeological record of this period.

The Archaeology of Domestication

A great deal of study has gone into trying to find the best criteria for identifying domestic animals in the archaeological record (Herre 1969; Bökönyi 1969; Davis 1987). The most obvious criterion involves the bones of the animals themselves. Our definition of domestication—"intentional genetic manipulation of plants and animals"—means humans were selecting those traits most beneficial to themselves. Often, however, there were unintentional results of intense animal/human interaction. One of these was that the animals became smaller with domestication.

Initial ideas on size decrease with domestication assumed that this was the result of intentional selection for smaller animals, but Davis (1987: 136) gives evidence that suggests that restrictions on nutrition may have had the most effect. Nutrition can affect fetal growth, and after birth the newborn has a reduced appetite, so never catches up with the size of larger conspecifics.

Reduction of the gene pool may also play a role. There is anecdotal evidence from farmers who say that restricting the breeding of wild game may result in animals of succeeding generations becoming smaller. This can happen quite fast, so that within the F3 generation, size changes can already be observed.

Davis also debates the possibility of environmental conditions at the end of the Pleistocene resulting in size decrease, noting that some animals did indeed become smaller (Davis 1987: 136). One control site in Pakistan, however, that showed a decrease in sheep and cattle sizes through time did not show a corresponding decrease in gazelles (Davis 1987: 139), suggesting that domestication was the factor conditioning the reduction in size.

Size reduction is quite dramatic in cattle. The data offered by Davis (1987: fig. 6.10) from Near Eastern sites show the astragali (heel bone) of wild cattle to range between 75 and 100 mm, and domestic cattle between 55 and 68 mm. Similarly, size indexes of sheep bones decrease with domestication in Neolithic times (Davis 1987: fig. 6.12).

Bökönyi (1969: 225) was convinced that transitional animals could be found in the archaeological record, and this would be the best evidence for local domestication. If the transition from wild to domestic is as rapid as suggested here, then there is a good chance that no transitional animals will be found. Even Bökönyi's own data (Bökönyi 1969: 224, table 1) show no overlap between wild and domesticated forms.

Other criteria for recognizing domestication can come from different ratios of age groups and sexes in wild to domestic populations; this may have a lot to do with animal husbandry practices and will be discussed below.

As with plants, the distribution of wild progenitors of domestic animals provides clues to where domestication could have taken place. Once animals or plants are moved to new environments, we can be sure that this was done with human intent.

An interesting dichotomy is offered by Bökönyi (1969: 227) between the animals kept by nomadic herders and those kept by settled peoples. Nomads have herd animals, which can be driven (cattle, goats, sheep, camels); villagers often have animals that can be confined (pigs, chickens). This separation is not exclusive, but the appearance of pigs on a site may tell us as much about what the people were doing as what the animals were doing.

The Archaeology of Animal Husbandry

How can we tell how people organized their herding strategies from the archaeological record? Seasonal variations, if they can be recognized in the faunal assemblages, are the usually the best clues to animal husbandry in the past. There are several ways in which an analysis of the bones of domestic animals reflects bias in the human selection of specific animals. The technique of husbandry would result in a domestic herd having different age and sex ratios from those of a wild population. In general, if production is to be maximized, then the herd need only include one or two breeding males, with the rest females up to the end of their reproductive age. A typical assemblage should consist of many young animal bones (young males), few reproductive age animals (mostly breeding females, but with a few males), and a number of older animals (the females beyond breeding age and older males).

However, as useful as these models are, they are not invariable. For example, in the Northern Hemisphere, these definitive ratios of mature to young animals may be altered, since an additional factor might be the decision to slaughter a herd in the fall in order to store the meat over winter, while keeping a small breeding herd alive for the next spring. This pattern has also been suggested for the husbanding of pigs in Iron Age Europe. However, at Trolsbjerg (Higham and Message 1969), people able to keep and feed their calves over the winter slaughtered an equal number of male and female cattle aged between 15 and 31 months, while 80 percent of those between 40 and 50 months were female, suggesting that not only meat but also milk was being used.

Analytical work by Balasse (1999) on prehistoric milking was expanded to look into seasonal variability and animal husbandry by shepherds in the Southwestern Cape (Balasse et al. 2002; 2003). Balasse was interested in testing Smith's model of seasonal transhumance (1992: 193–200). Smith suggested that cattle herders moved from pastures on the coast in winter to summer ones in the interior. This model was based, in part, on historic records that showed that early European mariners from the end of the fifteenth to the beginning of the seventeenth century met herders with stock at the coast if they arrived during April to September, but saw no domestic animals if they came in October or November. This model had an environmental component, since rainfall gradients drop off markedly during the summer months as one goes north, so that winter rains produce the best grazing at the coast. There are also differences in grazing across different geological substrates in the coastal forelands as one proceeds from the mountains in the east toward the coast, and it was thought that herders and their stock would have responded to these differences.

The analysis by Balasse involved oxygen isotope differences in tooth enamel over the growth period of a tooth during the year. By doing microsampling of the second and third molars, Balasse demonstrated that the $\delta^{18}O$ values shifted with season as a function of the vegetation available to the animal. She also measured the strontium values, as a reflection of the geological substrate in which the animals were feeding during the year. The result of this analysis was contrary to the Smith (1992) model, since it suggested that the animals were not being moved seasonally across different substrates, even though they may have grazed in different areas during their life.

The seasonal variation in the $\delta^{18}O$ values had an interesting spin-off. It became apparent that, even though all the teeth analyzed showed seasonal growth, the animals were not all in sync. Some animals grew at different times of the year than others. This suggested that there were two breeding seasons during the year. The question could then be posited whether ewes were producing two lambs each year, as suggested by Kolb (1731: 169), who said that the Khoekhoen let "the Rams (run) with the Ewes the Year round. By which Means their Herds encrease apace, their Ewes yielding them constantly Two Lambs in the year."

Current husbandry practices would suggest that breeding ewes twice a year would put tremendous strain on the animals and ultimately prove deleterious to their health. The alternative explanation is that, as with herders elsewhere in the world, there were two separate herds, bred at different times of the year, ensuring access to fresh milk production throughout the year, even though as Kolb (1731: 173) goes on to say, ewe's milk was drunk only by women (and presumably children).

Analysis of seasonality in seal mandibles by Woodborne (1996) suggested that during the later occupation of the Kasteelberg B site in the Western Cape there were two periods of occupation during the year. It is possible that these correspond to the two breeding periods for sheep. The isotope analyses suggest that sheep would stay in one area for most of the year. As this was contrary to the proposed model for prehistoric cattle pastoralism, it is highly probable that cattle, being bulk grazers, would have needed more pasture than sheep in an environment with low nutrient potential (Smith 1984). Herders needed to be more mobile and possibly more consistent in their residential mobility pattern to meet their cattle's needs. Therefore, the historically observed pattern of managing cattle seems likely to have been followed by prehistoric pastoralists in the Cape region. Unfortunately, we are now unable to do similar isotope analyses on cattle bones from the early historic period, since no pastoralist sites have been identified.

Discussion

Factors inherent in transhumance and hampering the accumulation of archaeological material are the size and duration of individual camps and the frequency of moves. As we have seen, the evidence they left behind of their camps was limited by the need to carry a light kit. The mobility of herding peoples was constrained not only by the nutritional needs of the herds or flocks, but also by the capability of pedestrian humans to haul the gear necessary to their maintenance. Stored foodstuffs might be necessary on the march, and heavier materials for hut construction would limit how much could be moved, unless their animals were used for draft. The logistical problem is always one of diminishing returns, since a large labor force, though it can carry more, also requires a larger store of food. Shepherds, lacking draft animals, would be severely restricted in their solution to moving camp and be required to leave many of their heaviest belongings behind or make rough shelters every time they moved camp. Once oxen came on the scene, mats could be rolled up and wooden frames of structures could be loaded on the animals to be taken to the next camp (fig. 2.2). Climatic patterns, pasturage availability, and on-the-march food and water sources are all factors determining not only the herdsmen regimen but also the types of evidence they left behind to be picked over by archaeologists, affecting their archaeological signature.

All these many contingencies are more than vexing problems getting between archaeologists and their observation of an extinct culture. These are elements intrusive upon the research process. The sparse nature of the herder's camps, as we have seen, obscures our ability to detect clearly and examine the lifeways in ancient encampments. The difficulty of discerning the earliest domesticated stock, or the problems inherent in interpreting the results of butchering practices and in identifying material culture indicative of domestication, impedes our ability to recapture the clues to the origins of herding regimes, a topic we turn to next.

3

The Advent of Domestication in the Old World

Perhaps, however, the earliest farming hamlets of all should be sought, not on the plain itself, but on the foot-hills and spurs overlooking it.

—V. Gordon Childe, *New Light on the Most Ancient East*

As the Earth warmed up, the glaciers of the Northern Hemisphere gradually began thawing after the glacial maximum 18,000 years ago. By 10,000 years ago, so much water had entered the ocean from these ice sheets that the sea level had risen by 130 m to its present level. The consequences were felt worldwide: corridors in the ice sheets of the New World opened up, large areas of the continental shelf were inundated, and many bodies of water were formed in Eurasia, all creating a new mosaic of ecological niches and causing people to reconfigure the patterns of their lives, altering what they believed about their relationship to the landscape; adapting to new foods, technologies, and increasing human populations; and settling places beyond their earlier range. Here and there, foragers who had long before engaged in a broad spectrum of food-getting strategies began experimenting with the control of the animals they stalked as game. Humans were taking the first steps toward food production.

Flannery (1969) looked closely at what was known of the human adaptation at the end of the Pleistocene in Europe and the Near East. He saw the shift to new foods as a crucial period in human cultural development, noting a wider exploitation of smaller food packages, including aquatic resources, such as mollusks, fish, and aquatic mammals (see Binford 1968), as well as birds, rabbits, and tortoises (see Stiner et al. 1999). There was also a focus on smaller ungulates, such as gazelles (Davis 1987). New hunting techniques, such as traps to capture gazelles, were developed to harvest these resources (Legge and Rowley-Conwy 1987), as were new technologies that allowed the processing of raw foodstuffs that were previously not available for human digestion, notably, grass seeds. This period in human development Flannery called the Broad Spectrum Wild Resource Utilization.

Not only were these new resources dependent on different procurement strategies from those utilized earlier, but they also resulted in new settlement patterns, encouraging new social formations intended to deal with denser, more sedentary populations, organized to manage an intensified extraction of resources and control access to and distribution of product. As population density increased in the most favorable habitats, the tendency was to stay longer and longer in one place, to protect and maintain access to resources against competition. Along with residential stability, people began to invest in more permanent settlements, constructing houses that could not only be occupied over long periods of time, but that also could house increasingly larger numbers of people. The ability to support larger communities ensured availability of the workforce required to produce the output necessary to feed and house the growing populations. The result was a conundrum where the formula for success decreed an amplifying equilibrium of an enlarging labor force and the means to sustain it. Over time, the social management within the long-established, simple kin-structured band formations grew somewhat more complex, investing authority in senior descent group stewards as agents of production and distribution.

None of this happened overnight. Nor did all people in the early days of the Holocene go down this path. Some remained foragers. Here and there is evidence that under environmental stress there were those who experimented with food production, only to abandon the extra effort required as conditions changed to accommodate the foraging lifeway once more. The advent of food-producing economies was never a forgone conclusion, but once the first steps were taken toward keeping game animals as stock and the social or other cultural changes were implemented, it would have been difficult to return, dismantling the cultural structure that now had these formative herders in its thrall. Considerable academic speculation and field investigations have gone into understanding this important period in the transition to domestication. As will be suggested, adaptations occurring in the Near East had affected cultural development over much of the Old World, as it was from this center that food production spread to Europe and North Africa.

Precursors to Food Production

In the Near East, early patterns of semi-permanent settlement were to be found on the coastal plain of the Levant and along rivers in the interior. As it became obvious that these villages were reliant on cereal grains for the bulk of their diet, it was assumed by Garrod (1932) that these were Mesolithic farmers. She even gave them the name Natufian, from her work in a cave in Wadi Natuf. Only later, analysis of the seeds demonstrated that the grains were wild forms of emmer wheat and barley and that they were still gathered rather than cultivated. As a result, Braidwood (1971) termed the Natufian gatherers "incipient agriculturalists," suggesting that though they were, presumably, experimenting with the management of plants and animals they were not true "food producers."

Like all hunter-foragers, the Natufians utilized a wide range of plant and animal foods, but they went to a lot of trouble in the gathering and preparation of cereal foods. In particular, they crafted specialized tools for use in the harvesting of the wild grains. The most characteristic and identifiable of these tools were sharp microlithic stone elements mounted in bone or wooden handles as sickles. Their function is palpable from the distinctive silica sheen or gloss on the blades that comes from cutting silica-rich grasses. The Natufians also used mortars and pestles for pounding the grains into flour. Though they may have engaged in an annual cycle that took them into the hinterland for some portion of the year, their investment in well-built architecture, such as stone buildings, enclosure walls, and bins for the storage of grain, suggests that they had long-term commitment to a semi-permanent residence in these nascent villages for at least part of the year. Indications of the first steps toward food production are scattered throughout the Near East and are summarized here as a prelude to their influence upon northeast Africa and beyond.

The Levant

The site that best demonstrates this is not the cave at Wadi Natuf, but the open-air site at Ain Mallaha (fig. 3.1), where three distinct levels

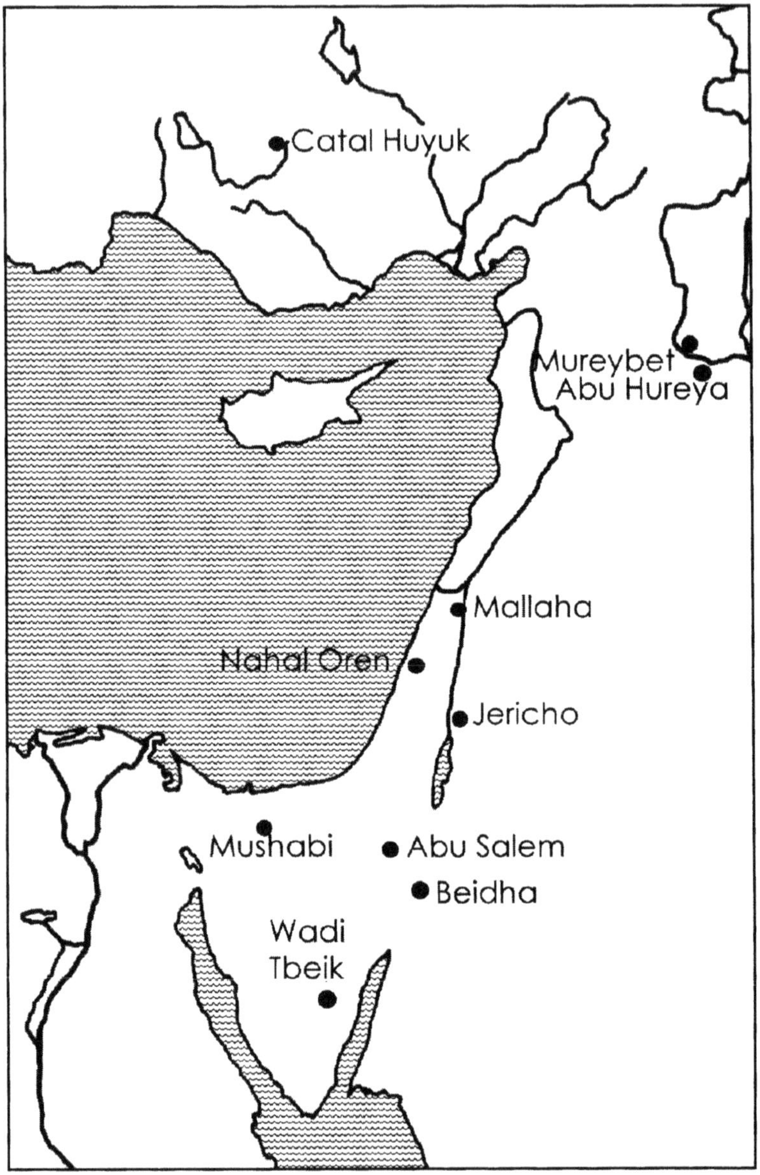

Figure 3.1. Map showing Near Eastern sites mentioned in text.

of occupation, dated from about 10,200 to 9,900 years ago, suggest residential use over a couple of hundred years (Valla 1981). It would appear that the site was originally chosen for its access to a nearby lake and spring. It is a big village covering a quarter hectare in area, with semi-subterranean, stone-founded circular houses ranging in size from seven to nine meters in diameter. Hearths were permanent and built into the well-constructed, stone-paved floors.

The sedentary nature of the village refuted earlier suggestions that only with "true" agriculture or food production were villages to be found. These, indeed, are some of the earliest villages known in the world, housing 200 to 300 people in 50 dwellings constructed close to one another and dug more than a meter into the ground with stone linings. The stone bases have survived, but the presumed reed superstructure for the roof has not. The entire community is constructed on a hillside, with the doors to the houses facing downhill.

The associated cultural material included some 50,000 pieces of flaked stone, 300 pieces of ground stone (grinders, mortars, pestles), as well as bone awls and needles. Finds of fishhooks and net sinkers attest to the collection of aquatic foods as important sources of animal protein. Inside one of the dwellings, the skeleton of a newborn infant was found buried under one of the stone slabs. Most of the other 200 burials were found outside the houses, associated with a variety of grave goods, mostly *Dentalium* shells or bone- and shell-bead necklaces and headdresses. Since not all the burials were primary inhumations, the inhabitants' mortuary practice may have included reburial.

In the interior, along the banks of the Euphrates River in Syria, the two Natufian sites of Abu Hureyra and Mureybet broadened our knowledge of these creative people even further. Mureybet is a mound, occupied from Natufian to Neolithic times, that is from between 10,200 and 8,600 years ago, is some 10 m high, and has an area of 250 by 125 m, located near an excellent source of fine brown chert used for tool making. The structures at the bottom of the sequence were all circular; only at the very top (in the later Neolithic levels) do rectangular dwellings appear (Cauvin 2000). The inhabitants utilized the river for catching catfish and collecting bivalves, but relied heavily on the wide range of mammals available on the flood plain (Maisels 1990).

At Abu Hureyra, a similar sequence of occupation and architecture was found to that at Mureybet, with round houses of the Natufian period dug into the parent basal soil and rectangular houses of the Neolithic (Moore et al. 2000). Of importance to us here is that the sequence at Abu Hureyra demonstrates the transition from the collection, or sowing, of wild grain to that of sown domestic cereals around 11,000 years ago. In addition, the site shows clear evidence of an intensive exploitation of wild gazelles as game throughout the Natufian until about 8,800 years ago, when the hunting of gazelles was replaced by the keeping of ovicaprids in the Neolithic. In this sequence, the use of domestic plants preceded the introduction of domestic animals by as much as 1,000 years (there is some uncertainty by how much, as the radiocarbon calibration curve around 11,000 years ago is very wide).

Researchers in the Levant have also recognized campsites on the coastal plain contemporary with the Natufian settlements, and it is supposed that the inhabitants practiced some form of seasonal transhumance. The settlement pattern associated with the Natufian seems to be one of semi-permanent occupation of the villages during the harvest part of the grain-growing cycle and temporary occupation of hunting camps in the hills and even beyond, in the desert. This model is intuitive in that it recognizes that it is probable that wild grasses would not support people for the entire year and that animal proteins other than fish would be available only if you went to find them in the hills or on the open plains of the interior.

While this is a useful model for explaining the residential and economic habits at the time, Perlès and Phillips (1991) show that there are other ways the archaeological data can be construed. They demonstrate that it is difficult to prove that it was the same groups occupying both the villages and the temporary camps. Gazelle hunters in the interior (Legge and Rowley-Conwy 1987) could just as easily have been specialized groups exchanging the product of the hunt for what the people on the coastal forelands had to offer. They suggest the possibility of interaction between groups, a prototype for the relationship between Solubba hunters and Bedouin herders that existed into the twentieth century in this same area (Dickson 1951; Jabbur 1995).

Zagros Mountains

Another area of importance to observing the progression toward food production is the Zagros Mountains area of Kurdistan. The terrain here is in sharp contrast to the coastal hills of the Levant, since elevations are much higher (above 400 m) with water supplied by only a few rivers. While many of the plants and animals found in the Levant also could be collected here, the densities and distribution were different. This hilly area is better suited to sheep and goats than to gazelles or cattle. Wheat and barley were available, though not in the thick stands found in the Levant.

The area best known for the preagricultural phase of occupation is Shanidar in Iraqi Kurdistan. Shanidar has long been known as a Mousterian site, but the upper levels, dated to between 11,000 and 10,500 years ago, are termed "Proto-Neolithic." But even better information from this period comes from the nearby Zawi Chemi Shanidar site. This site is relatively large, comprising an area some 60 ha, 112 sq m of which have been excavated to a depth of two meters. The excavation has exposed two stratigraphic levels, the lower of which contains remnants of a Proto-Neolithic village. The architecture is not nearly as well defined as that in the Levantine Natufian, but rough circular walls, four meters in diameter, were found.

The artifacts recovered—many upper and lower grindstones—suggest the inhabitants' reliance on plant foods. There were many bone tools, and the flaked stone industry was mostly of microliths, but silica sheen is rare. The plants exploited included wheat, legumes, acorns, and pistachio nuts. Faunal remains at the site consisted of red and fallow deer, sheep, goats, cattle, wolves (for skins?), and small rodents. These animals were probably all wild, although the excavators discuss the fact that the high proportion of young sheep remains may indicate either selective hunting or some control over the animals. However, there were no morphological changes that differentiate them from wild species.

Further southeast, in Iran, a series of sites has been excavated that show different seasonal use of the environment by preagricultural people. Karim Shahir is a hilltop site on a terrace above a small river at 800 m elevation. It produced a single shallow occupation of a pavement floor made of small stones, but no other architectural features.

Thirty thousand pieces of flaked stone were recovered, including some with silica gloss, as were grinding stones. Decorative items included stone rings, pendants, and two clay zoomorphic pieces, the earliest representational art from the Near East. The fauna was all wild: ovicaprids, cattle, wild asses, and wolves.

Contemporary with Karim Shahir, but at a lower elevation of 300 m, is the site of Tell M'lefaat, with round semi-subterranean dwellings with well-marked floors and some four meters in diameter and a meter below the surface. The flaked stone industry was the same as at Karim Shahir, though there were more grindstones at Tell M'lefaat.

At 1,400 m elevation is the site of Tepe Asiab, again culturally similar to Karim Shahir, but the one dwelling excavated was of semi-subterranean type, 10 m in diameter. The fauna here suggest that goats might have been kept penned, close to humans. As this elevation is snow covered in winter, this was probably a seasonal camp.

The settlement pattern inherent in the Zagros evidence suggests the occasional use of settlements or camps at different elevations as part of seasonal transhumance (nomadic movement). This suggests that the occupants moved from lower elevations in winter, where wild cereals were harvested and processed, to the higher elevations in summer to hunt. The availability of herd animals, such as goats and sheep, hunted as game, may have resulted in some control over these animals, perpetuating old habits at a lower cost. In this scenario, villages, once reoccupied seasonally after the conclusion of the hunt, could with the keeping of livestock be inhabited on a more permanent basis, encouraging greater sedentarization at the lower altitudes.

The Negev and Sinai

A separate industry, called Harifian, after the Har Harif Plateau, is recognized in the southern part of the Levant, in the drier areas of the Negev and Sinai. The excavator of many of the sites, Goring-Morris (1991), sees the occupants as full-time hunter-foragers on the periphery of formative agricultural economies to the north. Dated to between 10,500 and 10,000 years ago, this industry is a contemporary of the Natufian sites, already discussed. Some Harifian sites, for example, Abu Salem, have Pre-Pottery Neolithic B occupations on top, suggesting, if not an autochthonous transition from "incipient" behaviors to ones more common to food producers, an aptitude toward adaptation.

Harifian architecture has a great deal in common with Natufian. Both have semisubterranean dwellings, although the hearths are not as formal on Harifian sites. They also used shallow trash pits for their rubbish. The cultural overlap with the Natufian in other aspects of the material culture, such as lithic typologies and grinding equipment, begs the question: Should the Harifian be seen as a "distinctive regional" group or an "integral facies of the Natufian entity"? (Goring-Morris 1991: 210).

The game faunal remains consist for the most part of Dorcas gazelle, with wild sheep, ibex, wild ass, and the occasional wild cattle bone. Smaller animals include hares and foxes. Exotic raw materials filtered through to Harifian sites, including small quantities of Anatolian obsidian, suggesting participation in some kind of interaction sphere. Since cereals are much sparser in this region than further north, there would have been a greater reliance on hunting. This economic scenario continues into the later Pre-Pottery Neolithic B, when full-scale food production became available. Abandoned during a serious desiccation, the Harifian sites were resettled sometime between 9,300 and 9,000 years ago, by people associated with this late phase of the Pre-Pottery Neolithic (Bar-Yosef and Phillips 1977: 244; Mintz and Ben-Ami 1977: 243–44).

These settlements and their contents spread across the Near East suggest a transhumance pattern, perhaps a continuation of well-known foraging habits, in which the participants occupied camps with sufficient seasonal resources to be worth the effort of investing in the construction of permanent facilities. The progression toward full-time dependence on the produce of the garden and the stock enclosure had begun.

The Transition to Food Production

V. Gordon Childe (1936) recognized the importance of food production in human development, and since it was tied to the beginnings of pottery making, domestication was easily subsumed into the "stage" of development known as the Neolithic (New Stone Age). Childe even went further and coined the phrase "Neolithic Revolution," because so many rapid changes of a social and economic nature were inherent in the adoption of domestic plants and animals.

By the 1950s, Braidwood, on a combination of the distribution of wild progenitors of domestic plants and animals and the archaeological record, had defined the area of the earliest domestication as the coastal forelands of the Levant around through northern Syria to the Zagros Mountains of Iran, an area previously called the "Fertile Crescent" by Breasted (1916), referring to the grassland area separating settled agriculturalists from nomadic herders.

In 1968, Lewis Binford suggested that it was not in the most productive areas that food production was first practiced. His idea was that experimentation occurred among groups who were forced, by population pressure, to use the more marginal environments. Support for this idea came from the work of Braidwood et al. (1960) in the Zagros Mountains, followed shortly by Hole et al. (1969). The latter suggested that the earliest domestication was to be found in the hilly areas at Ali Kosh.

The keys to identifying early plant domestication are morphological changes in the way seed attaches to the stem of the plant, and possibly size, as well as the intentional movement of plants from where they would have grown naturally to new habitats.

As we have seen, while experimentation may well have taken place in the hills, the earliest record of cereal domestication so far recognized has been on the river banks at Abu Hureyra. Thus it is probable that existing interaction spheres spread the idea of people selecting, cultivating, and transferring economic grains into new areas over a large part of the Fertile Crescent.

Moore et al. (2000: 491–92) suggest changes in climate during the Younger Dryas was impetus for the people at Abu Hureyra to adopt agriculture if they wished to stay together as a community. However, not everyone is content to see climatic change as the prime mover in agricultural origins. Cauvin (2000: 66) suggests that changes took place as a result of a developmental process within the kind of sedentary preagricultural communities we have just been examining. It is suggested that a new way of life was emerging. This new emergent society is manifest in the archaeological record, as the beginning of new symbolic systems in the form of mobile art seems to indicate new social conditions. The political form of these societies was still rudimentary, since we have no evidence of social differentiation. Certainly, the markers of status in the grave goods all appear to be evenly distributed, and the similarity in house types suggests the lack of social hierarchies in the Natufian, or even in the early Neolithic at Abu Hureyra (Moore et al. 2000: 505).

Later Natufian Industries

After 10,000 years ago, many Natufian sites were abandoned, while others, probably due to their favorable locations, continued to be occupied. These later sites have become known as the Proto-Neolithic, or Pre-Pottery Neolithic A. However, their similarities to the characteristics of the preceding Natufian make it reasonable to think of them as a later form of it. Here we encounter the problems of pinpointing the exact beginnings of food production as a major characteristic of the Neolithic.

The average village grew in size, with more substantial architecture and varieties of building techniques. They are often built on artificial terraces. One such site is that of Nahal Oren, built on a terrace in front of a cave in a valley leading to the coastal plain from Mt. Carmel. The site had already been occupied since Upper Paleolithic times before the Natufians made use of it, since it had three springs close by. There are 14 houses some 9–15 m in diameter, on four terraces built against the steep slope. The floor is of pounded earth with a central, stone-lined hearth. Although the stone industry is similar to that of the Natufian, microliths are rare and were probably replaced by a new equivalent tool, the flaked arrowhead.

Another important site of this period is Jericho. The lower levels are Natufian, but not very substantial. The upper Pre-Pottery Neolithic A levels have massive architectural construction, resulting in an impressive site covering four hectares that probably had a population of greater than 2,000 people. Like many other sites, Jericho was located close to plenty of permanent water. In addition, the site may well have been on a crossroads in trade, as a range of exotic items and materials have been found. These include salt, bitumen, and sulfur from the Dead Sea, turquoise from Sinai, cowries from the Red Sea, and obsidian and greenstones from Turkey. Such early exchange activities may have been the reason for Jericho's size and apparent prosperity, although no direct evidence has been found of specialist traders and the quantities moving through the site were quite modest.

The impressive architecture included a stone defensive wall 1.9 m thick, over 2 m high, and probably 700 m in circumference, surrounded by an 8.5 m wide ditch, dug over 2 m into the bedrock. In addition, there was a stone tower over 8 m high, with an enclosed staircase leading down through the center of the tower to a passage at the base.

We can surmise that, as settlements grew in size and population, there would have developed the need for levels of authority greater than those implicit in family or band counsel leadership, both to mediate disputes and to control the use and distribution of arable land. Design and organization of the labor that went into construction, such as the walls and tower at Jericho, hint at new social formations taking place in the Neolithic.

An interesting feature of Jericho was its way of dealing with the dead. As in other settlements, the bodies were buried within the settlement, but the skulls were removed, and a plaster molding on the outside was used to replace the flesh, possibly even to resemble the face of the dead person. The skull was then ritually buried with other skulls. Perhaps this is one more indication of the rise of leadership, using ritual as confirmation of authority.

Another site in the Levant showing early farming societies is that of Beidha in southern Jordan. The site was first occupied about 9,500 years ago by Natufians, and later continued until 8,000 years ago by people who had a simple form of agriculture, although hunting was still practiced. There were six levels of house construction above the Natufian levels: Levels 6 and 5 had circular structures, while Levels 4 and above showed rectangular houses. The buildings in the top levels may even have had an upper story.

Although no pottery was found, clay objects were part of the cultural inventory. Imported materials included shell for beads from the Mediterranean or Red Sea and a few pieces of Turkish obsidian (from 900 km away). Many bones of young domestic goats were found, quite different from the adult skeletons of the hunted gazelles. The people also hunted wild ibex and cattle. Impressions of grains in the clay walls of the houses were of barley and a transitional form of wheat. Other plant foods included pistachio nuts and acorns, as well as legumes.

Analysis of the changes in species composition and richness by Horwitz (1996) shows that during Pre-Pottery Neolithic A times there was a wide faunal diversity that included small mammals, reptiles, amphibians, birds, and fish. By mid–Pre-Pottery Neolithic B times, there was considerable reduction in species richness and higher percentages of caprines, although there were no obvious morphological changes to indicate goat domestication. It is only in the late Pre-Pottery Neolithic B that the focus on these animals can be suggested as indicating domestication or introduction into southern Levant.

From the Zagros area, we have evidence of fully agricultural people beginning about 9,500 years ago. The site of Ali Kosh in the Deh Luran Plain of Khuzistan, a marginal habitat zone of Iran where domesticates could survive but not grow in any great abundance without human intervention, is 135 m in diameter. The seven-meter deep cultural stratigraphy produced three successive phases over a period of almost 2,000 years.

The bottom unit has been called the Bus Mordeh Phase and is dated between 9,500 and 8,700 years ago. It produced evidence of some crude rectangular houses of mud brick. The subsistence was a combination of wild and domestic foods, such as wild legumes and local grains; however, a small percentage of the seeds were barley and emmer wheat, neither of which is native to this area. The animal remains included goats (probably herded, since their natural habitat would have been in the mountains and not on the plain), a small number of sheep, as well as wild gazelle. Fishing was also practiced in the river. The cultural material from this unit included stone pestles, flaked-stone tools, bone tools, and personal ornaments of shell and bone.

The occupation at this time may have been seasonal, following the previous pattern of being at lower altitude to harvest plant foods in winter–spring, then moving up into the mountains in summer to find pasture for the animals.

The middle unit, called Ali Kosh Phase (between 8,700 and 8,000 years ago), was more substantial than what was found previously. The larger and better-constructed buildings suggest a more settled community with greater dependence on domesticated resources. Wheat and barley provided a greater part of the diet, with a concomitant reduction in wild legumes. Domestic goats were the most common animal represented in the faunal assemblage, although gazelles were still hunted. The cultural material included many sickle blades, containers such as stone bowls, and judging from impressions in clay walls of the houses, basketry. Clay figurines, especially of goats, were also found. There was evidence of exotic raw materials: shells from the Persian Gulf, copper from central Iran, turquoise from northeastern Iran, and obsidian from Turkey. A burial showed careful treatment of the corpse, which was covered in red ochre, wrapped in a mat, and buried with personal items below the house floor.

The final unit, Mohammed Jaffer Phase (between 8,000 and 7,600 years ago), showed even more improved building techniques, along with the introduction of pottery. The food base was the same as the previous phase, but as quantities seem to have dropped, this led the excavators (Hole et al. 1969) to suggest that resources were diminishing, and this may have been the reason for abandonment of the site.

At Tepe Sabz, 16 km from Ali Kosh, another site was located that showed a continuation of the Ali Kosh sequence. The bottom was dated to 7,600 years ago and may have been where the people went when Ali Kosh was abandoned. Occupation continued up to 6,000 years ago at this small village, by people who used irrigation for their agriculture and herded cattle, sheep, and goats. This is one of about 40 sites known from this period in the area, suggesting that a fairly dense population was beginning to appear on the edge of the alluvial plain.

Ideas of early domestication were easily transferred from Mesopotamia northward to eastern Anatolia. On a tributary of the

Tigris, at Hallan Çemi, hunters in sedentary villages had already appeared by 10,600 years ago (Rosenberg 1994). It is possible that these became established as a result of a widening of the trade in obsidian. The fertile Anatolian Plain further west became an obvious region for colonization by agriculturalists, and before 9,000 years ago domestic grains were to be found at Çayönü. The first domestic sheep and goats were to be found between 9,000 and 8,500 years ago, and cattle probably appeared about 8,000 years ago in south-central Anatolia. Agriculture and the obsidian trade laid the groundwork for further development and growth of early urbanism that was to be seen by 7,000 years ago at Çatal Hüyük. It is at this site that an early expression of a cattle cult was to be found in the form of shrines with sculpted ox heads (Mellaart 1975).

Advanced Farming Villages in Mesopotamia

The expansion out onto the alluvial plain more than 7,000 years ago was a function of improved effectiveness of domesticates and technological innovation, such as pottery. This meant a broader economic base that stimulated greater population growth. The size of the villages did not increase, there were just more of them, resulting from the need to colonize new areas. The lower elevations were hotter and drier, so the expansion required the selection of plants and animals that could take heat and aridity. The initial growth was into those areas where rainfall occurred, although not always reliably. Further expansion could only occur with the development of artificial irrigation systems. One of the first such areas to be colonized was the northern edge of the Mesopotamian Plain, an area of undulating hills cut by rivers but with an annual rainfall of only 200 mm, far less than needed for rainfall-dependent agriculture.

The transition to irrigation agriculture can be seen in several sites on the plain. Hassuna, dated to around 8,000 years ago, is a 200 × 150 m mound where the lowest levels show just temporary, seasonally occupied campsites with no house structures. The later levels gave evidence of settled agricultural communities. Similarly, the earliest occupation of Umm Dabaghiyah, around 8,000 years ago, showed small curved structures (possibly storage bins) within small farming villages. Immediately above these were substantial buildings arranged around large courtyards. The small rooms of the houses had thickly plastered walls painted on the inside with hunting scenes. The inhabitants' food consisted of cultivated wheat and barley, as well as domesticated sheep, goats, cattle, and pigs. Wild gazelles and asses were hunted. All the worked stone, primarily obsidian and flint, had to be imported: the value of this stone to these people is implicit in the fact that each piece was used and none was wasted. Other items of material culture included clay figurines, spindle whorls (used in spinning fibers), polished axes, bone tools, and both fine and coarse ceramics.

Throughout the Fertile Crescent, people were pushing the edges of technology and the environment: practicing transhumance from winter to summer camps; opening up new agricultural areas with irrigation; using storage bins for holding the produce of the fields; and because people were spending more and more time in one place, finding the leisure time to build fine houses (where heavy grindstones could be left for future use) and to create increasing amounts of mobile art. The art may be seen as a direct reflection of more than an aesthetic; it also reflected growing belief systems centered around domestic plants and animals (Cauvin 2000). There was also the labor to erect village walls, as at Jericho, or permanent hunting traps out in the desert. This labor would increasingly become important in digging irrigation canals as settlements grew across the Mesopotamian Plain.

The creation of facilities was a way of storing the group's effort and productivity. This set the stage for the development of food production (another way of efficiently storing labor), potentially exempting some people from agricultural work so they could become full-time craft specialists. It is not coincidental that pyrotechnics (ceramics, metallurgy, glass making) are all descendants of the use of clay for building and experiments with clay molding. Facilities such as ovens, kilns, or furnaces had to be developed, and this could only have occurred with increased sedentarization.

Environmental Conditions in the Early Holocene in the Eastern Mediterranean

Since the eastern Mediterranean and northeast Africa are areas with limited rainfall, any small changes in precipitation are bound to affect vegetation, and so human responses. Goodfriend (1991) has attempted to model rainfall patterns in this area using data recognized by Rindsberger et al. (1983), who were able to measure the isotopic composition of rainwater. As a result of their analyses, Rindsberger et al. have been able to show the isotopic differences of the three rainfall systems that affect the eastern Mediterranean. The most common rainfall regime produces rains that come from air masses originating in the North Atlantic and that pass west of the European Alps and travel southeastward to drop their rain in the Mediterranean basin. The rain from these fronts has enriched $\delta^{18}O$ values compared with the modern coastal average. The second system also originates in the North Atlantic, but passes east of the Alps, down to the Mediterranean. These rains have slightly depleted $\delta^{18}O$ values compared with the present coastal average.

The third system, and the least common, is one that comes from northeastern Europe, passing southward to the Mediterranean before turning eastward across Libya and Egypt, then northeast to the Levant. These rains are very depleted in $\delta^{18}O$ values, as "the result of intense evaporation over the Mediterranean and/or rainout effects along North Africa" (Goodfriend 1991: 422). Goodfriend, in turn, measured the $\delta^{18}O$ isotopes contained in land snails from the Negev, dated to the period between 10,000 and 3,500 years ago, as well as modern snails for comparison. He sees the $\delta^{18}O$ readings from the snails as a key to indicating the source and movement of air masses in the eastern Mediterranean in the past.

On the basis of his analysis, Goodfriend (1991: fig. 2) demonstrates a major depletion event beginning before 8,000 years ago and having its peak around 6,000 years ago. This he interprets as the result of the third Rindsberger rainfall system, which would have affected both the Levant and northeast Africa. The result of these rains was to allow the boundary between C_4 (tropical) plants to move northward at the expense of the more temperate C_3 plants. The modern boundary, as a result of the retreat of the C_4 vegetation, was attained only after 6,000 years ago. The rains at the height of the depletion event (between 7,000 and 6,500 years ago) were intense and can be correlated with both wadi runoff and the high level of the Dead Sea (120 m above the present level).

Evidence for climatic variation is also available from the Western Desert of Egypt (Schild and Wendorf 2001). Geomorphological data show a series of humid/arid events during the Early to Mid-Holocene that can perhaps be correlated with Goodfriend's rainfall sequence. As can be seen in table 3.1, the period between 9,800 and 8,200 years ago was generally wet, with a couple of dry intervals before and after the El Adam Humid Phase. A relatively long dry interval, undated but sometime between 8,200 and 7,700 years ago (the post-El Ghorab Arid Phase), was followed by a return to mainly wet periods, again with some dry intervals. The latter wet periods (between 7,700 and 5,800 years ago) would conform to Goodfriend's depleted $\delta^{18}O$ rainfall event. Schild and Wendorf (2001: 47) suggest the Middle Neolithic Humid Interphase (from 7,100 to 6,600 years ago) saw rains resulting in surface washes and a locally high water table. If the Goodfriend and Schild/Wendorf data are indeed correlated and the rainfall regime in the Al Jerar/Middle Neolithic Humid Phases were not the result of monsoonal influences, then the rains

Table 3.1. Geochronology of Nabta Playa

Phase	Time Period
Final Neolithic Humid Interphase	5700–5000 BP
Post-Late Neolithic Arid Phase	5800 BP
Late Neolithic Humid Phase	6550–5800 BP
Post-Middle Neolithic Arid Phase	6600–6550 BP
Middle Neolithic Humid Interphase	7100–6600 BP
Post-Al Jerar Arid Phase	7300–7100 BP
El Nabta/Al Jerar Humid Interphase	8050–7300 BP
Post-El Ghorab Arid Phase	8190 BP
El Ghorab Humid Interphase	8400–8200 BP
Post-El Adam Arid Phase	8560 BP
El Adam Humid Interphase	9500–8850 BP
Pre-El Adam Arid Phase	
Pre-El Adam Humid Interphase	

Source: Schild and Wendorf (2001).

penetrated deep into the Egyptian Desert, some 900 km south of the Mediterranean coast.

The Expansion of Domesticates Out of the Near East

As we have seen, agriculture with domesticated cereals and animals was well established in the Near East and Anatolia by Pre-Pottery Neolithic B times (between 9,300 and 8,000 years ago). From the rainfall data, we can infer that rainfall regimes of the eastern Mediterranean were, for the most part, the result of Rindsberger systems (1) and (2), but the establishment of C_3 vegetation in the northern Negev 10,000 to 8,000 years ago indicates rainfall significantly higher than present (Goodfriend 1991: 423). The change in rainfall patterns toward Rindsberger et al. system (3), with intense, but less equably spread rains, may have put some pressure on farming communities during the subsequent Pottery Neolithic period and so may have precipitated a need to find new areas for agriculture. The earliest occupation of Greece by food producers is dated to 7,500 years ago (Gkiasta et al. 2003), and the radiocarbon dates for the Neolithic get progressively younger as domestication spreads westward.

The geomorphological evidence from the Western Desert of Egypt between 7,700 and 7,200 years ago suggests that this was a wetter period, and this period has been named the El Nabta/Al Jerar Humid Interphase (table 3.1). By around 7,800 years ago, the first ovicaprids (presumably from the Near East) were to be found in Africa in the Al Jerar "Neolithic" of Nabta Playa (Gautier 2001: table 23.1).

If, indeed, conditions were changing in the Levant and herders were looking for new pasture territories, then northeast Africa would have been an obvious direction to head. Sinai of Egypt is a natural land bridge between Asia and Africa. Although the archaeological information coming out of Sinai has been limited, there should be no doubt that contact between the two continents probably existed from time immemorial. Modern humans probably used this route over 100,000 years ago, but it would be wrong to assume that it was only a one-way flow. Recent DNA studies suggest that there might even have been a back migration to Africa from Asia (Cruciani et al. 2002).

Sinai today is a desert with an annual rainfall of less than 100 mm. The area, however, is not uniform, with mountains in the interior and special microenvironmental conditions that include higher rainfall. Even today, the coastal strip connecting the Nile Delta of Egypt with Gaza has a distinctly Mediterranean flora, responding to rains that can penetrate about 40 km inland. Grasses dominate the flora of the coastal sands of Gaza, although these are currently heavily grazed (Danin 1983). Assuming these conditions pertained in the past, there would have been a convenient corridor for movement of domestic stock. In addition, there are other salty plants that, although usually ignored by grazing stock, nonetheless contain trace minerals that the animals need to prevent metabolic disorders, as well as against intestinal parasites carried by the annual grasses favored by the flocks (Bailey and Danin 1981). Bedouin botanical knowledge and pharmacopoeia are so thorough that almost every plant in Sinai has some use, whether it be grazing, medicines, or fibers for construction. Bailey and Danin (1981: 146) also note that over half the place-names in Sinai, including those for battle sites, are taken from some botanical landmark, indicating a wider identity with the landscape, as places get built into stories. This knowledge could only have been developed over centuries, if not millennia, and serves to support the idea that this dry area was never a barrier to pastoral use or passage.

As noted above, the equivalent of the Natufian in Sinai has been called "Harifian" (Goring-Morris 1991). There appears to be little evidence of early Neolithic sites (Pre-Pottery Neolithic A) in the desert; however, after 9,300 years ago, there are indications of hunters in the area (Mintz and Ben-Ami 1977) using distinctive Pre-Pottery Neolithic B arrowheads (Bar-Yosef 1981). At Wadi Tbeiq (Tubaiq), Bar-Yosef (1981) reported circular Pre-Pottery Neolithic B structures partially dug into the weathered bedrock, then built up of upright sandstone slabs, 2.5–3.5 m in diameter. The sites contained bone, seashells, and a lithic industry with large amounts of débitage. No storage bins were found, although a few grinding stones indicate some grain processing was probably done. By contrast, the site of Urjat el-Mehed (Igrat al-Mihad), near St Catherine's Monastery, had many more grindstones and complete granaries. It also had a stone industry that included serrated blades, although Rosen (1988: 500) says there has been an almost total absence of sickle blades in southern lithic assemblages. The faunal assemblage included goats (probably wild ibex), gazelles, fish, and wild donkey (Bar-Yosef 1981). These seem to have been hunters who harvested wild cereals.

If ovicaprids from the Near East were already in northeast Africa during Al Jerar Neolithic times, around 7,700 years ago, how did they get there? Rosen (1988: 500) states: "The preponderance of domesticates, especially goat and sheep, in contemporary sites in central and northern Israel stands in marked contrast to the southern picture. Of further note is the almost total absence of sickle blades in the southern lithic assemblages, in spite of the presence of numerous grinding stones." There are some similarities between the sites in southern Sinai and the sites in the Western Desert of Egypt at Nabta Playa. In both areas, there are semi-subterranean huts, presumably at one time with a skin tent superstructure and storage pits (Bar-Yosef 1981; Wendorf and Schild et al. 2001), a form of dwelling still seen in the Sahara today (Nicolaisen 1963: 331), although contemporary dwellings have a mud-brick structure above ground.

If we compare the identifiable specimens of ovicaprids from Nabta Playa in the Al Jerar Neolithic period with the numbers from later in the Middle and Late Neolithic (Gautier 2001: table 23.1), we see there is a fourfold to fifteenfold increase (depending on the sites) in the later periods. We might interpret this as reflecting the small numbers of animals brought in by the initial immigrant populations as they attempted to establish themselves in Africa. The archaeological visibility of the earliest entry would therefore not only be low, but also might explain why no sites with domesticates are to be found in the Sinai corridor between the Levant and Egypt in early Pottery Neolithic times. Another problem is the siltation effect in the Nile Delta, from annual flooding of the river, resulting in meters of deposit burying earlier sites that may have been occupied by immigrant herders.

There is a possible later connection with the Levant. The Pottery Neolithic site of Qatif in the Gaza Strip produced cattle and ovicaprid bones, dated to about 7,000 years ago (Oren and Gilead 1981; Epstein 1984). The stone tools from Qatif include flaked adzes with lateral polish that show up in the later pastoral sites in the Sahara and Nile Valley around Khartoum. Qatif is part of a coastal occupation of the southern Levant, where other sites, including Nizzanim, Ashqelon, Ziqim, and Giv'at Haparsa, have been recognized (Yeivin and Olami 1979) that would be contemporaneous with the Middle and Later Neolithic Periods in the Western Desert of Egypt.

4

Early Domesticated Animals in North Africa

It's bad to predict the weather.
Who can talk to the rain?

—Dodoth saying (from E. M. Thomas, *Warrior Herdsmen*)

As will become clear with succeeding chapters, the first African animal domesticates were to be found in North Africa, and the dates become increasingly later the further south one goes through East Africa and on to southern Africa. Based on the radiocarbon dates alone, we can be confident that herding societies and their domestic stock moved progressively southward over time.

Precursors to Domesticated Animals in North Africa

During the early Holocene, environmental conditions were such that freshwater lakes developed that were capable of supporting an aquatic fauna that included hippo, crocodile, and large catfish. The evidence for these lakes are balks of diatomites some meters thick found in depressions in the central Sahara, such as those from near Adrar Bous, Niger (figs. 4.1, 4.2, 4.3; Servant and Servant-Vildary 1980; Williams et al. 1987; Roset et al. 1990). Dates for these lakes are well attested between 9,600 and 8,500 years ago. Cultural material found associated with the diatomites are bone harpoons, microlithic stone tools, and the earliest pottery known from Africa or the Near East. This pottery, first described by Arkell (1949) from the confluence of the Blue and White Niles at Khartoum, has been called "wavy line" and "dotted wavy-line." Mohammed-Ali and Khabir (2003)

Figure 4.1. Tin Ouaffadene, 25 km southeast of Adrar Bous, Ténéré Desert, Niger, showing diatomite formation at foot of hill.

Figure 4.2. Diatomite balk at Tin Ouaffadene, with dead Addax below.

Figure 4.3. Catfish skeleton from the diatomites at Tin Ouaffadene.

have analyzed the distribution and chronology of these wares and show that the "dotted wavy-line" occurred over a huge area from the Nile to Niger during the early Holocene, but the "wavy-line" endured for much longer.

The ceramic microlithic industry at Adrar Bous (fig. 4.4) was recognized during work under J. D. Clark in 1970 (Clark et al. 1973; Clark et al. 2004). This cultural entity was given a local name, "Kiffian," after one of the locations at Adrar n'Kiffi (hill of the fish), an outlier at the south end of Adrar Bous, where microliths (fig. 4.5), bone harpoons (fig. 4.6), bone points (fig. 4.7), and aquatic fauna were found in situ. There is some debate over the definition of what the Kiffian comprises, due to the problem of possible admixture of surface collections. Subsequent to the work at Adrar Bous, Roset (1983; 1987) visited the area and was able to date the ceramic occupation at another location, which had been named "Diatomite 1" but Roset renamed Adrar Bous 10, to between 9,030 and 9,130 years ago. Roset also published his work at Temet on the northeastern edge of

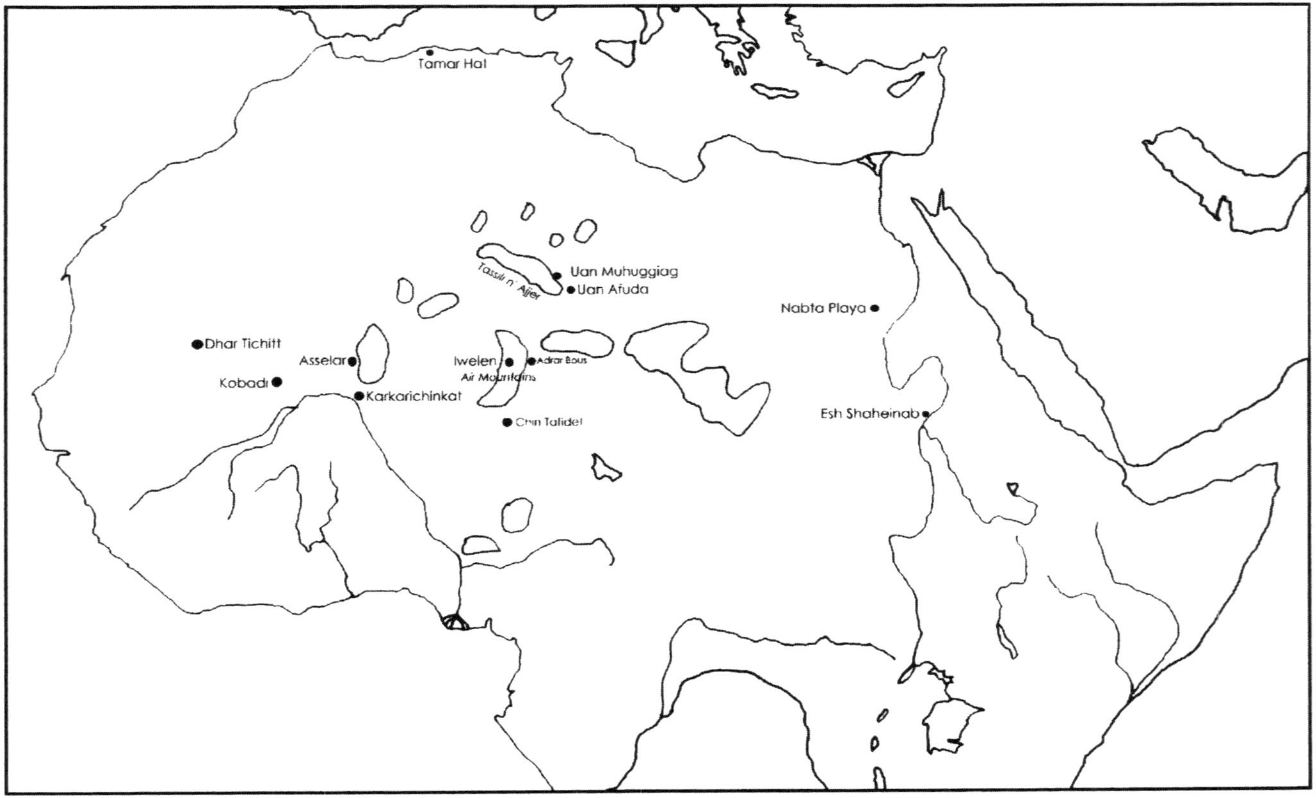

Figure 4.4. Map showing North African sites mentioned in text.

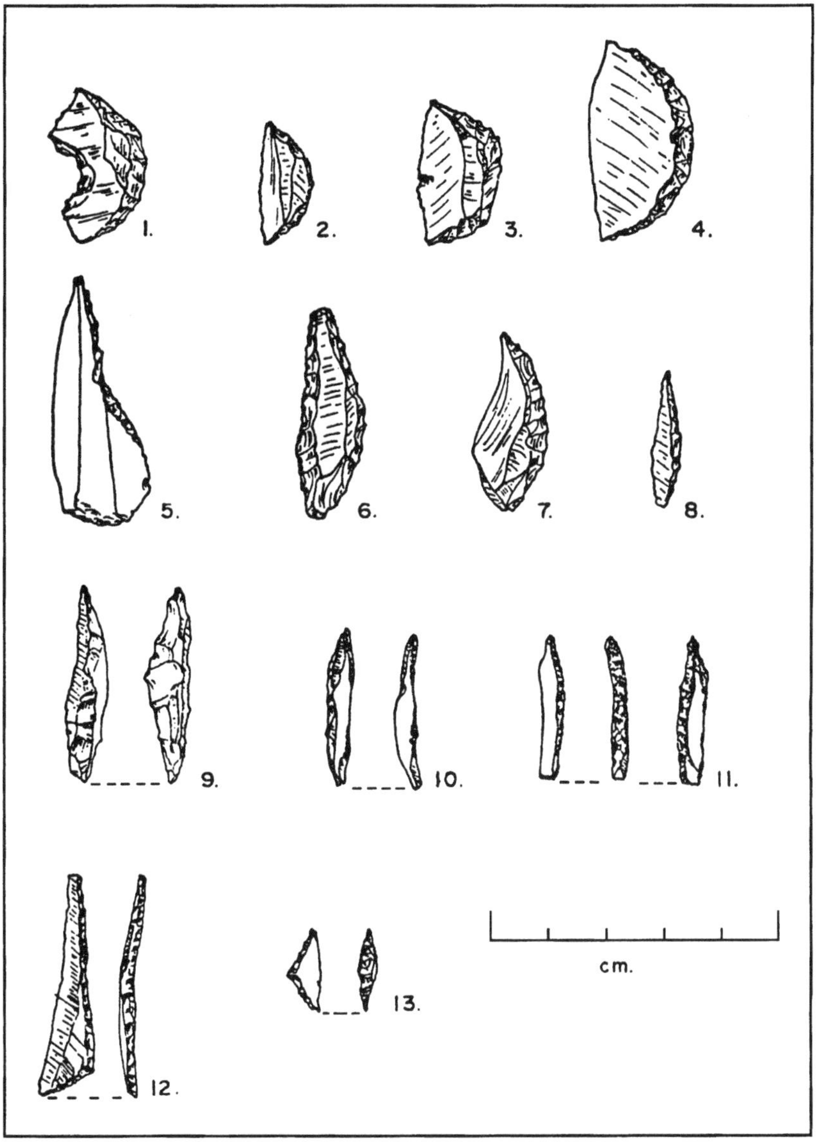

Figure 4.5. Kiffian microliths from Adrar Bous (Smith 1974).

Figure 4.6. Kiffian bone harpoon in situ on top of diatomites, Adrar n'Kiffi, Adrar Bous.

the Aïr Mountains, below Mont Greboun, some 60 km southwest of Adrar Bous, from which dates of between 9,550 and 8,565 years ago were obtained. These dates conform to others from Tin Ouaffadene, 25 km southeast of Adrar Bous, which showed that the site was occupied sometime between 9,610 and 9,080 years ago (Roset et al. 1990; Williams et al. 1987), and from Tagalagal, dated to between 9,370 and 9,330 years ago (Roset 1983). At Temet, Roset found ceramics and microlithic tools, but he also found associated projectile points and Ounanian points, which he proceeded to include in his definition of the Terminal Paleolithic industry.

Our initial definition of the Kiffian also included projectile points (Smith 1976), but we now believe that these are intrusive from the later Tenerian occupation (see below). What really indicates that Roset has a mixed assemblage is the inclusion of Ounanian points. The Ounanian is a macroblade and burin industry first identified at Bir Ounan in northern Mali. The type tool is a shouldered awl-like

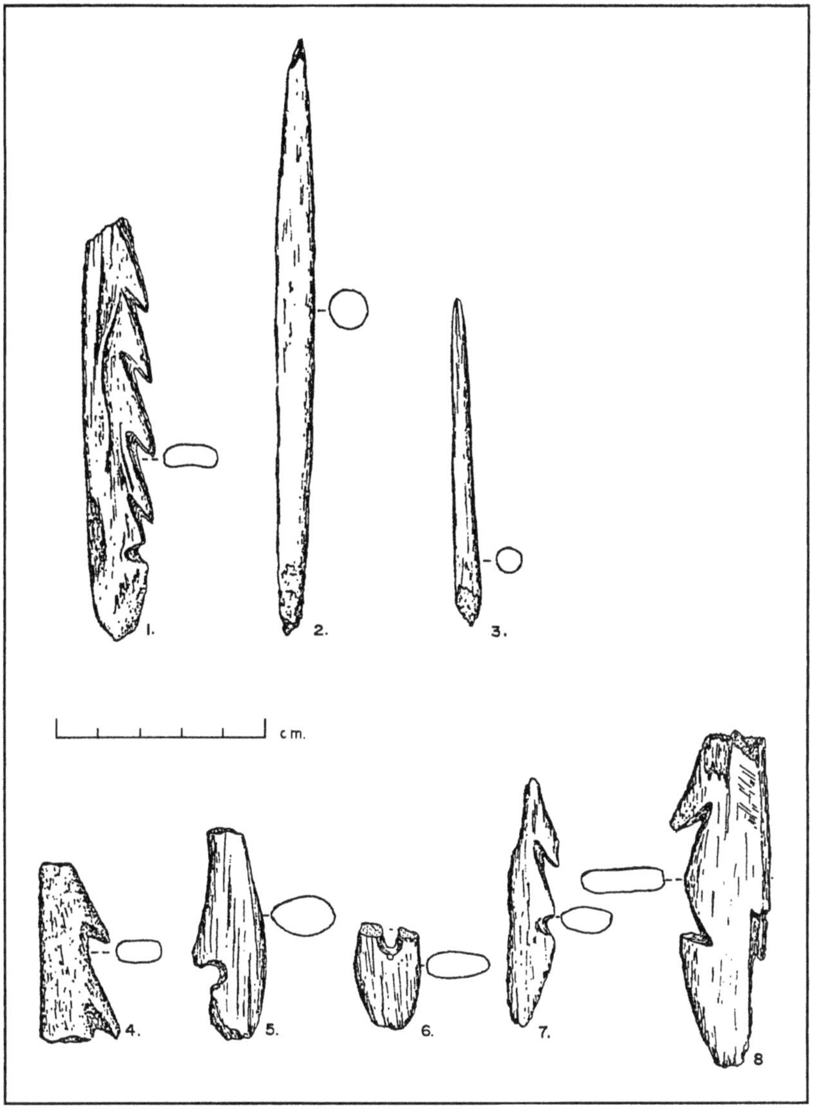

Figure 4.7. Kiffian bone harpoons and bone points, Adrar Bous (Smith 1974).

tool, which was among the formal tools located on the surface of a terrace below Mont Greboun (Clark 1976). Of the 84 formal tools in the collection of 439 pieces, 14.3 percent were these Ounanian points. Significantly, there are no geometric microliths in the assemblage. A similar site was found at Adrar Bous, which suggested it was discrete from the Kiffian.

Thus, contra Roset, there appears to be a cultural sequence at Adrar Bous: Ounanian (undated but probably around 12,000 years ago), followed by the ceramic microlithic (dated between 9,600 and 8,500 years ago), which in turn was replaced by the pastoral Tenerian (5,000 to 3,800 years ago) (Clark et al. 2004).

While the lakes of Niger and the Nile Valley in the Sudan were being exploited during the Kiffian period, hunters in other parts of the central Sahara were using resources in innovative ways. At Uan Afuda in the Acacus Mountains of Libya (di Lernia 1999a), the Barbary sheep (*Ammotragus lervia*) was a target prey species. In the cave at this site, however, a thick dung layer attests to these animals having been intentionally penned up for periods of time. Why should this be, and were the animals domesticated? An answer to the first part of the question may come from the rock walls above the excavation. On the walls are depictions of the Barbary sheep, along with human figures. There is good reason to believe that these drawings were part of ritual activities, and the animals may well have been kept for the ceremonies. Among the botanical remains are suggested several that were probably used as fodder for the sheep, but more interesting was the instance of *Echium* spp., a plant normally toxic to ruminants, found in the dung. Rather than assuming the animals were being poisoned (Mercuri 1999), it may be possible to argue that the plant was being used as a soporific to keep these skittish animals acquiescent. Thus, to answer the second part of the question, no, the animals were not domesticated but being controlled for a specific purpose. The faunal assemblages from a number of early Holocene sites excavated in the Acacus area consistently show frequencies of Barbary sheep of over 70 percent (di Lernia 1998: table 3). This is not the only area where large frequencies of Barbary sheep have been excavated. At Tamar Hat, just inland from the Algerian coast east of Bejaia, Saxon et al. (1974) also reported large numbers of these animals.

With control over wild animals by hunters, the conditions for domestication were therefore being formed in the early Holocene. This is when definitions of *control* versus *domestication* become crucial in arguing the beginnings of food production.

The Debate over Early Cattle Domesticates in North Africa

The earliest expression of animal domestication in North Africa is not without serious problems, which have to do with how the data are interpreted. There are two views of how animal domestication started in North Africa. One view has it that the wild ox, or aurochs (*Bos primigenius*), the wild cattle native to Europe and North Africa, was independently domesticated in Africa 9,300–9,000 years ago. The second view is that when sheep or goats (ovicaprids) were introduced to North Africa from the Near East, around 7,800 years ago, domestic cattle were part of the herding package and arrived at the same time.

From DNA analysis of modern cattle (Hanotte et al. 2002), there seems to be no doubt that there was a distinct African subset quite different from the European or Middle Eastern subsets. In essence, one would think that this should clinch the argument that there was an independent African cattle domestication event. Unfortunately, with current technology it is impossible to place narrow dates on when the African subset became domesticated.

Domestication of Cattle in the Early Neolithic of the Western Desert, Egypt

From intensive research carried out by Wendorf and his colleagues over the past forty years in Nubia and the southern desert areas of Egypt west of the Nile (Wendorf 1968; Wendorf and Schild 1980; Wendorf and Schildt, et al. 1984; 2001), there is some fine information on the Holocene sequence. Initially, the early Holocene material was called Terminal Paleolithic (Wendorf and Schild 1980), as it could be equated with other Epi-Paleolithic industries in North Africa, such as the Khartoum Mesolithic identified by Arkell (1949) from the confluence of the Blue and White Niles, as well as in the central Sahara at Adrar Bous, Niger (Clark et al. 1973); Tamaya Mellet, Niger (Kelley 1934); and Azaouad, Mali (Gallay 1966), all of which had produced ceramics of the wavy-line tradition.

Subsequent publications of Wendorf et al. (1984; 2001) recognized that not only were there ceramics, but also that the bones of cattle at Bir Kiseiba and Nabta Playa were from the Early Holocene. From an ecological argument, these cattle were deemed only to have survived in this area through human intervention and so must have been domesticated. The Terminal Paleolithic rubric was changed to Early Neolithic.

The core of the argument revolves around the animals in the faunal assemblages from Bir Kiseiba and Nabta Playa, dating from Early "Neolithic" El Adam to El Nabta/El Jerar times (sometime between 9,500 and 8,000 years ago). As table 4.1 shows, 72.5 percent of the bones come from gazelles (both *Gazella dama* and *G. gazella*), while 22.5 percent come from hares. The assumption is that the environment at the time was only capable of supporting such a fauna, and the 1.5 percent cattle bones must be from animals that could not have lived in such an environment without human help, possibly the digging of wells. This interpretation does not take into account that in the driest areas of Africa today (the Namib or the Sahara) there are always medium-sized bovids, such as oryx, hartebeest, and in the Sahara, the superbly adapted addax, as well as larger animals, such as giraffe and elephants. We can suggest, therefore, that the fauna assemblage is a selective one and is not necessarily a complete reflection of the environmental conditions in the Early Holocene.

Another part of the argument was assumed dryness of the environment at the time the early cattle existed. As Gautier (1984: 64) says, "this environment supported only a very poor vegetation, perhaps concentrated along the playas, while semi-desertic conditions prevailed elsewhere." In the same book (Schild and Wendorf 1984: 27), we read of the El Adam Playa: "The lower section of the sediments

Table 4.1. Nabta Playa/Bir Kiseiba Mammals (Number of Identifiable Specimens)

	MN, 7200–6500 BP	**El Jerar, 7800–7300 BP**	**El Adam-El Nabta/Jerar, 9500–8000 BP**
Desert Hedgehog			
n	10	9	10
%	1.1	0.7	0.5
Hare			
n	296	554	432
%	32.1	41.8	22.5
Ground Squirrel			
n	1	1	7
%	0.1	0.1	0.4
Field Rat			
n	66	36	12
%	7.2	2.7	0.6
Porcupine			
n	9	6	13
%	1.0	0.5	0.7
Jackal			
n	29	16	10
%	3.1	1.2	0.5
Striped Hyena			
n	—	3	7
%	—	0.2	0.4
Wild Cat			
n	8	14	6
%	0.9	1.1	0.3
Small Carnivore			
n	9	2	3
%	1.0	0.2	0.2
Dama Gazelle			
n	45	23	134
%	4.9	1.7	7.0
Dorcas Gazelle			
n	286	621	1,259
%	31.0	46.8	65.5
Barbary Sheep			
n	4	1	—
%	0.4	0.08	—
Ovicaprids			
n	120	13	—
%	13.0	1.0	—
Cattle			
n	35	27	29
%	3.8	2.0	1.5
Dog			
n	4	—	—
%	0.4	—	—

Source: Gautier (2001).

in the playa are the oldest dated beds of the Holocene wet period. Within them is a series of settlements containing the oldest Saharan pottery and the oldest domesticated cattle." Even if this was not an especially wet period, we also read in the book (Issawi and El Hinnawi 1984: 47) that the playas may be formed by groundwater and "(t)he formation of some of the Bir Kiseiba playas can probably be related to the truncation of the land surface by deflation almost to the level of the water-table during the Early Neolithic." Thus the environment seems to have been more than adequate for the movement of wild cattle away from the permanent waters of the Nile, if only periodically, as accepted by Schild and Wendorf (2001: 631), who note that "the playas carried little water and only for short periods."

From this, we can suggest the environmental argument supporting early domesticated cattle in the Western Desert is not quite as solid as first portrayed. There is no new evidence in Gautier (2001) for supporting the early cattle bones from Nabta and Bir Kiseiba as being domesticated. Gautier (2001: 633) continues to refer to these animals as "putative early domesticated cattle of the southern Western Desert," and he sees "no compelling reason to change the environmental evaluation published in the Bir Kiseiba (1984) faunal report."

Using Gautier's argument, then, in regard to all the eastern Mediterranean sites showing a preponderance of gazelles, and possibly in regard to all those showing a preponderance of hares, for example, Mureybet (Helmer 1991), Beidha (Hecker 1989), and Fayum (Brewer 1989) (see table 4.2), we would have to conclude that the low percentages of cattle found on these sites in the Natufian period were domesticated. This has not been suggested before now. In fact, the environmental conditions of the eastern Mediterranean during Early Holocene times, from a faunal perspective, are no different from those of Nabta Playa or Bir Kiseiba, so perhaps one might consider this whole area as a single faunal biome (Smith 1998a; see also Uerpman 1981) (fig. 4.8). Domestication of cattle in Greece, Anatolia, and the Levant is recognized only around 8,000 years ago.

Table 4.2. Faunal Percentages from Eastern Mediterranean and North African Sites

Faunal Percentages	**Gazella**	**Dama**	**Ovicaprids (1) Ammotragus (2)**	**Hartebeest, Oryx**	**Equids**	**Bos**	**Leporids**
Mureybet (Helmer 1991)	47–53	0.21–1.3	1.6–4.5 (1)	—	16–31	2.4–3.3	9–15
Abu Hureyra (Legge 1975)	65	—	11 (1)	—	15	—	9
Hayonim B (Davis 1982)	87	4	4 (1)	—	—	1	nd
Hayonim Terrace (Davis 1982)	83	14	1 (1)	x	—	x	nd
Mallaha (Davis 1982)	43	11	2 (1)	—	—	3	nd
Nahal Oren (Davis 1982)	83	3	x (1)	—	—	9	nd
Nahala EG II (Davis 1982)	94	—	x (1)	—	—	—	nd
Selabiye (Davis 1982)	94	—	1 (1)	—	—	1	nd
Hatoula (Davis 1987)	96	—	1 (1)	—	—	1	nd
Beidha (Hecker 1989)	22	—	70 (1)	—	2.3	6	x
Haua Fteah (Klein & Scott 1986)	2.8	—	78 (2)	2.3	—	16	x
Fayum B (Brewer 1989)	39	—	—	—	—	14	14
Nabta Playa/Bir Kiseiba EN (Gautier 2001)	65.5	7	—	—	—	1.5	22.5

Note: nd = no date; x = exist in assemblage.

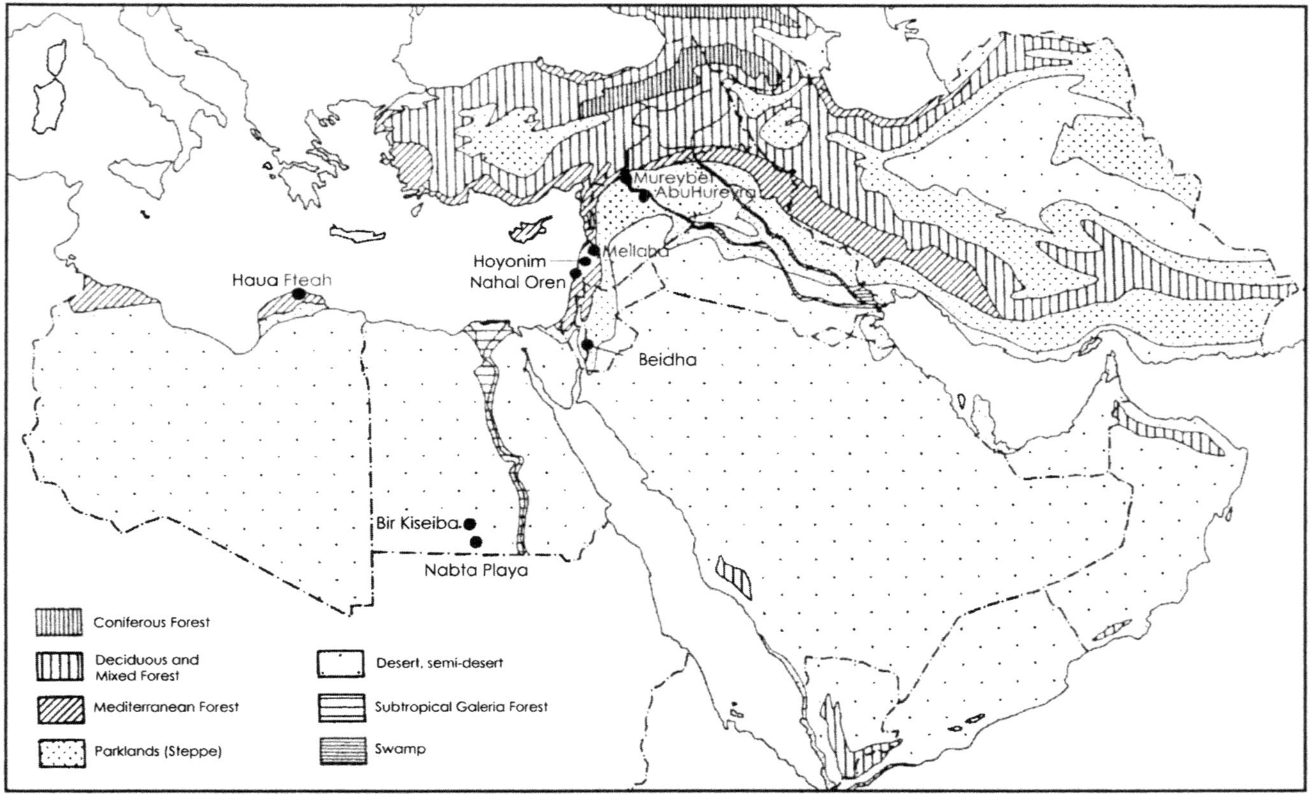

Figure 4.8. Generalized natural vegetation of the eastern Mediterranean, northeast Africa, and Arabia.

Domesticated Animals from the Near East

If the early cattle at Nabta Playa and Bir Kiseiba were not domesticated, when can we suggest that the earliest domesticates appeared in Africa? The most logical time would be when there is incontrovertible evidence of domestics. There is no dispute that the earliest ovicaprids in Africa are descended from wild progenitors in the Near East, which first appear around 7,800 years ago in the Al Jerar Neolithic at Nabta Playa (Gautier 2001: table 23.1) (table 4.1).

There are cattle bones in the Al Jerar faunal assemblage from Nabta as well. Elsewhere, Smith (1992: 41–43) has argued that the bones of these later cattle are smaller than those found at Nabta Playa around 9,300 years ago, which would support the idea that the cattle associated with the ovicaprids were also domesticated. There is little reason to doubt that if small stock were being brought into Africa from the Levant, then cattle could have come at the same time.

By 7,400 years ago, the ovicaprids and cattle had dispersed across the Sahara to the Acacus Mountains of southern Libya (di Lernia 1999b), and by 7,000 years ago they had dispersed to the Red Sea Hills (Vermeersch et al. 1996). Because of the siltation effects in the Nile Delta, we are unsure about the early animals in the Nile Valley. We do know that wild *Bos primigenius* lived in the valley in the Pleistocene (Churcher 1972), so there would have been a wild gene pool that ultimately could have contributed to the African domesticated cattle whose descendants have been analyzed by Hanotte et al. (2002).

Early Domesticated Animals in the Sahara

From his work in the central Sahara, di Lernia (1999b) refers to the Early Pastoral Period (7,800 to 6,400 years ago). The archaeology of the Acacus Mountains suggests that hunters descended from the Epi-Palaeolithic, or Mesolithic Late Acacus, Tradition continued to live side by side with new herding economies. The sites can be separated on the basis of the pottery of the herders, which was different from that of the hunters. The settlement patterns of this early herding economy were based upon a movement between the mountains and the lowlands, but with the greatest concentration in the highlands. Di Lernia makes the point that nowhere on the hunter sites does the faunal assemblage include wild cattle. These animals do not appear to have been indigenous to the central Sahara.

Between 6,400 and 6,080 years ago, there was a dry spell in the central Sahara when no pastoral activity can be detected. After 6,080 years ago, there was a resurgence of pastoral life, and di Lernia refers to this as the "Middle Pastoral Period." The intensity of occupation at this time indicates a period of pastoral consolidation. Environmental conditions seem to have been very favorable for a herding lifestyle. Freshwater lakes reached some of their highest levels, and the large pastoral sites found in the dune fields along the lakeshores may have been semi-permanent. Transhumance is also suggested in the use of dry-season camps in rock shelters in the mountains, where the fauna is almost exclusively ovicaprids. Cattle were kept to the well-watered lowlands near the lakes. This pattern of seasonally dividing the different herd components and sending them to separate grazing areas is well attested in the ethnographic literature (Gulliver 1955). Some animals can graze, and others browse. Sites are to be found in all the interdune corridors and mountain terraces, indicating a wide use of all available resources.

The Middle Pastoral Period lasted until around 5,000 years ago, when the climate of the Sahara started to destabilize, making conditions increasingly more precarious for herding, particularly cattle herding. In di Lernia's chronology, this is followed by the "Late Pastoral Period," which lasted until 3,500 years ago. Cattle bones on the sites decreased in numbers, while the small stock numbers remained high. People probably had to be more mobile than in the previous period and had to travel longer distances to fulfill the needs of their animals. Funerary monuments became much more elaborate, with a great deal of effort going into their construction.

At the end of the Late Pastoral Period, small villages appeared in the central and southern Sahara (Paris 1992; Holl 1993), and these were associated with fields where the first domesticated grains in the Sahara were grown (Amblard 1996). Graves clustered around these villages, forming cemeteries, which indicates a new social landscape.

Analysis of pottery from prepastoral and the three pastoral periods by Garcea (2003) shows clear distinctions in fabric, temper, and decoration in sherds excavated from Uan Telocat and Uan

Muhuggiag. The Early Pastoral ceramics have rocker stamped impressions, but different tools were used from those used in making later ceramics. The technique of fabrication was based on clay coils built up and smoothed with a surface layer of clay, and the inside was burnished. The Early Pastoral pottery has mica inclusions. As the nearest known source is seventy kilometers away, this may give an idea of the area the herders covered.

What separates the Early from Middle and Late Pastoral pottery is the inclusion of dung in the latter two periods. Setting the boundary between Middle and Late Pastoral pottery relies upon dating, as this is based on di Lernia's pastoral sequence, which suggests the Late Pastoral period begins around 5,000 years ago. As noted below, the Tenerian is probably the Middle Pastoral Period, but it extends to about 4,500 years ago; therefore the top of Uan Telocat might fit better as Middle Pastoral than Late, while the upper levels at Uan Muhuggiag are from the Late period.

From further south of the Acacus Mountains, in Niger, comes information on herding societies of this period known as "Tenerian," from their distribution on the edge of the Ténéré Sand Sea. This cultural entity, first named by Reygasse (1934), is typified by stone tools made from a characteristic green vitric tuff, a fine-grained material that permitted high-quality stone flaking. The best known of the Tenerian sites are located around Adrar Bous. On the southwest side of this granitic ring complex is a valley called Agorass n'Tast (valley of the cow), where the complete skeleton of a shorthorn cow was excavated (Carter and Clark 1976) (fig. 4.9) and dated to 4,145 years ago. This skeleton seems to exhibit the classic bowing that occurs as a dead animal dries up and the skin tightens. It is possible that it died in a drought, and that is why it remained whole. It would subsequently have been buried in lake-margin silts, possibly in the next rainy season. If this is true, then, even though conditions in the Sahara were generally favorable for cattle pastoralism, there were years when things got rough, probably toward the end of the Tenerian.

Agorass n'Tast is the richest area of Tenerian occupation, although smaller sites were to be found all around the massif. The rich scatters of stone tools, pottery, and other remains, including stone circles (figs. 4.10, 4.11), were on the surface or immediately below, embedded in the brown sandy loam that probably resulted from the

Figure 4.9. Alan Pastron excavating the Tenerian "cow" from Adrar Bous.

marshy conditions around the time of occupation. Certainly the basin on the south end of Adrar Bous held a freshwater lake that produced diatomaceous silts during the earlier part of the Tenerian period.

Initial dating of the Tenerian produced radiocarbon dates of between 5,800 and 5,000 years ago (Clark et al. 1973), but 14 more

Figure 4.10. Stone circle, Adrar Bous.

Figure 4.11. Stone circle, Adrar Bous.

recent Accelerator Mass Spectrometer (AMS) dates on bone gave a range between 5,430 and 3,880 years ago, with a median age of 4,770 years ago (Clark et al. 2004). The Tenerian would therefore straddle the boundary between di Lernia's Middle and Late Pastoral Periods, but would probably fit better with Paris's Néolithique récent (5,500 to 4,400 years ago; Paris 1996) (see fig. 4.12). Paris dated 19 graves at Adrar Bous ranging from 5,360 to 2,965 years ago, with a median date of 4,059 years ago.

The Tenerian industry gives a reasonably clear picture of what pastoral life was like in the Sahara during the good times of the Middle Pastoral Period. Freshwater was available from the lake at Adrar Bous, and wild grains could be collected from the edges. One *Sorghum* and one *Brachiaria* impression were identified from potsherds from the site, and *Celtis* seeds were found in a pot. Many large, deep-dish lower grindstones and their hand-held upper grinders were found that would also suggest that grains were important food. Ten whole pots and thousands of sherds of well-fired ware of a range of types—pots, bowls, and jars—were analyzed by Roset (1978). Figure 4.13 shows how these can be broken down by size.

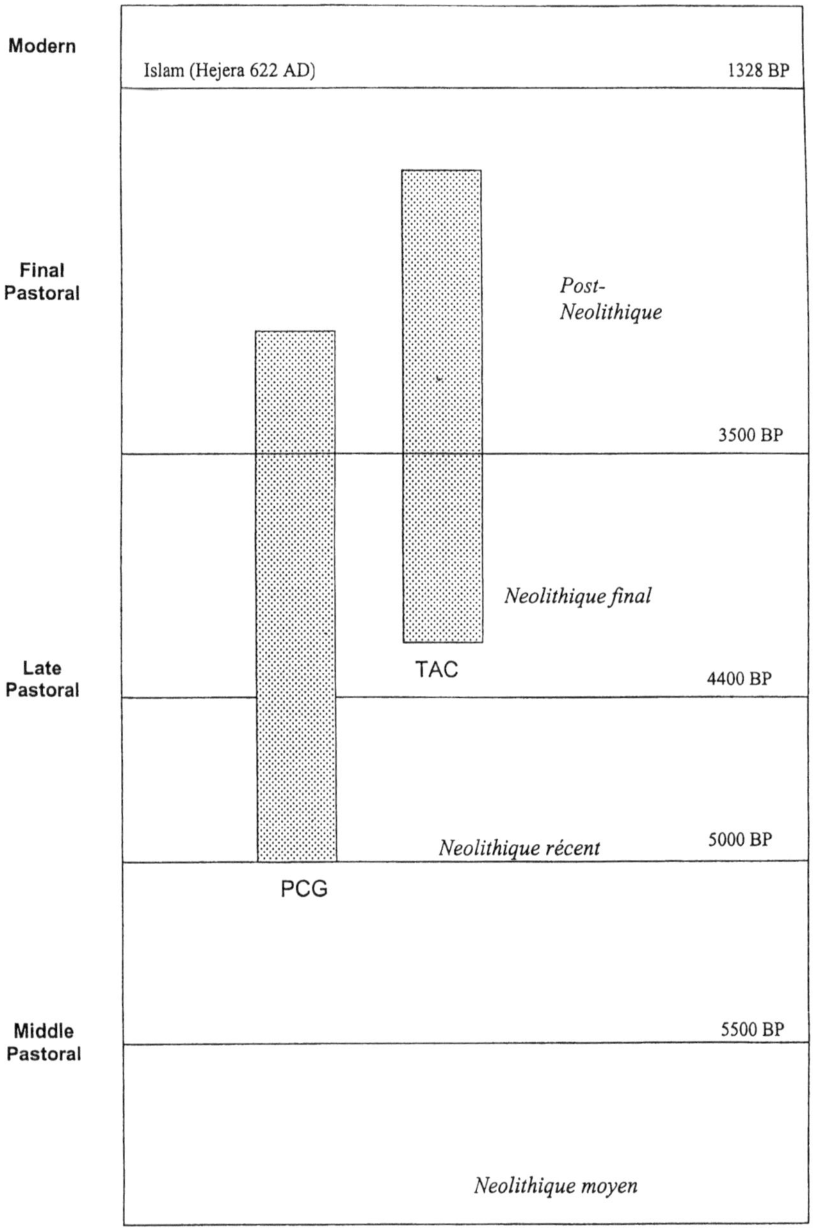

Figure 4.12. Funerary monuments from Sahara (after Paris 1996) against Pastoral Periods (after di Lernia 1999b).

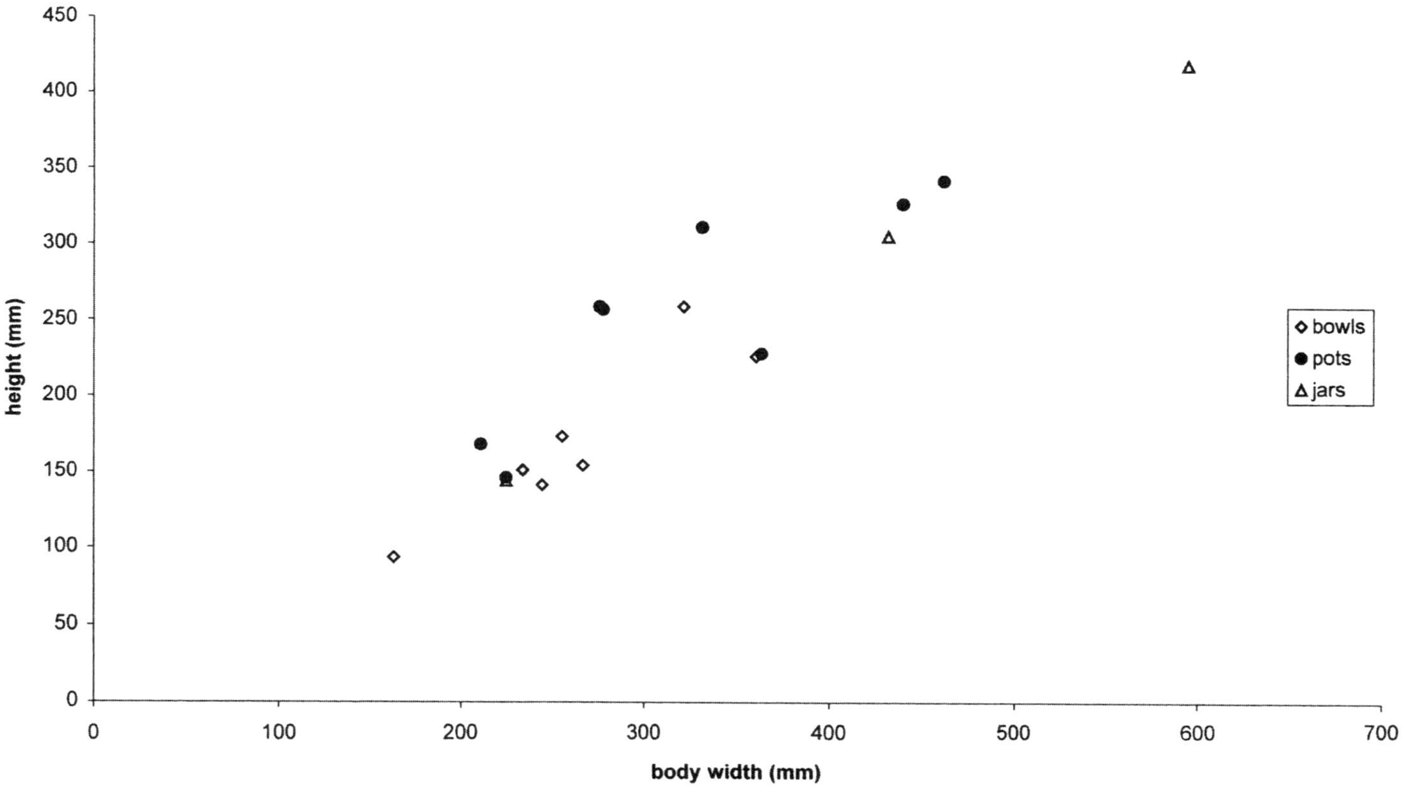

Figure 4.13. Tenerian pottery types (from Roset 1978).

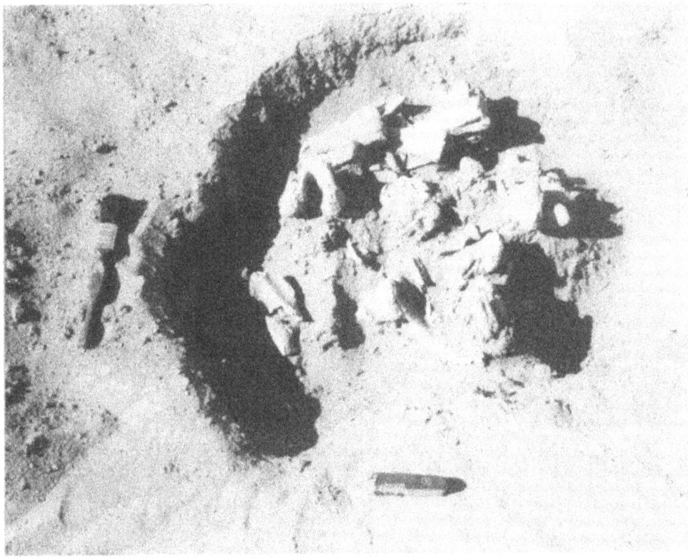

Figure 4.14. Burned cattle bones in pit, Tenerian, Adrar Bous.

Cattle remains, in the form of the whole cow and other burned features (see Paris 2000: fig. 7.13) (fig. 4.14), indicate the probable center of the economy. Wild animal bones (gazelle, hartebeest), along with the numerous projectile points (fig. 4.15), attest to hunting. The range of stone tools would be impressive from any stone-using industry. These include thin, round disk knives with deep invasive flake scars (fig. 4.16), flaked and polished axes, and a specific tool that has been used to suggest a connection between the central Sahara and the Nile Valley around Khartoum: the adze or gouge (Arkell 1953). This tool is shaped by flaking, then is partially polished (figs. 4.17, 4.18). It also shows lateral polish along the edges, which might be from use. The working edge (seen from the side) is asymmetrical, thus its ascription as a wood-working tool. Lateral polish is found on similar tools from the Neolithic of the Gaza Strip in the Levant. Cultural connection with the Nile Valley is also suggested by the decorative motif of diamond rocker-stamping on pottery (fig. 4.19; see Arkell 1953). Pottery repairs were effected by drilling both sides of a crack with a stone drill and then, presumably, binding the gap with a cord. Polished drill tips are found in the tool kit (fig. 4.18) that fit the size of the holes found in pottery. Personal

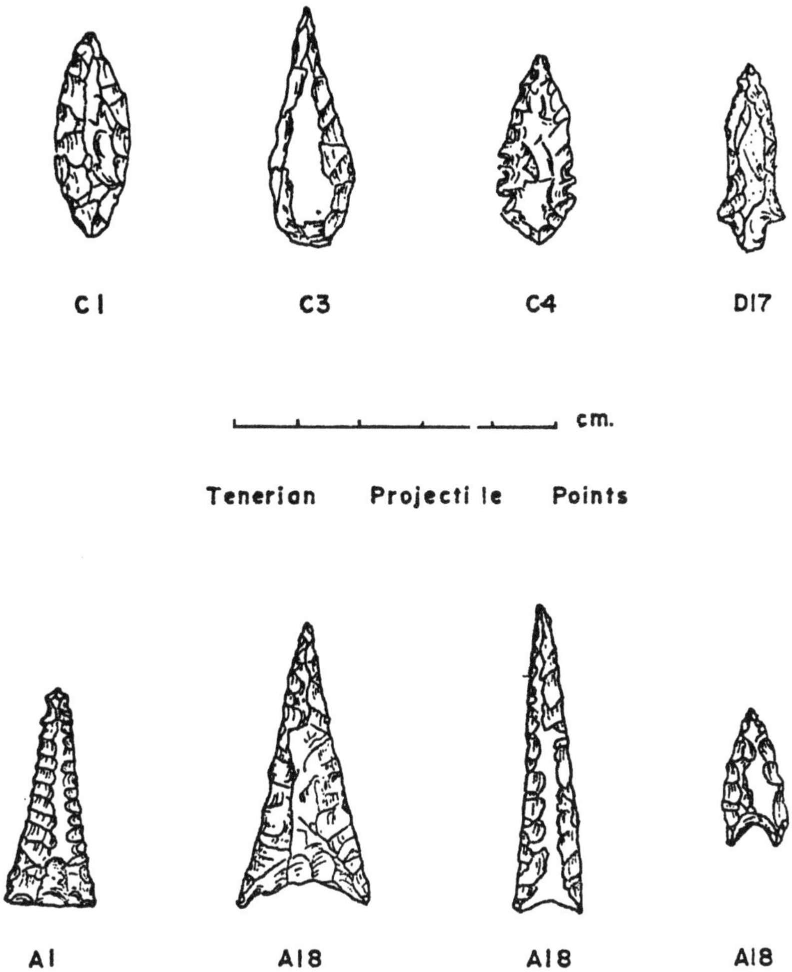

Figure 4.15. Tenerian projectile points from Adrar Bous (Smith 1974).

decoration can be seen in the number of stone beads found, as well as in the decorated ivory bracelet (fig. 4.20).

The kind of shelter used is uncertain. Modern Saharan nomads use portable skin or mat tents, and the rock art of the Tassili n'Ajjer shows just that type of shelter (Lajoux 1963: 121). There were circles of large stones, but of small diameter (one meter; fig. 4.11), and a semicircle of 1.5 m; but since all were totally devoid of associated

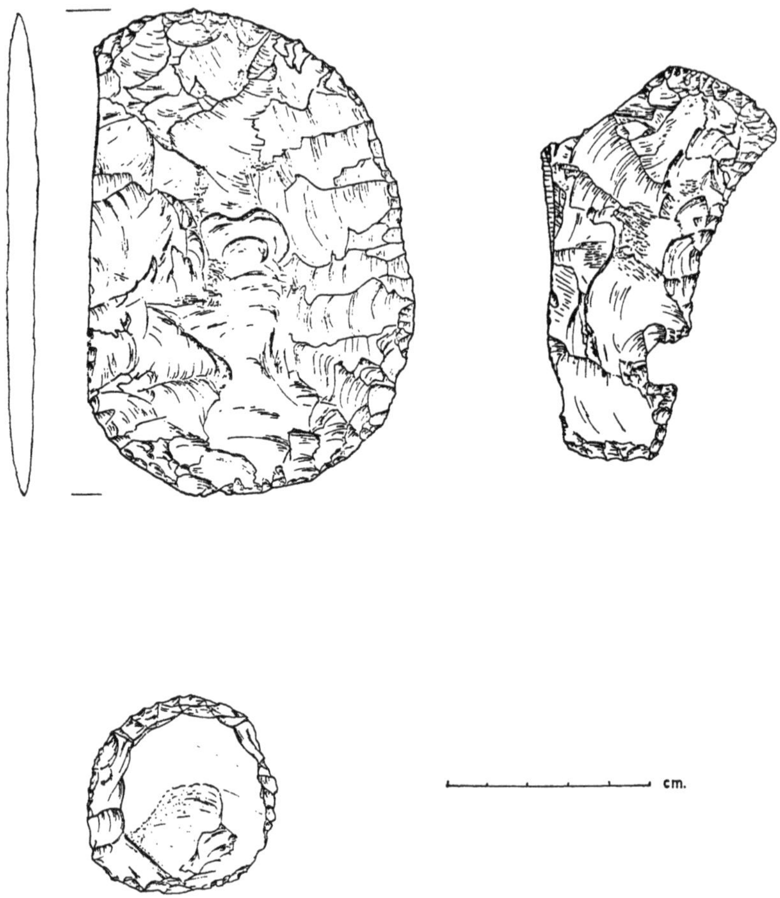

Figure 4.16. Flaked Tenerian stone tools from Adrar Bous. UL: Disc knife; UR: Miscellaneous bifacial knife; LL: Small convex/circular scraper (Smith 1974).

cultural debris, they can only be theorized to have been the base of storage structures.

Cattle Cults

An extraordinary development in the Sahara was the intentional burial of whole skeletons of animals, in particular cattle. The earliest date for these is probably from the site E-94-1 ceremonial complex,

Figure 4.17. Flaked and polished Tenerian adzes from Adrar Bous.

Nabta Playa (Applegate et al. 2001) of 6,470±270 years ago. This dates a skeleton whose bones are still articulated; five other burials produced bones that are disarticulated. At Nabta, these monuments continued until at least 5,500 years ago. A cow burial at Adrar Bous dated to 6,200 years ago (Paris 2000) and another at Mankhor (Ferhat et al. 1996) show that the activity was widespread throughout the Sahara at this time. At the village of Chin Tafidet further south in Niger, Paris

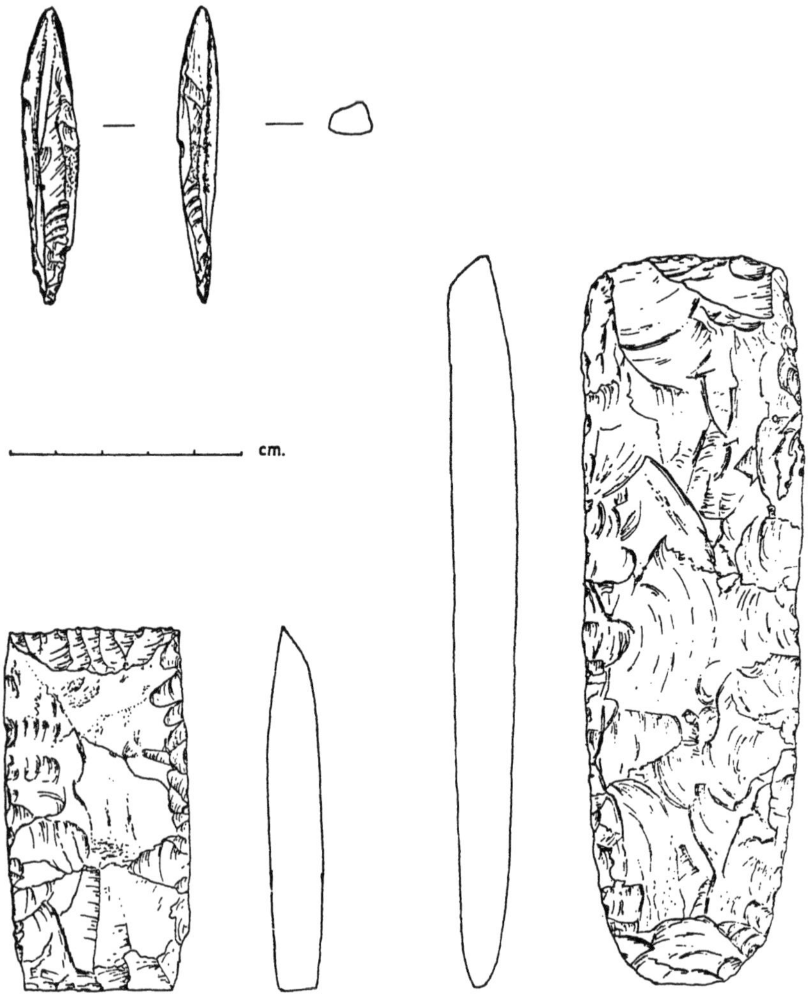

Figure 4.18. Polished stone drill tip and flaked adzes, Tenerian, Adrar Bous (Smith 1974).

(1984; 1996) excavated twenty-five more of these complete animal burials, dated between 4,555 and 3,325 years ago, of which eighteen were cattle. That these were probably sacrificed before burial is suggested by three of the animals having their necks turned back and eleven having been buried in an east–west orientation. These burials

Figure 4.19. Diamond rocker-stamped Tenerian pot from Adrar Bous.

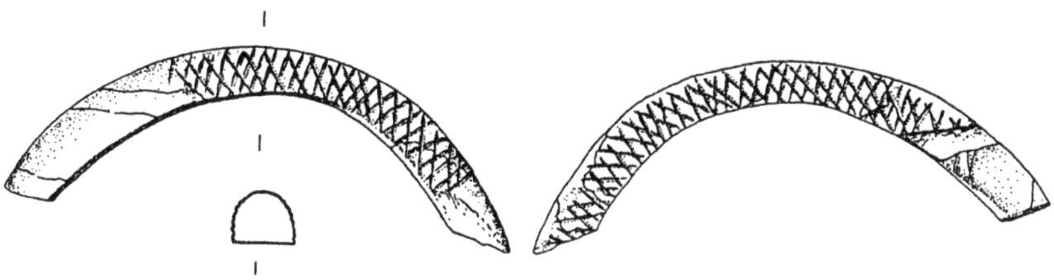

Figure 4.20. Ivory bracelet, Tenerian, Adrar Bous (Smith).

were close to human graves, but a direct connection was difficult to make.

Bovidian Rock Art of the Sahara

Not only are there indications of ritual sacrifice of cattle in the Sahara, but there are also beautiful paintings of cattle on the rock walls of shelters. There are two quite distinct genres of these paintings, which has led to a separation, probably chronological, generally known as Bovidian I and Bovidian II periods, although dating rock art is notoriously difficult.

Bovidian I

The art of this period has also been referred to as that of the "black-faces," since it is quite easy to recognize African faces (Smith 1993b) in the art. Cattle tend to dominate the realistic images (fig. 4.21). The loving depiction of coat colors of individual animals (Lajoux 1963) is in keeping with what we know about cattle keepers' detailed knowledge of their herds. Not only are the herds shown, but ritual activity involving cattle is evident as well. Two such depictions have been interpreted as having cultural connections with Fulani (Peul) herders of the Niger River area and further east.

Bovidian II

This style of painting is quite different from the Bovidian I style and can be considered to be later. The people depicted have long hair and a more Mediterranean look (fig. 4.22). Again, cattle have an important place in the genre, although small stock are also shown. While on the surface this style might recall a narrative of events, there are indications that the art is more than just a story. One panel appears to show people dealing with fire while striped cattle look on (fig. 4.23). There are other examples of these striped animals from Tassili n'Ajjer (Kuper 1978: 425, 431; Lajoux 1963: 110; Aumassip 1980–1981: 124) (fig. 4.24), but this is the only picture where there might be a connection with fire. Striped cattle appear elsewhere in the Sahara, for example, from Chad in the Ennedi Mountains (Bailloud 1997: fig. 25) and from northwest of Fada (Rossi 2000: fig. 2). In the Ennedi, there are also cattle with what look like zig-zag motifs (Bailloud 1997: fig. 24; Allard-Huard and Huard 1983: fig. 36:7; Simonis et al. 1994: figs. 13–14). The striped motif on cattle paintings continues eastward to the Nubian Nile Valley, possibly associated with C-Group sites (Allard-Huard and Huard 1983: fig. 26: 1–4). There are also cattle with dots painted on them, a motif that extends from the central Sahara to the Nile Valley (Gauthier et al. 1996: figs. 64, 75; Allard-Huard and Huard 1983: fig. 26:5). There are occasions when the Fulani today

Figure 4.21. Bovidian I period "black-face" people in cattle cleansing ceremony, Uan Derbaouen, Tassili n' Ajjer, from Colombel (after Kuper 1978).

Figure 4.22. *Bovidian II period "white-face" people in camp, Iheren, Tassili n'Ajjer, from Colombel (after Kuper 1978).*

Figure 4.23. *"Fire ritual," Uan Derbaouen, Tassili n'Ajjer, from Colombel (after Kuper 1978).*

Figure 4.24. "Striped" cow, Tadjelamine, Tassili n'Ajjer (after Lajoux 1963).

will paint their cattle before they cross the Niger River on their transhumance cycles (Dupuy 1998: fig. 18).

Funerary Monuments of the Sahara

Around 5,000 years ago, graves with formal funerary architecture started to appear in the central Sahara. Prior to this time, graves had simple cairns, many of which cannot be recognized, built over the burial, and they are only found when erosion takes place (fig. 4.25).

The most comprehensive study of these monuments was done by Paris (1996) in Niger, where he was able to identify sixteen types. The largest sample came from two types, which seem to be in chronological sequence, but with some overlap. In fact, in at least two cases the later form was constructed on top of the earlier. In both types of sites, the body was flexed.

Type *Plates-Formes Cylindriques à Gravillons (PCG)*

These monuments consist of a shallow hole dug into the parent substrate, into which the body was placed and covered with large

Figure 4.25. Excavated skeleton, Agorass in-tast, Adrar Bous.

boulders (fig. 4.26). A flat platform of stone rubble, retained by a round wall of large boulders (fig. 4.27), was then built above. The range of dates for PCG monuments extends from between 5,020 and 3,540 years ago. The orientation of the body was mostly with the head toward the south or east, occasionally to the north, but never to the west. In general, female skeletons from these graves tended to lie on their left side (83 percent), while males were more often on their right side (72 percent; Paris 1996: 294). Grave goods are rare or absent. In the skeleton in figure 4.26, a single stone bead was found around the neck, and there were traces of skin around the wrists.

Type *Tumulus Tronconiques à Cratère (TAC)*

The second major type is a mound of smaller stones covering the body, with a crater, or depression, above the skeleton. It is not clear whether the crater was formed by slumping as the body disintegrated through time. The oldest TAC grave provided a date of 4,050 years ago, and the youngest 1,160 years ago. The dated sample was twenty-four graves, nineteen of which (79 percent) were dated

Figure 4.26. Excavated skeleton, Agorass in-tchissiskan, Adrar Bous.

between 3,595 and 2,395 years ago. In regard to body orientation, the largest percentage of heads were toward the east (60 percent), but burials oriented in other directions were also found (Paris 1996: 301). More ornaments were found in this type of site than in type PCG, but no special preparation of the body was done before burial other than to place it in what appears to have been an ox skin bag. There were more traces of ochre in these later graves than found earlier, and in one case a bowl containing ochre was found with a child burial. Similarly, although pottery was found with burials in all periods, it is in the later burials that the idea seems to have spread.

Figure 4.27. Funerary monument type PCG, Adrar Sirret.

Funerary monuments are scattered across the Sahara, often isolated, which would suggest that these were graves of nomadic people. In sites less than 3,500 years old there are larger groupings of graves, and in a number of cases these are around small villages. Thus the idea of a cemetery is probably associated with a more sedentary lifestyle. It is possible the flat-topped graves were purposefully made so people could lie upon them. Camps (1961) suggests that lying on a grave was part of a ritual whereby the dead could be consulted by the living.

Villages and Post-Neolithic Pastoralism

Less than 4,000 years ago, a new phenomenon, in the form of large settlements, appeared as people moved to the southern edge of the Sahara (see fig. 4.28). At Dhar Tichitt in Mauritania, this takes the form of complex stone walling (Holl 1993). Elsewhere, large funerary complexes exist, such as at Iwelen (Paris 1990) and Chin Tafidet (Paris (1992) in Niger, in association with rich scatters of stone tools and pottery.

The growth of such settlements less than 3,500 years ago may well have been a function of the need to adapt to unstable climatic conditions by widening the food base. Certainly, this is when we see the first use of African domestic grains in the archaeological record in Dhar Tichitt (Munson 1976; Amblard 1996) and Karkarichinkat, Mali (Munson pers. comm.), and not too long thereafter, just less than 3,000 years ago, we see it in the Lake Chad basin (Neumann et al. 1996) and in the Sahel south of the great bend of the Niger River (Vogelsang et al. 1999). It is tempting to suggest that this was the time that nomadic pastoralists aggressively sought access to plant foods by raiding African people in the Sahel and capturing slaves that they brought back to the desert oases to work the fields for them. The people of the oases are known as Harratin (fig. 4.29), who are racially distinct from the Tuareg nobility today (*Immagaren*). The Tuareg also have low-status former slaves (called *Iklan*) who still serve their former masters as part of a paternal caste system. Their history is still the subject of some debate (Froment 1999).

MacDonald (1998) would go even further and say these settlements were an indication of a widening network of political units across the Sahel, based upon exchange of rare objects and raw materials. He refers to them as "mobile elites" and suggests they are an indication of social stratification. This may be the beginnings of interregional caravan trade networks that later developed in the Sahara and that the Romans capitalized upon, such as between the Garamantes state and salt sources in the desert (Liverani 2000). MacDonald bases his argument on the appearance of what seem to be nonfunctional items, such as small, polished stone axes (Smith 1974), and items of personal decoration, such as bracelets and beads made

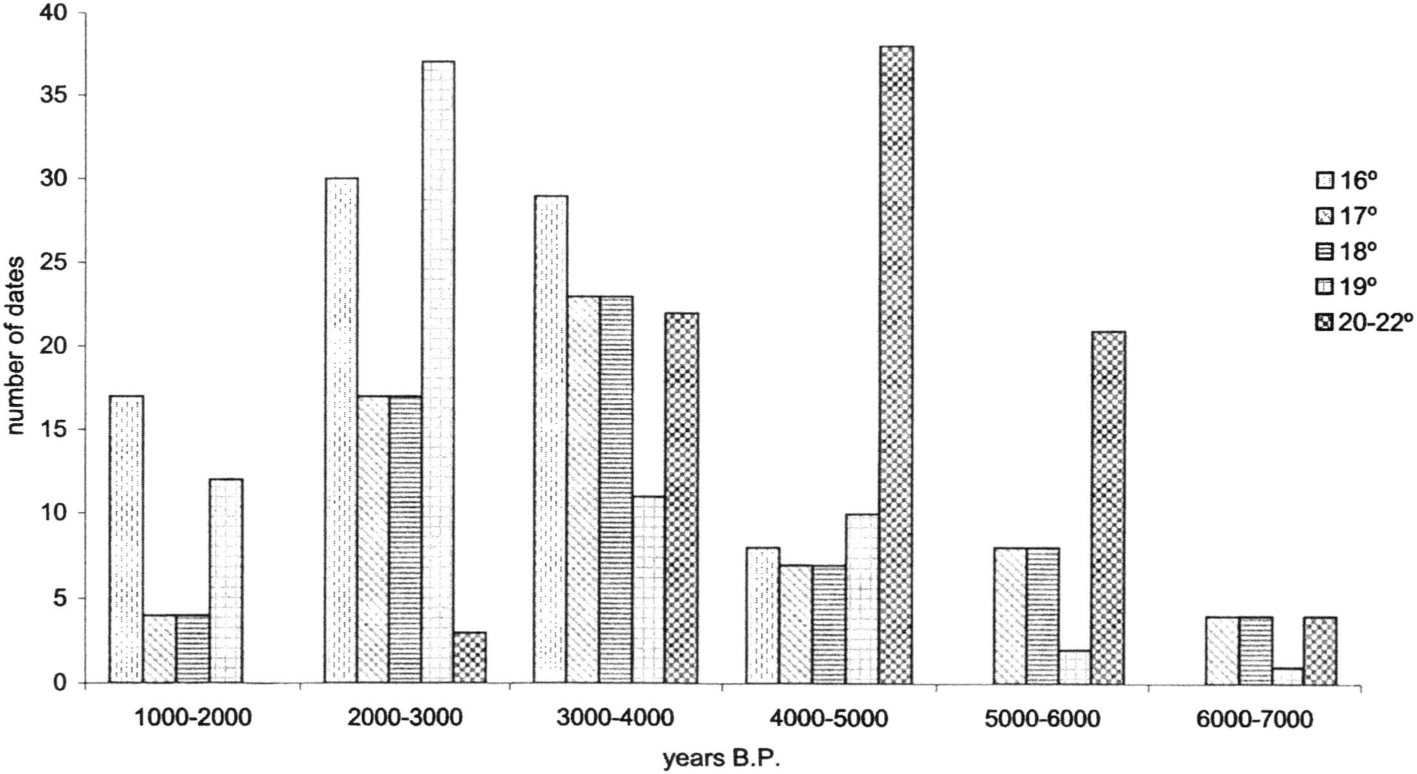

Figure 4.28. *Radiocarbon dates from Niger by latitude (data after Vernet 1998).*

Figure 4.29. Two Harratin women from Iferouane, Aïr Mountains, Niger.

from materials found over a wide area of the Sahel. While there is some disagreement on whether the small axes were really as pristine as MacDonald would have it, there is no argument that these items probably represent specialized tools, to be used for specific (if not ritual) purposes. Gaussen and Gaussen (1988: 114) found a cache of 17 beautifully made, flaked-stone axes at Lagreich in the Tilemsi Valley, north of Gao, Mali (fig. 4.30). The skill of the artisan is undoubted, and one wonders if indeed these axes had been intended less as functional than as aesthetic.

In support of MacDonald's contention are several scenes in the Bovidian II rock art of the "white face" people that seem to be of individuals on their knees giving obeisance to someone of high status

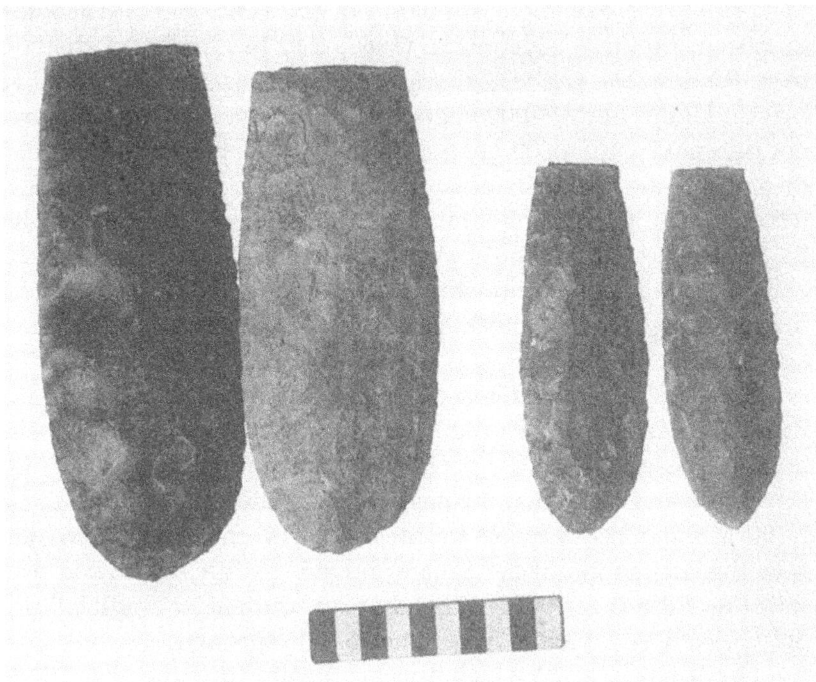

Figure 4.30. Four flaked axes from a cache found in the Tilemsi Valley, Mali.

(Kuper 1978: fig. 10 and fig. 15) (fig. 4.22). Making up part of the composition of the panel are striped cattle looking on at the scene with their herder kneeling. One cow in particular is remarkably similar to those in the fire scene (fig. 4.23), with chevron markings on the horns. We might interpret this as a demonstration of authority among pastoral elites, with the power of the chief encapsulated in the symbolism of the "fire" cattle.

Spread of Pastoralism Southward into the Sahel

By 4,000 years ago, the environment in the Sahara was considerably drier. It was at this time that the first signs of occupation of the Sahel by herders took place (Smith 1974). There is every reason to believe that prior to this date there was plenty of grass and water in the south to sustain the herds. Neumann (1989: 156) has analyzed charcoal from Fachi in the central Sahara and found that it represented "a rich Sudanian flora" 7,000 years ago. Why was the southern area not occupied until 4,000 years ago? One probable barrier is tsetse flies, which are the hosts of trypanosomiasis, or sleeping sickness, which is fatal to cattle. Stenning (1959) has shown how during his fieldwork the Fulani would migrate north and south as the tsetse belts expanded and contracted with the rains. This same pattern might be suggested of the Saharan–Sahel zone prior to 4,000 years ago (Smith 1979).

With the southward retreat of the Intertropical Convergence Zone, rainfall belts from the Gulf of Guinea necessary for tsetse breeding places no longer penetrated far into the Sahara, opening up a grassland niche that the pastoralists readily filled. The suite of radiocarbon dates available for the Sahara (Vernet 1998) shows just how the occupation of the Sahara moved steadily southward over time (fig. 4.28). It can be seen that the area south of 16^0 north latitude only became occupied in Niger after 4,000 years ago.

The Tilemsi Valley, which runs northward from the Niger River in Mali at Gao, would have been a natural route of entry for herders in the Sahara to penetrate southward. The work of Gaussen and Gaussen (1988), while based on surface collections, can give us an idea of the prehistoric connections between the Sahara and the Sahel. The site of Asselar, about 230 km north of Gao, has been well known for many years, as it produced a human skeleton that was studied by Boule and Vallois (1932). The skeleton was dated at 6,390 years ago, and it was one of the first Saharan skeletons to be dated. Asselar produced good samples of projectile points, which Gaussen and Gaussen call facies "A." There are several forms, but the dominant one is the hollow base point, common to many sites in the Sahara. There are also leaf-shaped points and tanged forms.

Further south, at Karkarichinkat, about eighty kilometers north of Gao, there are two mounds standing about six meters above the valley floor. The sediments of the valley floor are fluvial, showing that in the not-too-distant past this was a floodplain. In fact, excavation of the mounds shows they were islands during the rains and that the people living on them were herders who used them for fishing

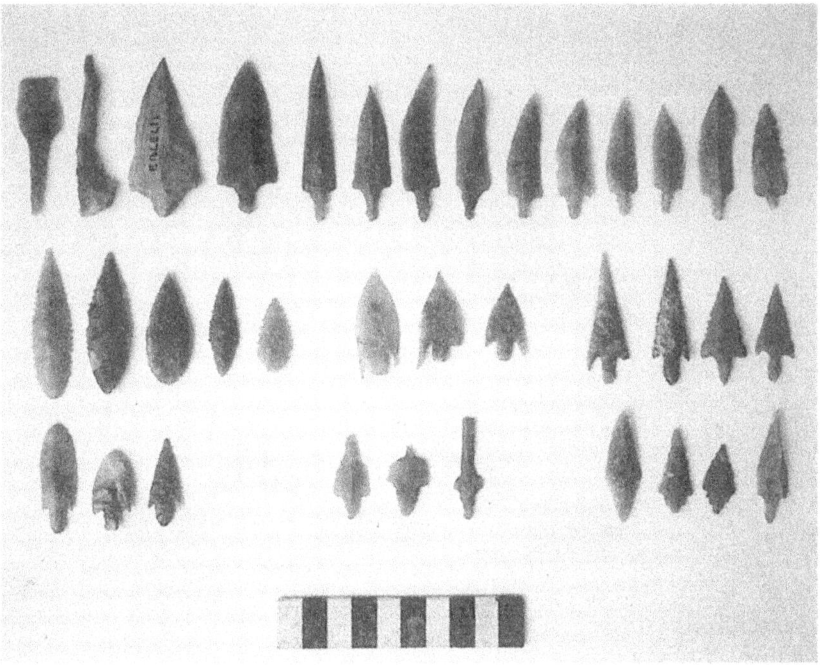

Figure 4.31. Tanged projectile points, facies K, Tilemsi Valley, Mali.

(Smith 1974; 1975). The sites were occupied between 4,000 and 3,300 years ago, and the nature of the cultural material shows affinities with sites in the Sahara. Gaussen and Gaussen (1988) call the industry from Karkarichinkat facies "K." There are leaf-shaped and tanged forms (fig. 4.31), not unlike in facies A, but the dominant form is a simple blade with a naturally sharp point given a denticulate tanged base. The pottery decorations are much more varied in the facies K than in facies A, but they have a few motifs in common. A contribution to our knowledge of the economy of the Karkarichinkat groups comes in the form of sun-dried clay figurines of cattle (Smith 1978). The delicate horns of the animals were found but broken off. Two of the figurines were just little round clay blobs with a head and horns on top and little udders below (figs. 4.32, 4.33). Along with pouring lips on the edge of some of the pottery bowls (fig. 4.34), this is strong evidence for the use of milk. We can with some confidence assume that these were toys made by children emulating their elders, similar

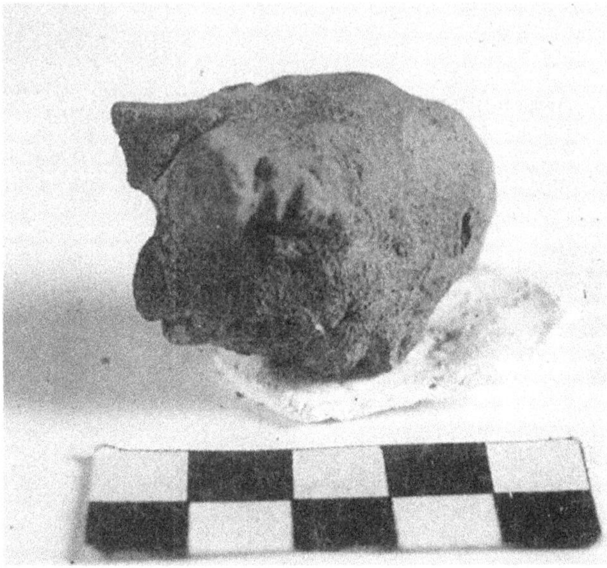

Figure 4.32. Unfired clay figurine (top view showing face and broken horns), Karkarichinkat, Tilemsi Valley, Mali.

Figure 4.33. Unfired clay figurine (same as fig. 4.32; bottom view showing udders).

Figure 4.34. Bowl with pouring lip and knotted string roulette decoration, Tilemsi Valley, Mali.

in many respects to what one finds among herding people elsewhere in Africa (cf. Evans-Pritchard 1940: 38 and fig. 7).

Other similarities with Saharan pastoral material culture can be seen in flaked axes (fig. 4.30) and flexed burials in which single beads were placed around the neck (fig. 4.35).

By way of contrast, but not dated, from the sites of In Begouen and Tin Aoukert, only a few kilometers from Karkarichinkat, comes a collection of stone artifacts, including many crystal quartz labrets and projectile points (fig. 4.36), a large proportion of which are hollow-based, reminiscent of the facies A types. In many other ways,

Figure 4.35. Flexed burial, with single bead around neck, Karkarichinkat, Mali.

however, facies K and facies B are very similar, and all three facies produced small polished axes.

It would appear that there were at least two different cultural groups who inhabited the lower Tilemsi Valley, and both show affinities with facies A to the north. It is unfortunate that the facies B has not been dated and that no decorated potsherds have been found, so we don't know if it was contemporaneous with facies K. There can be little doubt that the southern facies are derived from the north and that the way of life, revolving around herding, would have been similar.

Elsewhere in the Sahel, we have good evidence for another southward spread of herding people in the Méma, the area to the west of the Central Niger Delta of Mali. As happened further east, the affinities of people who lived at Kobadi (MacDonald 1996) seem to have their antecedents to the north, in this case from Dhar Tichitt in Mauritania, where similar pottery can be recognized on Kobadi sites. As at Karkarichinkat, the bones of cattle and ovicaprids, along with small clay figurines of the animals, were found, and the earliest dates are from 3,365 years ago.

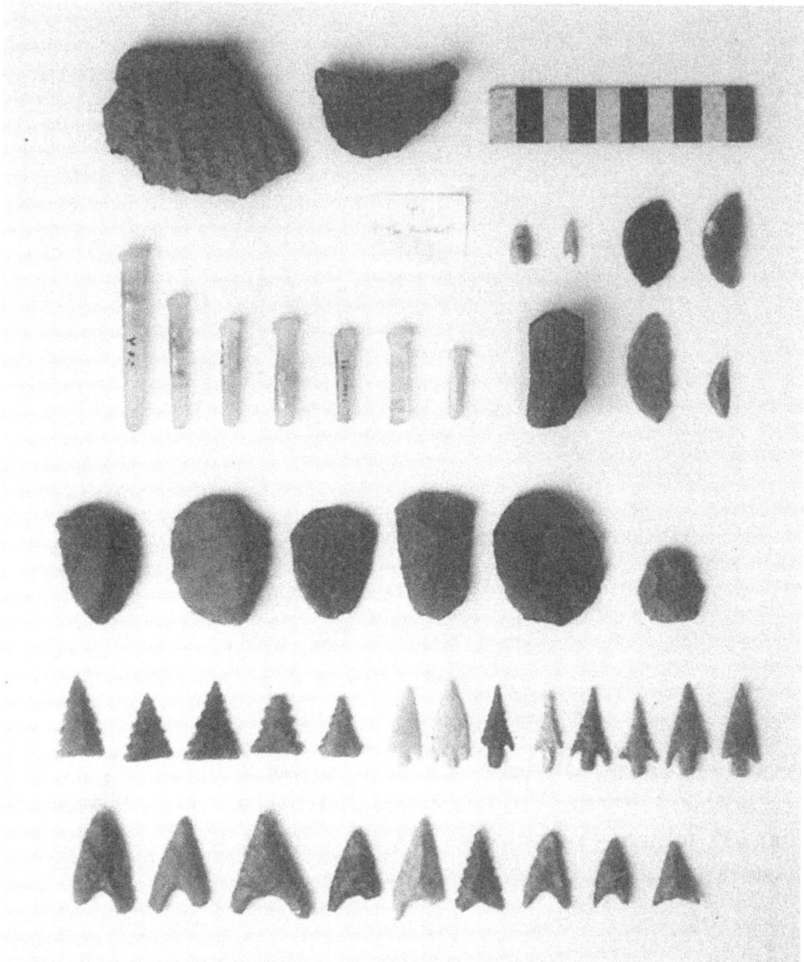

Figure 4.36. Artifacts of facies B, from top: decorated pot rims, quartz labrets, stone beads, microliths, end scrapers, projectile points.

Today, there are breeds of cattle that are trypano-tolerant; that is, they are not affected by sleeping sickness and can live in an area with tsetse flies. These animals, variously known as N'Dama, Baoule, and Bambara shorthorn (fig. 4.37), would appear to have been exposed to trypanosomiasis for such a long time that a degree of immunity has developed. They are small humpless animals, and the bloodline has

Figure 4.37. West African shorthorn cow, Ivory Coast.

probably continued where they occur down to the present without replacement by more modern breeds, such as the humped zebu (*Bos indicus*), which is common in the Sahel today. Until recently, zebu were not found in tsetse-infested areas.

Discussion

The relationship between *Homo sapiens* and hunted animals has a longer history in Africa than anywhere else in the world, and as we have seen, there were early Holocene attempts at controlling wild animals in the Sahara. This does not automatically mean that animals were independently domesticated in Africa, but it does suggest that the social conditions for domestication were in place once domestic animals appeared on the scene. It is just too coincidental that smaller cattle appeared in North Africa at the same time that ovicaprids entered from the Near East; there must have been cattle immigration as well. That separate African cattle DNA can be recognized in modern African breeds suggests that wild African cattle may have interbred with those from the Near East just less than 7,500 years ago.

By 5,000 years ago, environmental conditions began to destabilize, putting pressure on cattle that need to drink at least every two days. By 4,000 years ago, herders moved south into new areas opened up by tsetse retreat. At the same time, villages started to appear in the southern Sahara, and grain agriculture began shortly thereafter. Sedentary conditions were conducive to the growth of cemeteries, which were probably new identity points in the landscape.

5

Toward a Prehistory of Modern Saharan Pastoralists

I've lost their tracks, the loved ones
Perhaps my singing will bring them

—Bedouin ghinnawa (from L. Abu-Lughod, *Veiled Sentiments*)

In the previous chapter, I laid the groundwork for the beginning of pastoralism in North Africa and the Sahara. While our understanding of the prehistory is reasonably well grounded in archaeological data, the connections between the distant past and modern herding societies in the Sahara are vague and poorly researched. Although the ethnography of Saharan pastoralists has been used to explain the way of life and patterns of site layout of herding societies of the past (Smith, S. E., 1980; Smith 1992), there has been little attempt to push the archaeology of modern pastoralists back in time.

When Cavalli–Sforza et al. (1994: 172–73) noted the anomaly that the Tuareg (Kel Tamasheq), a Berber-speaking pastoral people of so–called Mediterranean stock, were estimated to be genetically closest to the Beja, a Cushitic-speaking pastoral group from further east in the Sudan, this went against the assumed history of Saharan people. This lead MacEachern (2000: 364) to correctly note, "there are no other data I know of that indicate such a link."

But perhaps this indication of possible links is not as outrageous as it first seems. I have already shown that there are good archaeological reasons to support large-scale cultural connections over huge areas of the Sahara, and present-day herders both in the Sahara and the Sahel are distributed across large regions, so perhaps we should not be so surprised to find their imprint in the present.

In regard to rock art, a large proportion of the paintings of the central Sahara come from pastoral societies where cattle were important. The Bovidian I rock art of the Tassili n'Ajjer of southern Algeria of the "black-face" style shows a range of pastoral activities, some of which have been suggested as ritual or ceremonial. A wide range of cattle coat colors clearly indicates not only a keen sense of individual animals being depicted, but also the stock lineage and a probable identification of the herders with their animals. The paintings show people who are clearly of "African" physical type (Lajoux 1963: 170), as opposed to the more "Mediterranean" people of the Bovidian II period (Lajoux 1963: 171). The people of the Bovidian I genre are suggested here as being the first wave of immigrant herders south of the Sahara to enter the West African Sahel after the Saharan climate became unstable around 4,500 years ago.

The later Bovidian II "white-face" style has yet to be adequately published and analyzed. Fortunately, Kuper (1978) managed to bring together the Saharan exhibit catalogue in Cologne, which included many of the panels transcribed by Pierre Colombel (Lhote 1976). These paintings are marvelously detailed, and Holl and Dueppen (1999) have used one of the larger examples from Iheren to suggest it depicts the entire pastoral way of life through a series of interlinking vignettes. Holl (1994) has also offered another interpretation, suggesting one of the large panels from Tikadiouine can be broken up into different segments that can be read as stages in a young man's growth toward manhood.

It is also notable that, in almost all the paintings with human figures, women are included, and there is considerable attention given to the dress and coiffure of females. Among the "white-faces," women are also shown riding oxen. These depictions would indicate the importance of women's roles within the society.

While the elements of most panels might appear recognizable to a Western eye, the striped fire cattle appear in several panels. The possible ritual importance of these animals has been suggested in fig. 4.23 as part of a "fire ceremony" (Smith 1993b). Among the Berbers of North Africa, there is a pre-Islamic fire worship. The people who practice this are referred to by the Arabs as *madjus* (Monès 1988: 229). Thus such beliefs might have a time depth of as much as 4,000 years. The wavy-line cattle may have been a metaphor for the fire-*djinns,* and their appearance in what might superficially seem to be simple narratives may take the paintings to a higher symbolic/ritual plane. These cattle may have been holy animals or animals imbued with contact between the living and the spiritual world, much like the "cattle of the ghosts" among the Nuer (Evans-Pritchard 1956: 164).

The fire cattle may be only one element of many that link these drawings. In fact, a number of these panels may have been part of a much larger, sequentially arranged visual landscape in which each panel led on a path to another as a series of mnemonics for ritual.

Modern People of the Central Sahara

The two major groups of the central Sahara today are the Tuareg (Kel Tamasheq) and Toubou (Teda, Daza, Zaghawa). Within the last centuries, they have been traditional enemies, separated by the Ténéré Sand Sea in Niger. Both groups have a social hierarchy, with endogamous castes of artisans who are feared and despised. The descent system of both groups is patrilineal, although there are conditions under which matrilineal descent exists among the Tuareg. The latter has led to great debate among scholars (cf. Rasmussen 1995: 162, note 6), some of whom believe that matrilineal descent may have been the original social organization. Although most writers today recognize a bilateral kinship relationship (Nicolaisen 1963; Murphy 1967), more than a thousand years of Islam must have had some effect upon the previous kinship patterns. Rasmussen (2000: 200) notes that postmenopausal women are, "seen as closer to pre-Islamic matrilineal forces in ritual, myth, symbolism and healing contexts."

The Teda occupied Kufra Oasis in the eastern Sahara for at least 2,000 years, until Arabs mostly displaced them at the beginning of the nineteenth century. Chapelle (1955: 109) believes that the Toubou were the Ethiopian Troglodytes hunted by the Garamantes described by Herodotus in 430 BC, or 2,300 years ago (Book IV: 183), but Chapelle (1955: 104) is the first to admit that the historical sources on the Toubou are extremely poor, saying: "les Toubous placent leur historiographie devant un vide inquiétant" (The Toubous situate their historiography within an uneasy emptiness).

There is obviously a great deal of conjecture about how to relate the early records with modern people. The /BèRi/ (Zaghawa) may be the same group mentioned by lbn Qutaiba in the eighth century (1,200 years ago; Tubiana and Tubiana 1977: 1). From oral traditions, Bernus (1981: 59) can give a time depth of only 1,000 years to the

Tuareg of the Aïr. He describes several "waves" of Berber-speaking immigrants from the north, indicating the open nature of the land and the permeability of pastoral territories. Equally, Levtzion (1973: 30) has to rely upon Arabic sources to describe the contact with the Sanhaja in the tenth century (1,000 years ago). This limited time depth begs the question of who lived in the central Sahara before AD 1000 (more than a thousand years ago). The caravan trade between Awdaghost and North Africa appears to have been well established long before the first Arabic observers and presumably was carried out, if not by, at least with the help of Saharan nomads.

The appearance of camels and *tifinagh* (the script of the Tuareg) in the rock art of the central Sahara may be late, but it does require us to know how long the camel has been in the area. Donkeys were used up to the Roman period, as evidenced by donkey dung in association with Roman era pottery southwest of Dakhleh Oasis (George 2000), and there is new genetic evidence to suggest donkeys may have been domesticated in northeast Africa (Beja-Pereira et al. 2004). The earliest camels in Africa may have been introduced across the Red Sea from Arabia, as by the second and first centuries BC (c. 2,100 years ago) there already existed a well-documented camel-borne trade route 500 miles south of the Nile Delta (Bulliet 1975: 116). Bulliet is convinced that the initial introduction was via poor desert dwellers on the African coast of the Red Sea who later transferred the animals southward to the Beja in the Sudan (Bulliet 1975: 134). There was certainly early trade across the Red Sea for several centuries before the rise of Aksum in the first century AD (2,000 years ago; de Contenson 1981: 343), and camel bones were recovered from the Kenya–Ethiopia border from a site dated to about 3,000 BC (4,400 years ago; Phillipson 1993: 150).

Ritual Behavior among Modern Saharan Pastoralists

Tuareg

Rasmussen's study (1995) of spirit possession among the Tuareg of the Aïr Mountains, Niger, offers a possible connection with much earlier people of the Sahara. This work adds to her earlier paper (Rasmussen 1992) where she describes the role of smiths (*Inadan*) as ritual specialists within Tuareg society. In both these reports, it is clear that the smith's marginal position in the society is due to their perceived access to the fire-*djinn* spirits. Through this power, they then become unofficial negotiators for marriages and within the politics of the group.

Spirit possession plays a somewhat ambiguous role within Tuareg society, as it is seen as being both pre- and un-Islamic, since it is predominantly women who go through these curing rituals. Rasmussen (1995: 8) suggests there is tension between male dominance (through Islam) and female power (through pre-Islamic beliefs). This does not mean that the religious specialists (*marabouts*) are hesitant to use spirit possession for their ends when the situation warrants it. It does point to an earlier, powerful belief system over which Islam is laid as a veneer, where women may have had greater political power than exists today, and there is even the possibility of matrilineal descent being more important in the past.

Among the Kel Ewey Tuareg, older women, "once culturally defined as post-childbearing . . . are therefore believed safer from spirits and able to approach Islamic rituals more closely with men. But they are also closer to matrilineal ancestresses, in particular, the twin-founders of herbal medicine and *maraboutique* medicine" (Rasmussen 2000: 196).

Support for either matrilineal descent or female power in the past exists in the tomb of Tin-Hinan at Abalessa in southern Algeria. A radiocarbon date of 1,480 ± 30 years ago came from the tomb (Brett and Fentress 1996: 208), and the rich grave goods of this woman would indicate her privileged position in Saharan society, possibly related to the trans-Saharan trade of the mid–fifth century. "In the Berber world there were several examples of supreme authority being attributed to a holy woman" (Salama 1981: 521). As legend has it, Tin-Hinan is linked directly with Tuareg history. A recent study of the oral history of Essuk in the Adrar des Iforas also hints at an earlier period when, "this city was under the command of a powerful Berber chief of the female sex" (Badi 2002: 53).

Other clues to pre-Islamic beliefs among the Tuareg can be seen in marks carved on the trunk of the tree *Maerua crassifolia* to placate or chase away the *djinns* that live in it. As Bernus (1996: 14) notes, "On ne se repose à son ombre sans tailler le tronc avec un couteau ou lancer des pièrres avant de s'en approcher" (One does not rest in its shadow without carving the trunk or throwing stones before approaching it).

The Kel Ferwan Tuareg will orient their tents so that the back is always into the wind (i.e., to the north), where the spirits, *kel esuf,* lurk at night (fig. 5.1). The layout of the tent by the cardinal points will protect the owners from evil spirits: "If one lifts any of the lateral mats during the day, one must be very careful, when night falls, to drop those which face north, because a tent opened to the north will be exposed to the worst dangers" (Casajus 1987: 56). Of the cardinal points, the south is the least dangerous and the source of divine benediction. The south and north of the tent are thus spatial opposites that lead to other binary separations, such as benediction/danger or ostentation (pride, or *faste*)/bad luck, solemnity (*nefaste*). Inside the tent the bed is oriented east–west, with the head to the east. The husband sleeps to the north, thus protecting his wife against the *kel esuf.* Such an orientation in turn leads to the idea of north (*nefaste*) being masculine and the south (*faste*) feminine (Casajus 1987: 57). Entry to the tent is through the door in the west side. It is unfortunate that Striedter and Tauveron (2002–2003) have named what they perceive to be the oldest rock art of the central Sahara *Kel Essuf,* which if they are correct in their dating, is unlikely to have anything to do with Tuareg history.

The ideology behind the spatial orientation of the Tuareg tent is a nomadic analog to the equally comprehensive and symbolic layout of the Kabyle house (fig. 5.1) of the Atlas Mountains of North Africa. The house is divided into "a dark part (the west and north sides) and a light part (the east and south sides)" (Bourdieu 1973: 109). According to the Kabyles, this reflects the division of the year into wet and dry seasons. Bourdieu orients his reader to the house by reference to the threshold on the light (east) side, across which one enters the abode. This is the entry that men or visitors would be expected to use. The back, or west, door is a private portal used by women, and it is closest to the loom that is the domain of the woman of the house. As Bourdieu (1973: 110) states, "The orientation of the house is fundamentally defined from the outside, from the point

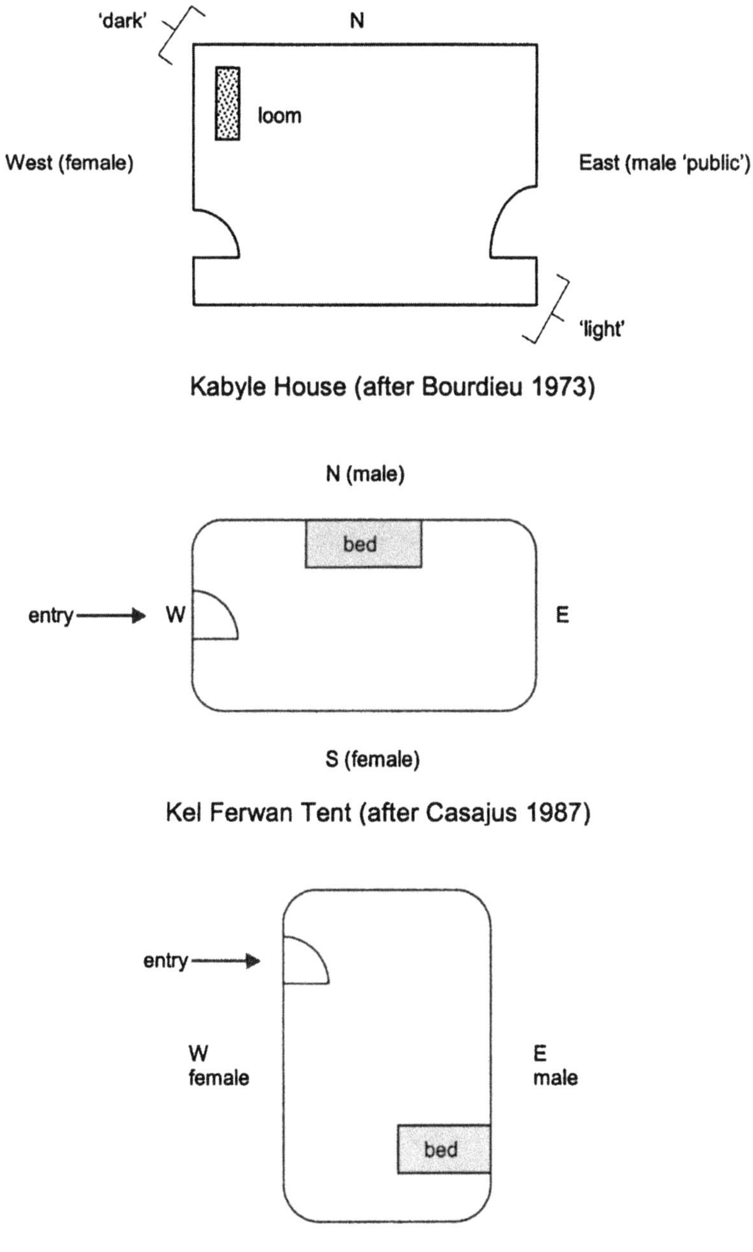

Figure 5.1. Comparison of layout of three domestic spaces: (1) Kabyle; (2) Kel Ferwan Tuareg; (3) Toubou.

of view of men and, if one may say so, by men for men, as the place from which men come out." The eastern orientation of the house is similar to how the Bedouin of Arabia orient their tents, that is, toward the rising sun (Jabbur 1995: 255). The Kabyle house would probably conform to an Islamic format, as far as the men are concerned.

Bourdieu, as a man, got the male perspective on Kabyle cosmology. If he had been a woman interviewing women, perhaps a slightly greater emphasis would have been given to the world from the female side. In the 1977 translation of his book *Outline of a Theory of Practice*, there is no mention of the woman's door in the section dealing with the Kabyle house (Bourdieu 1977: 90–91). In the 1973 paper, his reference to the door is almost in passing: "the low and narrow door, reserved for women, which opens in the direction of the garden, at the back of the house" (Bourdieu 1973: 106). Berber women in towns also use the back door to their houses, never the front, or public, entrance (Courtney-Clarke 1996: xxiii).

The Tuareg tent is owned and made by a woman (often with her mother's help before marriage). Thus the domain of women is the domestic sphere, while the domain of men is the herd and public life. As with the Kabyle house, there is only one appropriate approach to the dwelling; but in the case of the Tuareg tent it is from the west, where the door is located.

Is there a connection between the two? If so, which influenced the other? The woman's entry from the west might be a clue. In addition, both groups speak a Berber language. The archaeology of grain agriculture in the Maghreb suggests that it arrived quite late and as in the rest of North Africa was preceded by nomadic pastoralism. As Camps (1974: 276) states, "There is no analytical element which will allow us to affirm that agriculture was being practiced before the 5th millennium B.C. [5,200–6,100 years ago] on the African littoral." Domestic animals were already in the Aurès Mountains of Algeria in the sixth millennium BC (Roubet 1978). Thus fully sedentary communities such as the Kabyles probably have their ancestry in mobile herding societies. If this is indeed the case, then the tents of the nomads, which existed before Islam, may have been the original structures on which the houses of the Kabyles were later modeled.

Toubou

Pre-Islamic religious beliefs also exist among the Kanuri-speaking Toubou (Teda, Daza, Bideyat, Zagawa) of Chad and Libya. Today, like the Tuareg, most Toubou are adherents of Islam, but where *djinns*, or spirits, are part of the religion. A number of these spirits live in the mountains, on dunes and lakes, and protection against them can be achieved through sacrificing an animal or wearing amulets. There are dangerous spirits (e.g., Fada Manda) and kind spirits, such as Deli Manda. To ask for the protection of Deli Manda against harm requires placing a rock on the ground and surrounding it with small stones. The rock is covered with flour, salt, and dates. Two weeks later, a goat is slaughtered on the rock, and the entrails are placed there. Part of the animal is roasted and placed on the rock, while the skin is put on a branch of the tree "dirigée vers le lieu où habite le génie" (directed toward the place where the genie lives; Chapelle 1957: 387). The amulets may contain Koranic writing, or they can be special pieces of wood, other vegetal matter, or fragments of animal or human residues. These activities all point to an animist past overlain by Islamic beliefs.

Water points are also potentially dangerous places. The Toubou believe that crocodiles surviving in waterholes of their regions are the spirit protectors of the water, and it is forbidden to kill them. The ancient Libyans, according to Desanges (1981: 431), attributed supernatural power to geographical features, such as rivers and mountains, believing that *djinns* lived there; they also worshipped certain freshwater pools and trees for their ability to increase human fertility.

Tubiana (1964) has reviewed the literature on survival of pre-Islamic religious practices among the various pastoral groups of the eastern Sahara and compared these with the Zaghawa. There are a number of common threads that appear among most of these people. These include the importance of mountains, groups of boulders, trees, and wadis where spirits are believed to live and where rituals are performed, mostly for rainmaking; but other fertility rites are also observed. Involved in these rites are always sacrifices (in some cases in the past, human sacrifice), and although mostly men officiate, older women are prominent in many of the activities. Among the

Zaghawa, the clan chief and his uterine nephews maintain authority by performing sacrifices. Tubiana (1964: 197) suggests that the historic reason for this was the selection by the chief of a wife, followed by all of his followers from a conquered clan, that is, taking their procreative power and maintaining it within male hands. He does not consider the possibility that this is a leftover from a time of a more powerful matriarchy, where women controlled more than just the domestic space. As it is, the Toubou have mat tents of similar construction to the Kel Ferwan that they use during the wet season, and they have also made the cardinal directions gendered. The tents are laid out in a north–south axis, with the door opening on the northwest (Lebeuf 1959: 18) (fig. 5.1). The woman's side of the tent is the west, closest to the door, and the man's is the east (Baroin 1985: 56). This layout would have resonance with the Kabyle house. The layout of the tents within the camp, however, places the girls to the north of the wives' huts and the boys to the south (Baroin 1985: 62).

As suggested above, so much of Tuareg and Toubou cosmology is pre-Islamic overlain with a veneer of Islam. There are a number of connections we might make between the present and the past. Among the Toubou, the tombs of revered religious men (*marabouts*) are believed to have supernatural powers, and the dead are asked for favors by giving offerings to them (Chapelle 1957: 390). Similarly, Tuareg *marabouts* are thought to possess holiness, and when a respected *marabout* dies, his power is believed to increase, as he is now nearer God. His grave becomes a shrine, and people will come to his grave during the day and pray (Rasmussen 1992). In the late nineteenth century, Bruun (1898: 298–99) noted among the Berbers of Tunisia: "The Khrumis are musulmans only in name. . . . [T]hey own some Marabout tombs, enshrining saints to whom peculiar influence is attributed, and who are worshipped like positive idols. . . . In short, all these Marabouts are worshipped as lesser gods. Beneath Islam, idolatry flourishes as in the olden days: the gods have merely changed their names."

The rock art of the later Saharan pastoral periods showing a fire ritual is evocative of the modern Tuareg belief in fire-*djinns* and of the despised endogamous caste of artisans (Inadan) as intermediaries between the real and spirit worlds. Spirit possession and altered states of consciousness, while today restricted to women, may have been more universal in the past. Men have a stronger identity with Islam, as their power and authority are embedded in Islamic belief (Rasmussen 1995). Women, who may have been more powerful in the past, can use the pre-Islamic belief in spirit possession as a counterfoil against male-dominance to establish their own political and social space. Bourdieu (1977: 89) makes the point that Islam also affected the Kabyles, among whom religion is male and magic female.

It is not only among the Tuareg that artisans are reviled and feared. Like the Tuareg, the Toubous have a distinct hierarchy, with three separate levels: Teda/Daza, Aza artisans, and slaves/domestics. As early as 1871, Nachtigal (1974), the first European to enter the Tibesti area and to spend time with the Toubous, noted how the blacksmiths were segregated from the larger populace and seen as contemptible. They are feared as sorcerers for their knowledge of magical potions and black magic. No Teda/Daza would think of marrying a blacksmith. They are a caste apart, marrying only among themselves (Baroin 1985: 70–71). Also, they are never insulted or attacked; in fact they are protected by the Teda/Daza that they work for against others who would attempt to abuse them or steal their animals.

Fulani

While the Fulani (Peul, Fulbe, Woodabe) are not strictly Saharan pastoralists, their proximity to the Tuareg and Toubou is such that they should be considered as possible descendants of prehistoric Saharan pastoral groups and as part of the wider pastoral network of West Africa.

Islam has massively impacted much of Fulani religious belief (Riesman 1977), and it was a holy war (or *jihad*) that propelled the Fulani of the nineteenth century under Uthman dan Fodio on their conquest of Bornu. The degree of Islamization tends to vary, as the more sedentary the group, the more Islam is central to life, while the pastoral nomad end of the continuum has, at least until recently, maintained a semblance of their more ancient belief structure. This is highlighted in the detailed description of Woodabe initiation given by Amadou Hampaté Ba, a Fulani philosopher and historian trained in the intricacies of their beliefs (Hampaté Ba and Dieterlen 1961).

The history of the Fulani is shrouded in myth and overshadowed by Islamic history. The myths of origin of the pastoral Woodabe give no clear indication of where they came from before Islam (Stenning 1959: 20). The closest we can get is via linguistic reconstructions that indicate that the language spoken by all Fulani is closest to Serer-Wolof, found in Senegal. Migration of the Fulani eastward is suggested as starting in the eleventh century, presumably following pastures, but as Stenning (1959: 22) describes: "Pastoral Fulani have always formed minorities within wider societies, and intolerable political conditions within these have been countered by a more dramatic form of movement—migration from the scene of war, excessive tribute, and the like. Pastoral Fulani have remained pastoralists . . . only by continuous seasonal movement, which develops imperceptibly into migratory drift, and by periodic migration. They have left behind them Fulani populations more closely wedded to the soil, the semi-permanent and sedentary populations." This has resulted in their distribution across most of the savanna of West Africa, from Senegal to Nigeria and Cameroon.

While their recent history is relatively clearly understood, their more distant past is not clear, and there is no archaeology to elucidate their existence. Intriguing suggestions of a Saharan past have been raised regarding perceived similarities between depictions in the rock art of the Tassili n'Ajjer and Fulani ceremonies. Figure 4.21 from Uan Derbaouan has been suggested as representing the Fulani *lotoori* cleansing ritual (Hampaté Ba and Dieterlen (1966: 150). Another example from this period, also from the Tassili n'Ajjer, shows heads of cattle around a sun motif (fig. 5.2) that Hampaté Ba and Dieterlen (1966: 149) interpret as one of the seven suns where initiates receive training from the god, Koumen, during "clairères," or stages of initiation, on their path to ritual elder status.

Such interpretations are not without their critics. There is nothing within Fulani origin myths to support these contentions. On the one hand, Le Quellec (2002) maintains that there are none of the recognized Fulani symbols, such as the important calf rope symbol, while on the other hand, there is the long time between the execution of the painting, perhaps some 5,000 years ago, and the present (Vansina 1984). To Le Quellec (2002: 149), the ceremonial attributions

Figure 5.2. "Pastoralist initiation," Tissoukai, Tassili n'Ajjer (after Hampaté Ba and Dieterlen, 1961).

are too exact, and some of the arguments for equating the paintings with the Fulani need not be specific to just the Fulani but rest on a "level of generalities common to all pastoral cultures."

However, there are too many other such coincidences in the paintings with modern pastoral Fulani society, such as the layout of the camp from Tissoukaï (Lhote 1976), where the male and female domains are clearly separated by the calf rope, and the *kaakul* display of containers (Kuper 1978: 426: fig.11), not to at least consider the possibility that we are dealing with similar cultural patterns. It is possible that the Tassili paintings depict a formative West African pastoral society whose best fit today may be the Fulani, but the detail that Hampaté Ba and Dieterlen claimed to see in the paintings is perhaps what they wanted to see to support their thesis. Time depth, however, should not be used as an argument against the survival of deep meaning in any society. We know that the history of the Judeo-Christian Bible goes back several thousand years, and only part of this history was maintained in written form.

The Landscape of Saharan Pastoralism

Using Tilley's idea of a landscape (1994: 34) as "a series of named locales, a set of relational places, linked by paths, movements and narratives," we can situate the cultural space of pastoralism in the Sahara through key symbols, such as rock art and funerary monuments, that have survived in the archaeological record of the Later and Terminal Pastoral Periods. While di Lernia (1999b) has given a general account of the transhumant responses to climatic shifts, we should ask what role the symbolic elements played within the wider landscape. The transhumant orbit of pastoral people follows known and repeated paths. Various points along these paths are named and become referents for giving information to others, as well as being embedded in the historical narratives. The fact of naming is a means of control and identity. This can be for claiming rights, but it is more for enhancing the mental map of territories that is learned at a very young age.

The landscape is equally a place of referents that are built into the oral histories, myth, and stories of the people repeated around campfires. This accumulative knowledge of places becomes a synergic fabric through which actions and events are woven.

Even the most monotonous landscape to an outside observer is rich in historical events, the significances of which are passed down through the generations. Tracks linking points are avenues among which people, animals, goods, and information are passed from person to person. As Tilley (1994: 27) notes: "All locales and landscapes are . . . embedded in their social and individual times of memory. Their pasts as much as their spaces are crucially constitutive of their presents. Neither space nor time can be understood apart from social practices which serve to bind them together." The landscape, therefore, has real meaning in identity and is more than just a backdrop for social and economic activities.

Mostly, the places are natural features in the landscape, such as water pools or rock formations, but there are also man-made sites, such as rock art sites, kraals, or graves, each belonging to individuals or families who may be remembered for many generations. Marking places with signs or symbols, such as the Tuareg sign for water, or writing in *tifinagh*, adds to identity points. Other symbols may be encoded in rock paintings or engravings. Select areas or points may be places where rituals take place, and they may be considered to have more power for successful outcome of desired effects. Such holy places may even become centers of pilgrimage for a large area, if they are associated with important ritual figures. This is particularly true of cemeteries in modern Islamic belief.

If paths constitute a narrative of linking points, we might suggest that in the period after 4,000 years ago important locales would have been the rock art panels on the walls of caves in the Tassili n'Ajjer and Acacus Mountains. The paintings reproduced in Kuper (1978) show most of the "actors" facing to the left, particularly the traveling scenes showing women riding oxen from two sites: Iheren and Uan Derbaouen. This might be construed as some linearity in a progression, and may represent a continuous line connecting one panel with another. Thus each panel may be read as a continuation of the previous one, and not in isolation. The narrative would unfold as the individual viewer moved along the paths. There are some variations in dress, which suggest the paintings were done over a period of time. However, these paintings are finished pieces and so are the work of skilled artists. This would indicate a tradition of training art specialists, possibly in conjunction with other ritual training. The incidence of wavy-line cattle in several paintings of the white-face style would take them out of the simple narrative and raise them to a higher plane of ritual and belief that would be understood by anyone who knew the "code." It is tempting to think of the wavy-line motif as representing the flickering of fire to those practicing spirit possession, and that the "big men" to whom obeisance is being offered were using the fire motifs to demonstrate their power.

Human Biology

Studies of human skeletal material from Neolithic sites in the Sahara indicate a robust African "mechtoid" population inhabited North Africa from possibly Aterian or even earlier times, until around 4,000 years ago (Petit-Maire and Dutour 1987: 279). After this, in the Malian Sahara, the skeletons no longer show the traits that identify them as aboriginal, and the multivariate analysis (Petit-Maire and Dutour 1987: fig. 13.16) shows that there is considerable overlap with measurements from skeletons from northeast Africa, that is pre-Dynastic Egypt.

The historian Salama (1981) arrived at a similar conclusion, that the history of Mediterranean people in the Sahara goes back at least to "proto-historic" times. He goes on to say, "it seems that the origin of this physical type is no longer to be looked for towards the Maghreb but rather towards the north-east of the African continent" (Salama 1981: 520).

Similarly, an earlier study of blood groups among the main Saharan groups by Briggs (1957) suggested that the Teda (a Toubou subgroup) show distinct differences compared to other sub-Saharan African groups, even though they physically look similar. Briggs (1957: 196) also posed the question whether there was a connection with people "who came into the area from the North-East in early Neolithic times."

It would appear, therefore, that around 4,000 years ago there was a shift in the population of the Sahara. This generally appears to have coincided with other cultural changes, such as the appearance of well-constructed funerary monuments.

A tiny, and insignificant, piece of evidence that might connect northeast Africa with pastoralists of the central Sahara is to be found in burials. Merimde beni-Salame on the edge of the Nile Delta had what the excavator Junker described in the 1920s as a very "un-Egyptian" burial practice: almost no grave goods were placed with the skeleton, except an occasional bead or amulet (Hoffman 1980: 174). A similar pattern was found during the excavation of one of the burials at Adrar Bous in Niger (fig. 4.25): a single stone bead around the neck. Paris, who continued the work at Adrar Bous, says "ornamentation is rare and there is nothing we can consider to be especially funerary" (Paris 1996: 299). Like these two localities, the burials at Karkarichinkat in Mali also had very limited grave goods, and in one case only a single stone bead around the neck (Smith 1974) (fig. 4.35).

Central Saharan Connections

Since the early Holocene, there have been cultural connections between the Nile Valley, at its confluence of the Blue and White Niles, and Nubia, all the way across the Sahara to Niger (Smith, A. B., 1980). This can be seen in the similarities in the wavy-line and dotted wavy-line pottery and bone harpoons, dated between 9,300 and 8,500 years ago. Pottery continued to be an indicator of cultural exchange in the later periods, with "diamond" rocker stamped wares appearing in both the Nile Valley at Es Shaheinab (Arkell 1953, see also Caneva 1989) and in the Tenerian of Adrar Bous, around 7,000 to 4,500 years ago (Smith, A.B., 1980).

From this we might suggest that the mobile aspect of, first, nomadic hunters and, later, pastoralists had set up a series of connecting links that manifested itself in the water points across the lowlands and most of the highland areas (Ennedi, Tibesti, Aïr, Hoggar), facilitating movement, if not of commodities, at least of ideas. This belt of connection, roughly 16°N–22°N, would have as its southern limit the most northerly extent of the 500 mm rainfall isohyet conducive to tsetse breeding places, and thus difficult for pastoralism (Smith 1979).

These routes, possibly embedded in the landscape of nomadic movement and memory, seem to have had continuous use well into the seventeenth century or later. Funerary monuments from the Nubian Desert containing cattle horns and dated to about 5,000 years ago (Sadr et al. 1994) are very similar to those found in Niger after 4,500 years ago (Paris 1996).

MacDonald (1998) elaborates on these connections by suggesting that long-distance trade in highly desirable commodities existed across the southern Sahara. He further suggests that this trade resulted in monopolies that underpinned the more complex social formations seen at Kerma on the Sudanese Nile (Bonnet 1992) and at Dhar Tichitt in Mauritania (Holl 1985).

History has divided the Saharan nomads into somewhat smaller groups, but even if we look at the present-day Tuareg and Fulani, we see they are equally spread over vast areas of land. We might suggest that the linkages between the different groups of present-day nomads, although broken, might be reconnected by looking at the later influences upon them. For example, in the recent past, the Tuareg have been archenemies of the Toubou who live to the east beyond the Ténéré Sand Sea. Both share a great deal in common, even though they don't look alike or speak similar languages. Not only are they camel herders, but both also have a hierarchical social organization of nobles, vassals, and slaves. Like the Tuareg, the Toubou have an endogamous caste of artisans who are feared as the intermediaries with the spirit world but considered unclean and of low status. In comparing approaches to medicine among the Tuareg and Toubou, Beltrami (2002: 65), while noting that their approaches to disease may be different, asserted that "their use of natural drugs and treatment of traumatic events are the same."

As noted above, the historical connection of the Tuareg appears to be with the Berbers of the North African littoral. In his discussion of the derivation of the mixed populations of the central Sahara, Froment (1999) poses the question: Are the Tuareg indigenous people whom the Berbers found in the Sahara, and who were admitted into their culture, or were they later immigrants?

The Toubou are Kanuric-speaking people who have more in common with the Sahel and Bornu to the south around Lake Chad. Both Tuareg and Toubou were well connected with trade routes to their respective neighbors. Cordell (1977: 22) indicates that the trans-Saharan trade from the Mediterranean at Benghazi to Wadai was opened up only in 1809/1810. Previous contact between the oases of Libya and northern Chad (e.g., Kufra) was with Bornu (Cordell 1977: 27).

What all this may mean is that the almost inherent needs of nomadic pastoralism, of pasture and water, across large tracts of open country from the Red Sea to the central Sahara resulted in complex movements of people and cultural material over considerable periods of time, and that they have left a sizeable genetic imprint wherever they went.

Saharan pastoralists are notorious for their personal aversion to agriculture. They are, however, quite happy for other people to grow grains for them and to extract their tribute at harvest time. It may well be that around 3,500 years ago, with the first appearance of domesticated grains from sedentary villages, slaves were being brought from the south to work the fields for the nomads. This could have been the origin of a hierarchical system where there was a social separation between the nomads and the agricultural Harratin people of the desert oases (see Froment 1999).

Toward the end of the Later Pastoral Period, pressure on agricultural people on the southern fringes of the Sahara may have been one significant reason for the development of organized states, such as Ghana and Mali, for defense against pastoralist depredations (Munson 1980; MacDonald 1998).

Beja Archaeology and History

At the beginning of this chapter, we looked at possible biological connections between Tuareg and Beja. Where might the Beja fit in this grand scenario? With its early consolidated power, Dynastic Egypt raided Nubia for cattle around 4,700 years ago, forcing A-group people away from the Nile Valley (Sadr 1991: 93). These raids disrupted use of the river by people with cattle and may have led to the A group becoming nomadic. With the onset of drier conditions after 4,500 years ago, and with the riverine pastures closed to the herders, nomadism would probably have been an acceptable strategy.

By 3,700 years ago, the Medjay appear in the written records in the Eastern Desert, synchronous with C-group people along the river. The Medjay are identified as early Beja (Sadr 1991: 99), who have been given the name "Pangrave" by archaeologists working in Upper Egypt and Nubia. They may have been mercenaries in Northern Atbai and influenced the Mokram groups of Southern Atbai by 3,600 years ago (Sadr 1991: 47). Thus, we can tie the Beja with nomadic groups south of the confluence of the Blue and White Niles, which in turn means they could have been part of the pastoral connections further to the west.

The Beja are later identified as the Blemmyes of the Roman period, but although many different groups came into contact with these nomadic people, very little information has come down to us about their early culture or social organization. What is obvious is that the contact the Beja have had with other groups throughout their history involved them "in long distance trade as guides, middlemen and desert brigands" (Hjort and Dahl 1991: 14). Hjort and Dahl further note that, unlike the other Cushitic camel herders, the Beja use their camels for riding, and they state that: "even if the ancestors of the Beja ever were closely related to other Cushites, they broke away from them at least 6000 years ago, i.e. long before their particular adaptation of combining caravan service, durra cultivation and pastoralism was developed" (Hjort and Dahl 1991: 15). While this date may be arguable, it would appear that there has been sufficient time depth for the language of the Beja and their techniques of camel rearing to be significantly different from those of other Cushites.

As with agrarian products among the Zaghawa, especially millet (Tubiana 1964: 198), introduction of sorghum cultivation was probably late among the Beja and is suggested as occurring after the separation from other Cushites (Hjort and Dahl 1991: 15, following Ehret 1976). The archaeological evidence so far suggests that domesticated plants did not appear in Africa until after 3,000 years ago (including probably the return of *Sorghum durra* from India; Kajale 1988). The suggestion that durra cultivation was introduced to the Beja around 2,000 years ago would be acceptable (Bulliet 1975: 116).

From Arabic texts, the Beja are thought originally to have been a matrilineal society (Murdock 1959: 317), with women playing a central role (Clark 1938: 3). We have already noted that there is some suggestion that the Tuareg also were matrilineal in the past (Nicolaisen 1963: 153), and there is no question that older women among the Tuareg have considerable say in camp affairs behind the scenes.

Using Cavalli-Sforza et al.'s genetic tree (1994), Holden and Mace (2002) compare lactase persistence—the ability to digest lactose, or milk sugar—among various African pastoral populations. Table 5.1 shows that Beja and Tuareg have levels of lactase persistence over 80 percent, as do Saudi Bedouin. While there are some anomalies in the data, for example, the unexpectedly low lactase persistence levels in the Nuer and Dinka (both Nilotic pastoralists from southern Sudan), generally, the levels of lactase persistence are a reflection of the degree of pastoral activities within the society (compare the pastoral to sedentary Fulani). The high lactase persistence levels among the Tuareg, Beja, and Bedouin may indicate a historical link, although Berber and Bedouin are closer in the Cavalli-Sforza et al. genetic tree than are Beja and Tuareg (fig. 5.3). Bedouin are quite distinct from other Asian populations (Cavalli-Sforza et al. 1994: fig. 4.15.1) and cluster with Yemeni and Saudi groups, thus an Afro-Arabian genetic link might be proposed.

Table 5.1. Lactase Persistence in African Herder Populations

Population	% Pastoralism	# Individuals	%LP
Baggara (2 groups)	50.5–70.5	39	40–47
Bedouin (SW Asia; 2 groups)	80.5–93.0	197	76–83
Beja (4 groups)	60.6–93.0	281	80–87
Dinka	50.5	213	24
Egyptians	30.5	742	36
Fulani (pastoralist)	80.5	9	78
Fulani (sedentary)	40.5	24	29
Ganda	10.5	27	4
Hausa	30.5	17	24
Herero	60.5	37	3
Hutu	30.5	51	49
Igbo	10.5	16	19
Nama	50.5	18	50
Nubians	93.0	21	33
Nuer	50.5	23	22
San	0.0	63	5
Shilluk	20.5	8	37
Sotho	30.5	23	35
Swazi	20.5	12	25
Tswana	40.5	24	17
Tuareg	60.5	118	87
Tunisians	20.5	43	17
Tutsi	40.5	59	93
Xhosa	30.5	17	18
Yoruba	10.5	100	9
Zulu	40.5	32	19

Source: Holden and Mace (2002).

Another study of genetic distance that seems to reinforce the Cavalli-Sforza et al. study is by Knight et al. (2003). Figure 5.4 shows the distance in selected African groups and how the Tuareg and Kanuri are firmly within the "African" group, while Berber is out on a limb.

Discussion

Increasing aridity in the central Sahara after 4,500 years ago forced pastoralists to adapt their herding strategies. This period coincided with a shift in populations, with the "black-face" people of the Saharan rock art being able to move south with the retreat of the

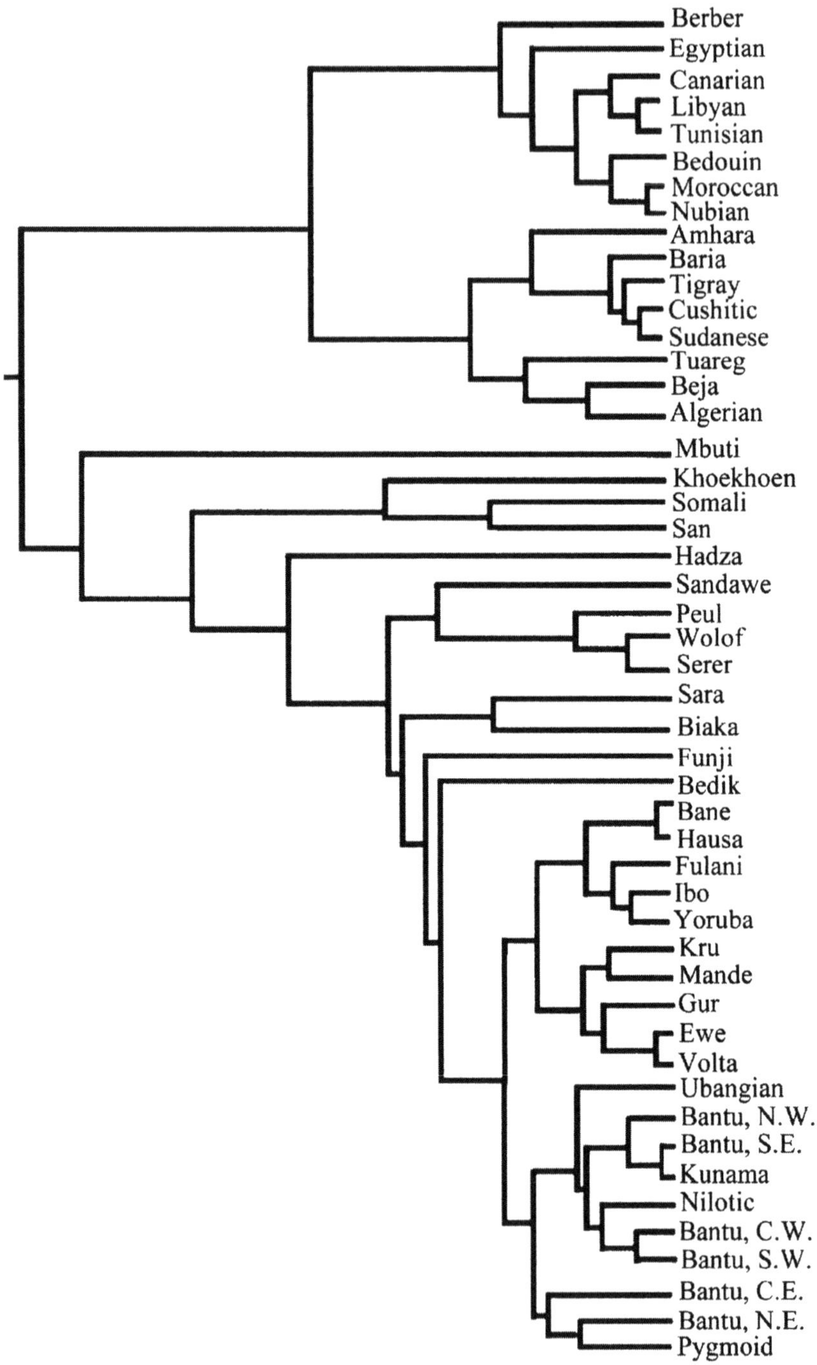

Figure 5.3. Genetic tree of 49 African populations (from Cavalli-Sforza et al. 1994).

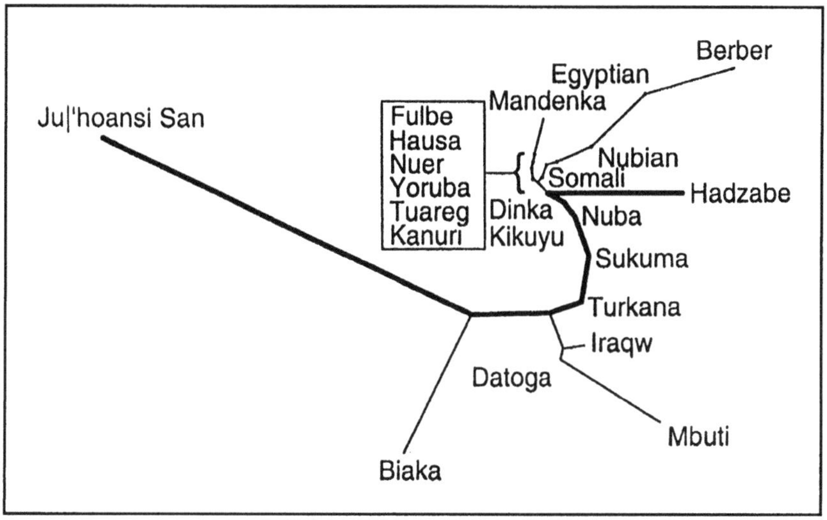

Figure 5.4. Population relationships as a summary of genetic distances (Knight et al. 2003; reprinted by permission).

tsetse belts as the rainfall associated with the Intertropical Convergence Zone moved toward the Gulf of Guinea (Smith 1979). The pastoral niche in the central Sahara was filled by people of Mediterranean stock, seen in the "white-face" people of the rock art. These arrivals brought a new tradition not only of rock art, but also of finely constructed funerary monuments that were to be found scattered across the rocky parts of the desert.

After 4,000 years ago, with increasing instability in climatic conditions and corresponding pastoral resources, villages with gardens appeared, reflecting a more sedentary lifestyle. This may have been a response of widening the food base to include domestic grains in the diet. This is also when large collective graveyards began to appear in Saharan prehistory. This may also reflect greater hierarchization, with slaves being taken from agricultural communities in the south and being brought in to work the gardens. A new population group would have been added to the central Sahara: the ancestors of the so-called Harratin in desert oases (Briggs 1957). The southern Sahara was probably where experimentation with African grain crops, for example, sorghum and millet, began (Harlan 1971). The earliest direct evidence for domestic grains is late and comes from Dhar Tichitt in Mauritania, c. 3,000 years ago (Munson, 1976; Amblard and Pernès 1989). Wild grains were harvested prior to this date.

It should come as no surprise that cultural connections have been made over large sections of the Sahara for the past 9,000 years. The present distribution of the Fulani, from Senegal in the west to Cameroon and beyond in the east, and the Tuareg distribution in Algeria, Mali, and Niger offer us modern examples of how widespread pastoral societies can be in the Sahara. It does force us to think how such connections are maintained, and here the landscape of transhumant pastoralism is one way of modeling their world. The two basic resources that drive much of the distribution at any moment in time throughout the year are water and pasture. The fluctuating climate, and thus environmental conditions, produces a lowest common denominator of severe droughts, which today occur roughly every 30 years. These are long enough intervals for the cultural memory to forget the hardships and loss of livestock, but an awareness of alternative strategies, such as growing grain or choosing to raise cattle for beef instead of camels, is still required.

Water points must always have been major landscape referents, but the archaeology would suggest that it was not only economic variables that determined distribution. Cultural and ritual points in the landscape were probably just as important. The location of rock art display centers or important grave sites of revered holy people could have become part of the folk memory and would thus have become centers for ceremonial activity.

The assumption has always been that Berber influences came from the Maghreb and entered the Sahara via the Tuareg from the north. While this might be true of the language affinities, the long time depth of the Saharan rock art and related ritual activities suggest it may have been pastoral people living in the Sahara practicing their religion that had influence on Berber beliefs. Thus the genetic relationship suggested between Tuareg and Beja (Cavalli-Sforza et al. 1994) may indeed be a real one, indicating associations among Saharan pastoralists from the Red Sea to the central Sahara that had already existed from earlier Neolithic times. We might suggest that formation of many of Berber cultural ideas came from the lands to the south. Formative Tuareg links with the north may have heightened the traditional enmity between groups, especially when the Toubou sought their connections with Bornu and black Africa to the south.

Wilkinson (2003: 107) has recently suggested pastoral links between the Eastern Desert of Egypt and the Nile Valley on the basis of rock engravings. Wilkinson recognizes in the art precursors to Dynastic traditions involving cattle. Although rock art is difficult to date, Wilkinson sees the art as coeval with the cattle burials at Badari, about 5,000 years ago.

The image of the Sahara as a desert land with few people who have to rely upon the more cultured societies of the north or south for both ideas and commodities needs revision (Vercoutter 1988). Long-distance trade across the central and southern Sahara, experimentation in grain agriculture, and religious ideas that spread to the Nile Valley and the Maghreb all point to innovative and dynamic pastoral societies whose stability existed over thousands of years, and whose genetic imprint can still be seen in the present.

6

Domestic Animals Spread to East and Southern Africa

Ox with diverging horns,
The horns are reaching the ground;
The horns are overflowing like a boiling pot.
I love the black pattern of the Pied Ox of my father.

—Dinka Praise song (after Deng 1972)

As far back as the 1930s, Louis Leakey found pottery at Stable's Drift in Kenya that he named "Gumban A" (Leakey 1931: 199). The pottery was later designated Nderit Ware, for which Bower et al. (1977: 133) claimed a date of 7,155 years ago from the lower levels of Salasun Rockshelter. Investigators of pastoralism in East Africa have generally rejected this date, and as with the discussion of the southward movement of domestic animals into the Sahel in West Africa, the best record we have of domestic stock in Kenya is around 4,000 years ago (Marshall 2000). As far north as Dongodien, near Lake Turkana (fig. 6.1), domestic animals, mostly ovicaprids but also some cattle, are dated to this time (Marshall et al. 1984; Barthelme 1985). Further south, in the Rift Valley, the earliest ovicaprids at Enkapune Ya Moto may date to 4,860 years ago (Ambrose 1998), with cattle appearing at 3,990 years ago, although these dates need support from other sources. Near the border with Tanzania, in Tsavo National Park, Wright (2003) has a date of 4,020 years ago for domestic animals.

This coincidence of dates with West Africa may indicate that similar environmental conditions influenced the expansion of domestic animals into both areas, that is, tsetse retreat as rainfall decreased. There is also the question of how influential the Ethiopian highlands were in the initial spread of domestic stock. At the moment, the dates from Ethiopia are younger than any for northern Kenya,

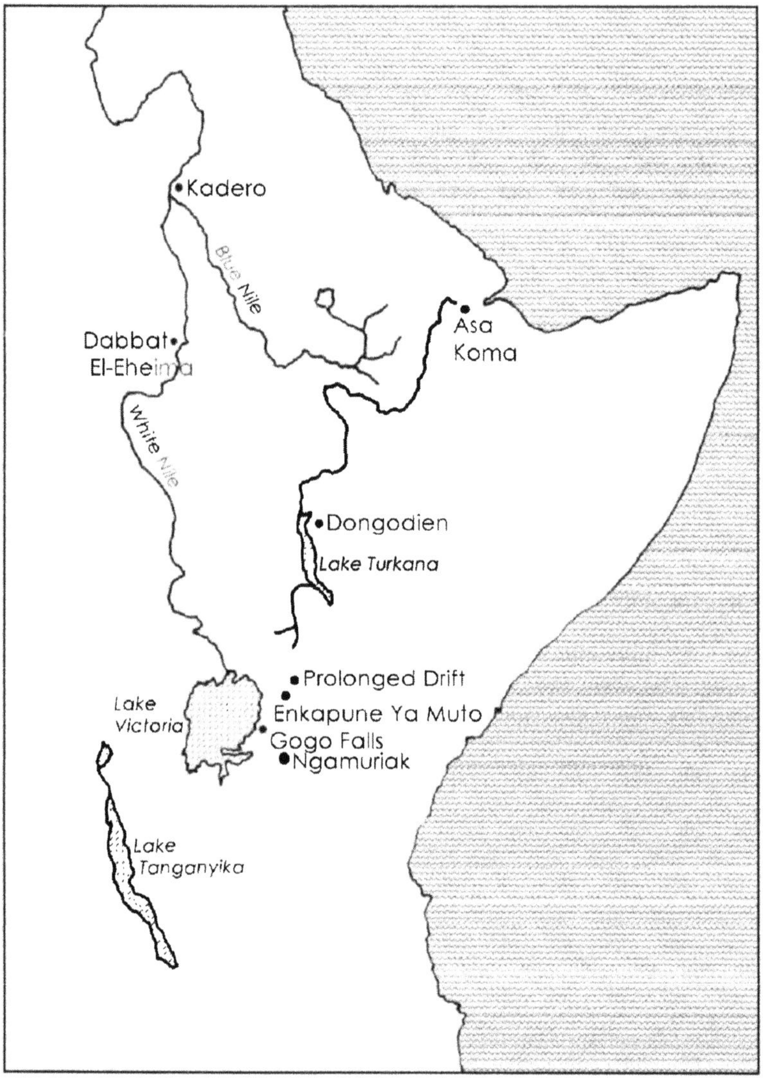

Figure 6.1. Map of East Africa showing sites mentioned in text.

so it is possible that the highlands were occupied by herders somewhat later, but there are few recorded sites from this crucial period (Marshall 2000).

We can suggest that the rainfall belts of the Intertropical Convergence Zone would have extended across the southern Sahara from the Atlantic coast to the Red Sea around Djibouti. With the drying up of the Sahara, the rain belts would have moved southwestward from the lower elevations of the Ethiopian plateau, taking with them the woodland savanna needed to support tsetse breeding and thus creating tsetse-free corridors permitting access by pastoral people into northern Kenya from the southern Sudan.

By 3,300 years ago, there was already significant cultural diversity in East Africa. Ambrose (1998) has created an ecotonal model showing coeval groups of pastoralists, each with a distinct material culture living on the Rift Valley floor, as well as foragers higher up on the edge of the Rift Valley. Since all these people were pottery users, Collett and Robertshaw (1983) have attempted to separate the different pottery traditions in East Africa, and Ambrose (1982) and Ehret (1998) have tried to place these within language groups. According to Collett and Robertshaw's analysis (1983: 120–21), the ceramics may be separated into four groups. They divide the Savanna Pastoral Neolithic into two of the clusters: Olmalenge and Oldishi.

1. The Olmalenge tradition has two phases: Nderit (found in northern Kenya around Lake Turkana and dated from 4,000 years ago) and the later phase, Maringishu (also found at Lake Turkana, but as far south as the Lake Nakuru basin). Ehret (1998: 98) would associate these pottery makers with Ma'a southern Cushite language speakers.
2. The Oldishi cluster, found from south of Lake Naivasha toward the Tanzania border. Ehret (1998: 98) sees these people as Rift southern Cushite speakers.
3. Elmenteitan, also found in southern Kenya, dated from around 2,100 years ago at Ngamuriak (Robertshaw 1990: 303). This cluster is considered to relate to southern Nilotes and is later found with the Iron Age at Deloraine Farm, around 1,100 years ago. Ehret (1998: 179) would see the patrilineal clans of these southern Nilotes as descending from a "more distant Eastern Sahelian ancestry."
4. Oltome (or Kantsyore) found at Gogo Falls on the eastern side of the Western Rift at Lake Nyanza. The pottery is reported to be similar to that found in Equatorial Province of southern Sudan (Collett and Robertshaw 1983: 121). Ehret (1998: 90)

> calls the makers "Eastern Sahelian" and gives them the more specific name of "Southern Rub."

The earliest East African herders utilized all the resources available to them, including the hunting of wild game animals and fishing for animal proteins. This lifeway may have been similar to that of herders in the Sudan who lived close to the Nile Valley. For example, the site of Kadero, located just north of the confluence of the Blue and White Niles, comprises a low mound standing some 1.8 m above the valley floor (Krzyzaniak 1984). It was occupied from 5,300 to 5,030 years ago, and the excavations have shown a people focused predominantly on cattle, with a much smaller number of ovicaprids for their meat. They also ate wild sorghum and millet that were prepared by grinding, along with wild arboreal fruits. The river provided food as well, in particular the large freshwater snail (*Pila*) and other freshwater mollusks, but only small amounts of fish bone were recovered. Wild animals, such as gazelles and buffalo, were hunted, and the bones also attest to the presence of hippopotamus, warthog, and a number of carnivores at the site (Gautier 1984).

Another potential connection between the Nile River in the Sudan and northern Kenya may lie in elaborate funerary monuments (Gifford-Gonzalez 2000). Cairn burials were described by Sadr et al. (1994), and they are also to be found around Lake Turkana (fig. 6.2).

Kleppe (1984) excavated on the Shilluk and Dinka ridges at Debbat El Eheima, roughly 450 km south of Kadero, in the seasonally inundated "toich" area of Upper Nile Province in southern Sudan, where occupation started around 4,000 years ago. She suggests the "fire-based ecosystem" from annual grass fires that maintain the open grass plains (Sherwood 1948: 816–17) that exists today started at this time. If this was an indication of drying up of the environment, it could have allowed a southward occupation of the flood plain by herders. Although, historically, bovine pleuropneumonia, sleeping sickness, foot-and-mouth disease, and particularly bovine typhus (or plague) all exist in this province (Sherwood 1948: 818), these conditions, at times desperate, are still managed by the local herders.

Marshall (1990a) believes that, by 3,000 years ago, herdsmen in East Africa were fortunate to live in an environment that had two

Figure 6.2. Grave tumulus, near Lake Turkana, northern Kenya.

rainy seasons in the year. Shortly after, around 2,600 years ago, herding societies in East Africa were starting to take advantage of these optimal conditions to specialize by maximizing milk production, similar to what the Maasai of Kenya and Tanzania do today. Unlike the earliest pastoral people of East Africa, these herders have little interest in hunting, fishing, or other foraging for food. Perhaps their knowledge of the threat epizootic diseases among wild animals pose for their herds makes them wary of contamination.

If Gifford-Gonzalez (2000) is correct in suggesting that herders need to keep their cattle separate from wild animals, in particular buffalo and wildebeest, to prevent disease transmission, then there are some enigmas in the faunal assemblages from several East African sites. Two sites, Prolonged Drift (Gifford et al. 1980) and Gogo Falls, Trench 3 (Elmenteitan levels; Robertshaw 1991) have both wild and domestic animal bones. The large numbers of domestic animals—22.5 percent of the bone, representing at least 20 individuals, or 1 percent of the individual specimens identified, at Prolonged Drift (table 6.1), and 42.2 percent of the bone, representing 53.6 percent of the individual specimens from Gogo Falls (table 6.2)—with

Table 6.1. Fauna from Prolonged Drift

	Minimum # individuals	Number of identifiable specimens
Cattle	22	250
Hartebeest	18	232
Wildebeest	17	241
Zebra	16	340
Thomson's Gazelle	15	165
Grant's Gazelle	11	106
Impala	7	35
Ovicaprids	5	50
Eland	4	37
Buffalo	2	11
Warthog	1	14
White Rhino	1	4
Giraffe	1	6

Source: Gifford et al. (1980).

Table 6.2. Fauna from Gogo Falls

	Minimum # individuals	Number of identifiable specimens
Ovicaprids	17	223
Cattle	10	105
Topi/Hartebeest	9	93
Oribi	8	72
Zebra	4	69
Reedbuck	4	17
Warthog	2	11
Eland	3	7
Roan/Sable	3	7
Bush Duiker	2	4
Hippo	1	3
Bushpig	1	1

Source: Marshall (1991).

the domestic cattle at Prolonged Drift constituting the highest minimum number of individuals of animals represented would suggest that these were camps of pastoralists. Modern pastoralists in East Africa, while they may hunt under special conditions (Robertshaw 1989), generally are averse to bringing any bush meat into their cattle camps (Hussein A. Isack, pers. comm.). The Nuer are not averse to hunting, but they regard wild animals more as a famine food. "The

Nuer are little interested in hunting. They speak of it as . . . beneath serious attention of a Nuer who can boast of a herd" (Evans-Pritchard 1956: 267).

At Prolonged Drift, both buffalo and wildebeest bones are present, while they are absent from Gogo Falls Elmenteitan levels (Marshall 1991). It is tempting to suggest, as Gifford et al. (1980) do, that Prolonged Drift was a hunter camp and the domestic animals were obtained by trade or theft. The Gogo Falls sample, by contrast, having twice as many domestics as Prolonged Drift and lacking the two animals most threatening to cattle, suggests that this was a pastoralist camp.

Many archaeological faunas from East Africa have almost 100 percent domestics (Gifford-Gonzalez 2000: 103), but there are several that have mixtures of wild and domestics and that include wildebeest; however, in none of those reported have buffalo been identified (Gifford-Gonzalez and Kimengich 1984). Wildebeest are only dangerous in the neonatal stage, so it is important to know if there are young animals present in the faunal repertoire (see below).

From the Elmenteitan site of Ngamuriak, Marshall (1990a) has offered an excellent picture of the way of life of East African herders in the archaeological record. The site, on the Kenyan side of the border with Tanzania, is a large one (8,000 sq m), but appears to be a single occupation horizon, although with spatial distribution of cultural material and bone refuse, including an area of compacted mud surrounded by postholes. This would indicate a settlement not dissimilar from that of a Maasai *manyatta* today.

The faunal material has been used to interpret the husbandry techniques of the early herders and to differentiate between how cattle versus small stock were used. In both cases, culling took place when the animals were well into their growth period, although the ovicaprids were killed slightly earlier than the cattle. This has led Marshall (1990a: 877) to suggest that there was little stress among the herders and that they were able to allow their animals to get to a reasonable size before slaughtering them.

The size of the site at Ngamuriak suggests that, like today, the grazing conditions were sufficient that the herders could stay in one place for most of the year or, if they moved, come back to reoccupy the homestead in the next season. Under normal conditions, final abandonment of Maasai homesteads today happens after a period of seven to eight years, when compaction around the settlement becomes so great that cattle urine will no longer penetrate the soil and living conditions become less tolerable (Western and Dunne 1979: 95). Movement may also be required due to disease or death of an occupant.

Marshall (2000) has surveyed the rather limited available evidence on early domesticated animals in the Horn of Africa. The data so far suggest that cattle arrived in the Horn somewhat later than in Kenya. In Djibouti, at Asa Koma, a date of 3,500 years ago is associated with cattle bones (Guerin and Faure 1996), while a similar date is suggested for the highlands proper around Lake Besaka (Brandt 1984).

It is from the Horn that some of the best rock art depicting domestic stock of East Africa comes. Longhorn cattle with their coat colors carefully drawn are shown in paintings from Ba'atti Sollum, Eritrea, while another from Zeban Ona Libanos, Eritrea, shows a cow being milked, surrounded by warriors holding spears and shields (Graziosi 1964). That all of these are humpless animals shows that the paintings predate the introduction of the humped *Bos indicus* (zebu) to the Horn. Another painting, from Serekama, Ethiopia, shows fat-tailed sheep, with their udders clearly depicted (Clark and Williams 1978). It is apparent from these paintings that milk and milk products were important to the herders.

If cattle in East Africa came from the Sudan, why are there no trypano-tolerant breeds like those of West Africa? Gifford-Gonzalez (2000: 121–22) offers two suggestions: (1) cattle were never exposed to tsetse and trypanosomiasis before entering East Africa or (2) if such animals existed in the past, they have been subsequently replaced by other breeds. From genetic research, it would seem that *Bos indicus* (zebu) ancestry is the most common among East African cattle today (fig. 6.3).

Trypanosomiasis is not the only epizootic disease that affects cattle. Just as virulent are other tropical diseases, none of which would have affected the westward spread of cattle across the Sahara. Once cattle moved south of the 16th parallel, they would have entered the domain of the African buffalo (*Syncerus caffer*), which is the host of east coast fever and foot-and-mouth disease

Figure 6.3. Zebu cattle, near Lake Turkana, northern Kenya.

(Gifford-Gonzalez 2000). Another conspecific that Gifford-Gonzalez identifies as having a potential fatal effect on cattle is wildebeest (*Connochaetes gnou* in southern Africa; *C. taurinus* in East Africa), whose young secrete a mucous that contains malignant catarrhal fever. Modern Maasai know to keep their cattle away from wildebeest breeding grounds. There is equal likelihood that pastoralists entering East Africa and points south would have had to learn to keep their cattle away from buffalo and neonate wildebeest, all of which would have taken time. Even though the distribution of the two animals overlaps, once herders realized there was a connection between disease and proximity to the wild animals, buffalo and wildebeest could be avoided. Trypanosomiasis, however, would require tsetse-free corridors, and these are limited. Figure 6.4 shows that they do exist, especially through the highland areas of the interior of Kenya, Tanzania, and Zambia.

Since small stock appear to be less affected by many tropical diseases than cattle, it is possible that ovicaprids preceded cattle into East Africa, as suggested by the early date from Enkapune Ya Moto of 4,860 years ago and the fact that ovicaprids preceded cattle to the southern tip of Africa.

It is as yet uncertain when zebu cattle were introduced to East Africa. There is little reason to doubt that this occurred more than a thousand years ago, when the Indian Ocean trade was at its height; a bronze figurine of a humped animal is reported from early Aksum times, about 1,800 years ago (Marshall 2000: 199). Also, epizootic

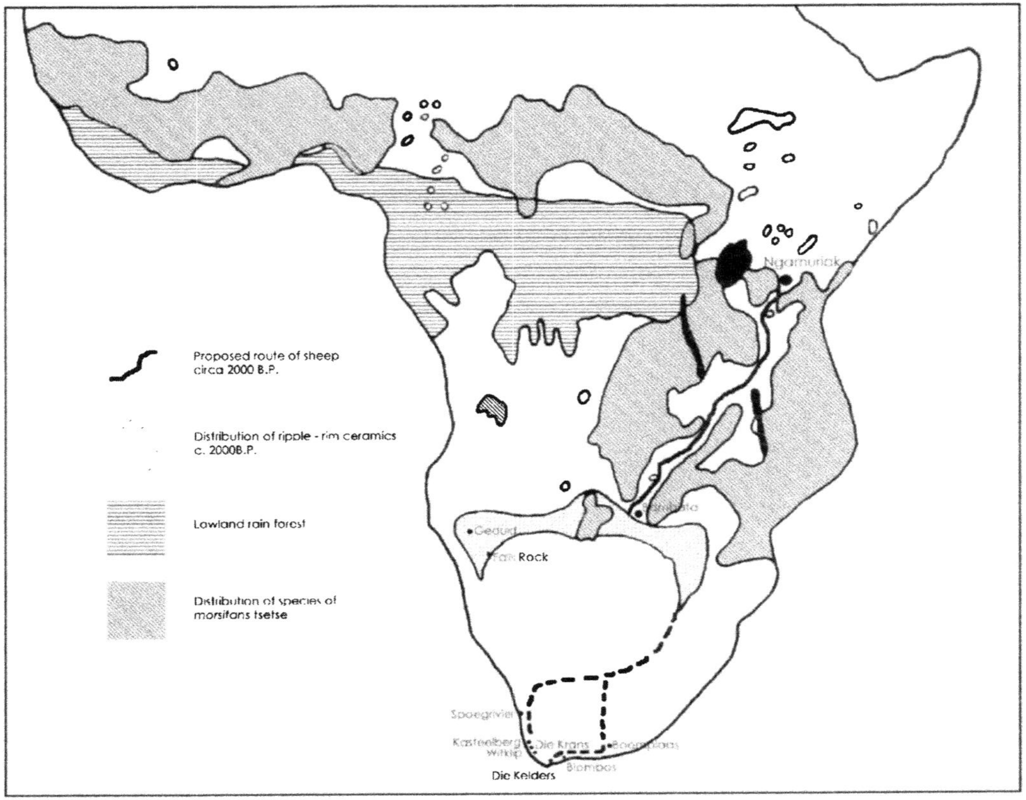

Figure 6.4. Distribution of tsetse and possible route of sheep diffusion from East Africa, c. 2000 BP (after Jordan 1986).

episodes within the last 150 years may have affected the genetic range of cattle presently found in East Africa. The rinderpest visitation of the late nineteenth century meant widespread loss of cattle, which had to be replaced. Zebu may be more rinderpest tolerant, and they are certainly very well adapted to the dry conditions of the grasslands of East Africa, so they were an obvious choice for rebuilding the herds. They probably were not exposed to tsetse, as they have no trypano tolerance (Gifford-Gonzalez 2000: 122).

Mixed agriculture would appear to have been a much later development in East Africa. Bantu speakers, bringing crop agriculture and iron technology into East Africa, adopted livestock as a convenient wealth-storage mechanism, along with many of the cultural attributes of the donor societies, such as cattle identification.

Backdrop to Khoesan Peoples of Eastern and Southern Africa

It is obvious from the models offered here that herders from several areas were entering new environments to which they and their stock had to adjust. There is no question that these environments were not empty spaces. The areas were occupied at the time by hunter-gatherers. The need to adjust to new ecological and social environments must have required a great deal of flexibility on the part of pastoral people, who are generally recognized as being opportunistic. The open grassland niche of East Africa must have been very attractive, which might have been the reason for the wide linguistic and cultural diversity seen in East Africa today.

Generally speaking, pastoralists could have had the economic and political edge over the indigenous hunters, pushing them more and more to the periphery of the Rift Valley. The lower elevations of the valley are better grazing, but it would also have been where the wild game animals, traditional resources of the hunters, would have quickly been in competition with, and disrupted by, domestic stock.

Who were the aboriginal people of East and southern Africa? From the historical record, it appears that there were a number of hunting people speaking various languages. It is possible that some of those speaking a Maa language, such as the cave-dwelling

Mukogodo, took on that language by long-term association with pastoralists with whom they shared age-set systems. They appear to have adopted herding only as recently as the 1920s (Cronk 1989). Gifford-Gonzalez (1998) suggests that forming marriage alliances with hunters would have been a risk-avoidance mechanism when droughts occurred, allowing herders to fall back on their hunting relatives until they could once more recoup their herds.

Click languages spoken by people who are believed to be descended from hunter-gatherers are widespread throughout East (Ambrose 1982: 111–12) and southern Africa (Barnard 1992). It is on the basis of their distribution that a correlation is made with Later Stone Age microlithic Wilton stone tool industries found throughout the southern part of the continent during the Late Pleistocene and Early Holocene (Ehret 1998: 92). This present distribution may not be as constant as it seems or reflect the dynamics of occupation by hunting people in the past; and there may have been several periods when the distribution was interrupted. Knight et al. (2003) analyzed the genetic material of click speakers in East and southern Africa. Their East African sample comes from Hadzabe hunters, while the southern African material is primarily from Ju/'hoansi. The genetic imprint suggests the separation between the two groups may be as old as the origins of *Homo sapiens sapiens*, which may mean something in excess of 70,000 years.

More recently, during the glacial maximum, some 18,000 years ago, the interior of southern Africa was cold and dry. Such a climatic scenario is used as a reason why few archaeological sites have been found, and the suggestion is that people may have mostly moved out of the interior toward the coastal forelands of the east and south. It was not until the end of the Pleistocene that conditions ameliorated and the interior was once more reoccupied.

While it must be accepted that, compared with the interior, more archaeological research has focused on the coastal area and immediate hinterland, which is rich in caves, and that the many widespread surface scatters seen in the interior are difficult to date, it is from the coast that continuous occupation sequences can be demonstrated. Significantly, prior to 12,000 years ago, the glacial advances of the Northern Hemisphere had sucked up water out of the oceans and resulted in a drop of up to 130 m in the sea level. This had particular relevance for the southern tip of Africa, which has a large continental shelf that would have been exposed at this time. Thus, not only was the coast more attractive than the interior, but also the coastal plain would have been enlarged manifold. This would have been an environment favored by large grazing animals, such as the extinct giant Cape horse (*Equus capensis*) and eland. It also means that much of the information about human occupation at the end of the Pleistocene is under water.

If all this is true, then the reoccupation of the interior in the Early Holocene must have been a northward and westward movement by populations who had occupied the coastal forelands. It is from the coastal areas that Morris (2002) suggests that Khoesan groups of the interior today, such as the Kalahari, may well have migrated, as c. 12,000 years ago sees an upsurge in dated sites away from the coast (Mitchell 2002).

If the interior of southern and East Africa was depopulated during the glacial maximum 18,000 years ago, then there was plenty of time for the speakers of the three Khoesan languages, which are mutually unintelligible, to have been pushed toward the coastal periphery and to have formed their distinctiveness. In Knight et al. (2003: table 1), Khwe and Ju/'hoansi are closer to each other than either is to Hadzabe. It is possible that Khoe (Khwe) speakers were a northern outlier of the diaspora of Khoesan groups in East Africa, and this separation that produced the three Khoisan linguistic groups today occurred long after the earlier Hadzabe separation.

One problem with this scenario is that no obvious Khoesan skeletons have been found north of the Zambezi (Ribot and Morris 2003). Admittedly, the sample sizes are small, but both Later Stone Age hunters and Iron Age skeletons from Malawi have been analyzed, with negative results. Does this mean the northern extent of Khoesan people was only as far as Zimbabwe and possibly southern Zambia?

Regardless of the indigenous populations of hunters, pastoralists need not have been hindered by their presence, and they may even have integrated somewhat with them, as suggested by the Nderit ceramics found on hunter sites (Ambrose 1998). Hunters probably constituted less of a barrier to southward movement than animal diseases. It seems that colonization of southern Africa by shepherds, some 2,000 years ago, was by people who probably spoke a click language. This means that small stock had to be taken up by people who previously would have been considered hunters.

Bantu-speaking Iron Age farmers, whom Ehret (1998) calls Mashariki, moved into the western Rift Valley around 3,000 years ago. During the next half a millennium, consolidating their tenure, they took up domestic cattle from their pastoralist neighbors further east. It was only when one subset of Mashariki, called Kusi (Nyasa, Makua, Shona, and various Southeast Bantu–speaking groups; Ehret 1998: 36), moved south after 2,000 years ago that cattle entered southern Africa along with grain agriculture. These Bantu-speaking farmers are known collectively archaeologically as Chifumbaze (Phillipson 1993) or by three Early Iron Age traditions: Kalundu (Western), Nkope (Central), and Kwale (Eastern)(Whitelaw 1997).

Southern Africa

The complexity and diversity of food-producing societies in East Africa meant that there was a plethora of potential donors of domestic stock to southern Africa. It has become clear, however, that sheep and ceramics preceded any Iron Age advance southward. Sheep arrived in the Cape of Good Hope, historically the home of the Khoekhoe (Hottentot) pastoralists, around 2,000 years ago.

For most of the colonial period, there have been questions asked about the origins of the Khoekhoen. Mentzel (1944), who was in the Cape in the 1740s, worked through a rational argument, built on biblical assumptions, that the "Hottentots" were derived from children shipwrecked on a voyage from the Near East (ibid: 274). Stow (1905) was certain that the Khoekhoen came from the Great Lakes region of East Africa. Such assumed connections with East Africa were taken up by Meinhof (1912), who was convinced that there was a relationship between the Khoe languages and the so-called Hamitic languages of northeast Africa. Maingard (1934) was able to squash the Hamitic linguistic connection, and from then on there was acceptance that the Khoekhoen were indigenous to southern Africa, as were the Bushmen or Soaqua/Sonqua (San-qua). But this has not resolved the relationship or perceived differences between the Khoekhoen and the Soaqua recognized in the historic period.

Elphick (1977) argues that they were the same people, only seen as part of a cycle of fortune (people with stock were Khoe herders; people who lost their stock fell back on hunting to become Soaqua). The confusion of ethnic identities was taken up by Wright (1996), who suggested that the distinction between the "Khoikhoi" herders and the "Bushmen" hunters seen in the historic period was not a neat one, so the names were problematic.

Questions of origin still remain, as the archaeological data show domestic sheep and pottery in the Western Cape by 1,900 years ago (Henshilwood 1996; Webley 2001), but little to suggest where they came from. Much of the argument around the origins of herding at the Cape revolves around the excavations at Kasteelberg and other sites on the Vredenburg Peninsula north of Cape Town.

Smith et al. (1991), while offering information on a wide range of sites in the Western Cape, nonetheless gave most attention to excavation at the small rockshelter of Witklip (fig. 6.5). Their paper offered an archaeological attempt to distinguish between hunters and herders and argued that each of these economic groups had distinct signatures.

Figure 6.5. Excavations at Witklip rockshelter, Vredenburg Peninsula.

The hunter signature was defined on the basis of the predominance of small bovids (*Raphicerus* spp.; fig. 6.6), high percentages of formally flaked stone tools on fine-grained rocks (up to 4 percent of total stone), small ostrich eggshell beads (<5 mm), and after 2,000 years ago, very low numbers of potsherds (10 to 20 per cubic meter of excavated deposit) and a few sheep bones. By way of contrast, herder sites produced large numbers of sheep (over 50 percent of bones from Kasteelberg A, or KBA, site; Klein and Cruz-Uribe 1989) (fig. 6.7), almost no formally flaked stone tools (0.2 percent), large ostrich eggshell beads (>5mm), and large numbers of potsherds (over 700 per cubic meter at Kasteelberg B, or KBB site; fig. 6.8).

The sequence showed that the hunters, primarily of small antelope (*Raphicerus* spp.), were little different culturally in the period before the appearance of domesticated sheep and ceramics than they were afterward. This is a pattern that played itself out elsewhere on the Vredenburg Peninsula, for example, at Die Krans (Mütti, forthcoming), lower KBC (Smith 1984), and more recently, at the Kasteelberg G site (KBG; Sadr et al. 2003), as well as in Namibia at Geduld (Smith and Jacobson 1995) (fig. 6.14).

Subsequent use of these signatures (Smith and Jacobson 1995; Smith et al. 2001) has avoided the ethnic labels, preferring to separate the signatures on economic grounds. So significant were the differences, however, that it was argued that hunters and herders were different ethnic groups and that the herders were immigrants who brought sheep and pottery to the Southwestern Cape around 1,900 years ago.

Sadr (1997) created a formal tool/ceramic index that was used to separate hunter from herder sites. In this index, sites exhibiting high numbers of formal tools, but which were low in pottery fragments, would fall into the hunter end of the spectrum. Those sites with large numbers of sherds but few formal tools would be herders. Sadr also gave examples of where some sites, such as Toteng 1 in Botswana (ibid: fig. 2) showed changes from one economic group to the other. In his graph, he clearly distinguishes between Witklip (as an example of a hunter site) and Kasteelberg A and B (both herder sites; fig. 6.9).

This is one way of estimating differences between economies. In a later article, Sadr (1998: 125) chooses another. He looks at the

3000 BP	1800–1400 BP	500–330 BP		2100 BP	1800 BP	1300 BP	900 BP	200 BP
35/2[a] 53%[b]	162/3 62.5%	26/2 55.3%	 Small Bovids	105/2 78.9%	238/7 7.0%	174/5 3.8%	532/10 6.0%	294/7 8.6%
4/1 6%	19/2 7.3% (includes *Silvicapra grimmia*)	4/1 8.5%	 Small to Medium Bovids	12/2 9.0%	1809/35 53.5%	1332/21 29.2%	1466/23 16.5%	354/10 10.2%
3/1 4.5%	1/1 0.4%	0 0	 *Arctocephalus pusillus*	8/1 6.0%	1218/24 36.0%	2646/30 58.1%	6085/72 65.5%	2391/31 70.0%

a. NISP/MNI b. Percentage of total fauna.

Figure 6.6. Main fauna elements from Witklip.

Figure 6.7. Main fauna elements from Kasteelberg.

KASTEELBERG	WITKLIP
Open air site	Small rock shelter
c.1800–800 B.P.	c. 3000–350 B.P.
Cultural Material	**Cultural Material**
■ Very few microlithic tools – 0.2% formal ■ Coarse-grained rocks ■ Potsherds: 750/m^3 ■ Grindstones ■ Ostrich eggshell beads: large	■ Microlithic tools ■ Fine-grained rocks ■ 4% retouched ■ Potsherds:10/m^3 ■ Ostrich eggshell beads: small < 5mm -increase in size after 500 B.P
Economic Material	**Economic Material**
Low percentage of small bovids	High percentage of small bovids (steenbok)
High percentage of seals	Low percentage of sheep
High percentage of sheep	No seals

Figure 6.8. Comparison between the archaeological assemblages of Kasteelberg and Witklip, Vredenburg Peninsula, South Africa.

percentage of domestic animals within the faunal assemblage as an indicator of a pastoralist site; however, because Cape fur seals dominate the assemblages from KBB, this gives the impression that the sheep numbers are low. In fact, although there is some variability in the sheep numbers in different levels at KBB (Smith and Mütti 1992), except for the very top level, small–medium bovids always outnumber small bovids.

This may offer a better indicator of a pastoralist site: the predominance of domestic stock (small–medium, Bov II faunal category) on herder sites, over hunted animals, particularly small bovids (Bov I faunal category). This distinction was seen during excavation of Kasteelberg C site, where two horizons were recognized. The lower horizon, dated to 2,160 years ago, exhibited a high formal tool component, along with small ostrich eggshell beads, and a dominance of small bovids in the faunal assemblage. Stratified above, the formal tools virtually disappear, to be replaced by crude flakes. The beads are larger, and the faunal component has many more sheep than small bovids. This horizon is dated to 1,270 years ago. These

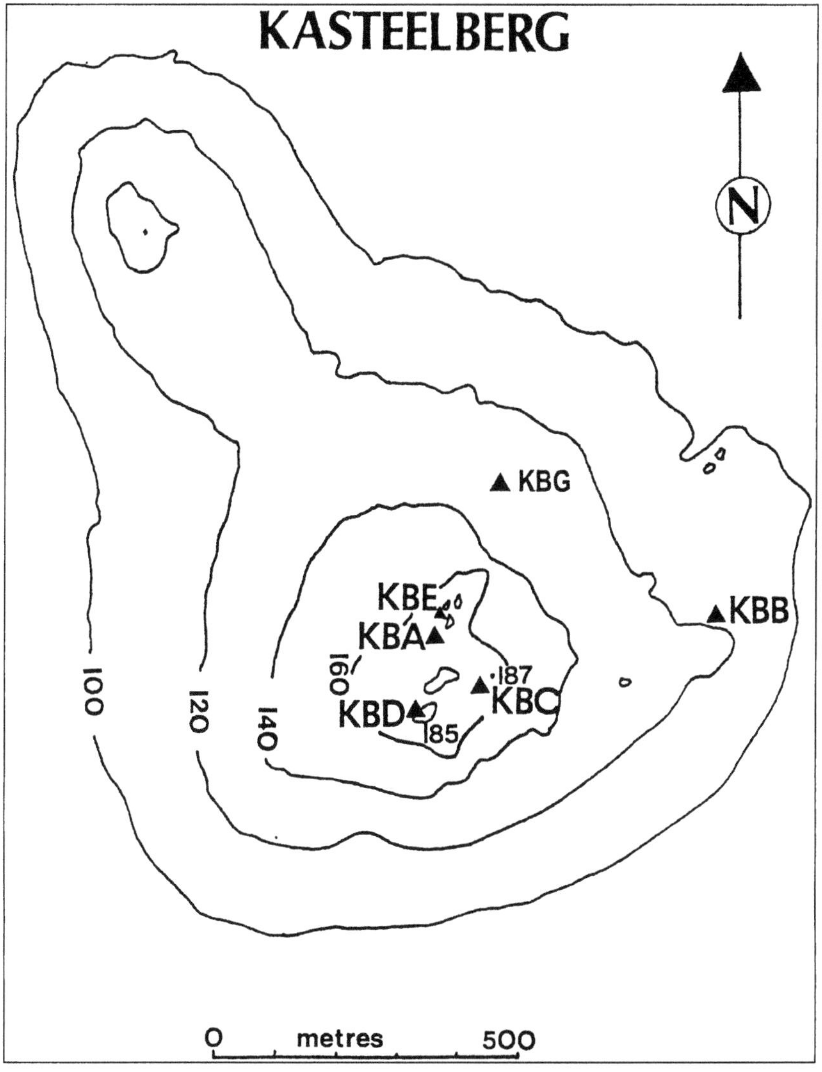

Figure 6.9. Map of Kasteelberg, Vredenburg Peninsula (Smith).

indicate quite different economic and cultural attributes, which we might say show a shift from hunting to herding occupations.

Whether or not we can use the criterion of the faunal differences to separate out other herder sites will depend on consistency in reporting what until now has been lacking. For example, the publication of the fauna from the upper levels at Boomplaas (Klein 1978; von den Driesch and Deacon 1985) only gives the minimum number of individuals for each species and level, and not the number of individual specimens. Von den Driesch and Deacon (1985: 43) state that domestic animals are much more numerous than hunted species, such as klipspringer (*Oreotragus* sp.) in the "herder" levels. However, if we compare the minimum number of small bovids (probably *Oreotragus* and *Raphicerus*) to the minimum number of small–medium bovids, there are more small bovids (34 to 29) (Klein 1978: table 1). There are also questions about why the small–medium bovid, *Redunca fulvorufula* (mountain reedbuck) should completely disappear in the herder levels, after reasonably high numbers in the Wilton levels. And if *Raphicerus* was hunted, why are there no indications of *Silvicapra* as well? Since there are also relatively high numbers of formal tools in the herder levels, this raises the question of whether Boomplaas was truly a herder site. The same pattern is also seen at Die Kelders (Schweitzer 1979: table 27). There, the minimum number of individual *Raphicerus* (295) far outstrips the sheep (34), even though, as at Kasteelberg, there are considerable numbers of seals (101). In the pottery levels at Spoegrivier, Webley (2001: table 17) produced minimum numbers of individuals for *Raphicerus* (43) and sheep (14), and for the large number of seals (40).

In the Smith et al. (1991) report, no sheep bones were specifically identified at Witklip, but small–medium bovids existed before and after the introduction of ceramics. In the preceramic period, these can be assumed to be from the common duiker (*Sylvicapra grimmia*). As *Raphicerus* are found both pre- and postceramics, there is little reason to doubt *Sylvicapra* was hunted in the same periods. It was only from subsequent excavation at Witklip that sheep bones were specifically identified in the ceramic period.

Sadr et al. (2003) published a note on new excavations of a number of sites around Kasteelberg (KBA, KBD, KBE open, KBG, KBM, and KBN; figs. 6.9, 6.10) and gave an interpretation of what these new data might mean. Rather than looking for immigrant herders bringing sheep and pottery to the Cape, Sadr et al. suggest local hunters adopted these commodities to become *herders* in their own right. Such ideas are in sharp contrast to the immigrant model; but

Figure 6.10. Kasteelberg from the east.

the older views of early herding societies have equally evolved as new data have come in.

Publication of the Kasteelberg monograph has been bedeviled by outstanding dating questions of the earliest herding societies on the kopje. Attempts to resolve these questions resulted in redating that brought into question the earliest dates from KBA of 1,860 and 1,790 years ago. The earliest AMS date on sheep bone from KBA was only 1,630 years ago (Sealy and Yates 1994: 63). The excavations during 2000–2002, which included KBA and KBE, were a further attempt to revisit the sites with the view to resolving some of the outstanding dating issues.

The existence of KBG (a hunter site) within 50 m of KBE (a herder site) raises interesting questions. The postceramic dates of KBG overlap the earliest herder dates from KBA (which has similar cultural material to KBE). What was the relationship between the occupants of both sites? Were they occupied at the same time, in serial fashion during the same year, or during different years? The position of KBG on the open terrace is similar to the other "hunter" sites of KBM and KBN: exposed to the southeast winds. In fact, we were forced to abandon the excavations at KBN due to the winds that made work there extremely difficult. This strongly suggests different seasons of occupation by hunters and herders, although the identification of KBM as a hunter site is problematic, as there are no small bovids in the small faunal sample. We might also question the assumption that all the bovid II bones from KBG need necessarily be sheep.

The idea that Sadr et al. (2003) raise of different groups exploiting different habitats is also questionable. All the late Holocene sites on Kasteelberg are shell middens; therefore both groups used marine resources. The fact that seals are virtually nonexistent on hunter sites may have less to do with differences in exploitation patterns, as in the different social purposes for which the sites may have been used.

That herders were using the hill for specific social reasons during the entire period that the herder sites of KBA, KBB, Upper KBC, and KBE were occupied is suggested by several unusual elements from the sites:

1. A small lamb skeleton, dated between 1,000 and 900 years ago, was found in the upper levels of KBB. The skeleton was covered in ochre (while all the surrounding bones were not). This suggests that at burial the lamb had been covered in ochre and possibly wrapped in a skin. The ochre permeated the bones before the skin disappeared. Thus, ritual slaughter, as later found among the Khoekhoen (Smith and Pheiffer 1992: 10–12), can be inferred.
2. Richard Klein (pers. comm.) noted the unusually high number of mongoose bones in the fauna from KBA and KBB (Klein and Cruz-Uribe 1989). Robert Gordon, in his travels in Namaqualand at the end of the eighteenth century, refers to ritual slaughter patterns of the Khoekhoen. Men usually performed sacrificial rituals, but if a woman was needed to be the slaughterer, she had to wear a piece of mongoose skin on her head (Smith and Pheiffer 1992: 12). This curious anomaly has support from Dunefield Midden (Parkington and Fisher 2004), also on the Cape West Coast, where several disarticulated mongoose skeletons were defleshed and intentionally buried in small holes across the site.
3. The inordinate number of bedrock grooves at Kasteelberg (fig. 6.11), especially around KBB, where there are almost 100, indicate a considerable amount of grinding took place.

Figure 6.11. Bedrock grooves, Kasteelberg.

All the portable versions of grindstones found in excavation were ochre stained, as were the upper grindstones. Among the large numbers of seal bones (figs. 6.8, 6.12), the majority are nine-month-old animals (Klein and Cruz-Uribe 1989: fig. 9). Their 25-kg bodies would have been easily carried whole to the site. They are also of an age when there is more fat relative to the mass of meat than at any other age. This suggests that fat may have been the main reason for collection. It is well documented in the historical literature that fat mixed with ochre was a symbol of Khoekhoe well-being and possible conspicuous consumption (Thom 1954: 367).

These features suggest that Kasteelberg may have been a ritual aggregation site for pastoral ceremonial purposes. This is also supported by the far greater amount of economic and cultural debris on the herder sites, which indicates intensive use of these spaces. Such intensity may have had nothing to do with being more sedentary, but with larger groups occupying the sites for limited periods.

Figure 6.12. Excavated floor, Kasteelberg.

The lack of seal bones at lower KBC and KBG (as well as at Witklip; figs. 6.6, 6.7) is probably because the occupants of the sites were focused on the hunting of small solitary antelopes (*Raphicerus* and *Silvicapra*). Shellfish and tortoises would have been more predictable resources, like plant foods that foraging women collect to feed their families. Butchering of seals and whales by hunters was done at the coast, where both seal bones and whale barnacles have been found (Robertshaw 1979; Jerardino and Parkington 1993).

While the Sadr et al. (2003) model tries to limit itself to dealing only with the archaeology of Kasteelberg, there are bigger issues that are being ignored. Not the least is the argument that herding was a locally derived economic activity. An attempt to find sources of the pottery, and by association the animals, was inconclusive (Sadr 1998).

The focus on Khoekhoe and Soaqua relations in Smith et al. (1991) really only dealt with the argument in the historic period. We tried to avoid cultural labels in the earlier periods, as we were unable to identify the cultural or linguistic groups. Rather than assume that the origins of herding at the Cape were a local phenomenon, and that the Elphick (1977) cyclical model was appropriate for precolonial hunter/herders, an alternative scenario suggests that the transition to herding had already taken place among Khoe-speaking hunters in a broad belt, stretching from northern Namibia to the Limpopo Province (Smith 2000a). The arguments supporting this are threefold: archaeological, linguistic, and social anthropological.

Archaeological Argument

The appearance of pottery in southern Africa predates the earliest Iron Age farmers on the Highveld. Bambata pottery is found in Later Stone Age contexts north of the Limpopo (fig. 6.13). Ehret (1998: 217) would relate this pottery to Eastern Sahelian settlement south of the Zambezi. Bambata, as an archaeological entity, is poorly defined. Walker (1983) sees the makers as a source of the early herding societies of southern Africa, but fails to define exactly what Bambata as a cultural entity might relate to. He allows Huffman's assumptions (1994) that Bambata is Iron Age ware to prevail, although in a later paper (Walker 1995: 61) he notes that there may be pottery with "thick undecorated rims and bands of oblique-incised neck decoration" below Bambata at several sites. While Walker (1985) takes issue with Jacobson's critique of Bambata (1984), Jacobson makes a credible point about different thick- and thin-walled pottery.

A unique pottery form that we call "ripple-rim" ware is decorated with incisions that have subsequently been smoothed by burnishing (fig. 6.14). Ripple-rim pottery is found in a broad band from Geduld (Smith and Jacobson 1995: fig. 8: l, *m* and *n*) and the Brandberg (Kinahan 1991: fig. 2.10: *e* and *f*) across to the Soutpansberg and Waterberg in Limpopo Province (Marie van der Rist and Simon Hall, pers. comm.) (fig. 6.4). All the ripple-rim ware is thin walled, with what appears to be a dark, burnished slip. Judging from the rim diameters, the few fragments we have of this pottery would appear to come from small pots. It is not clear what the precursors to this thin-walled, high-fired pottery might be, nor have

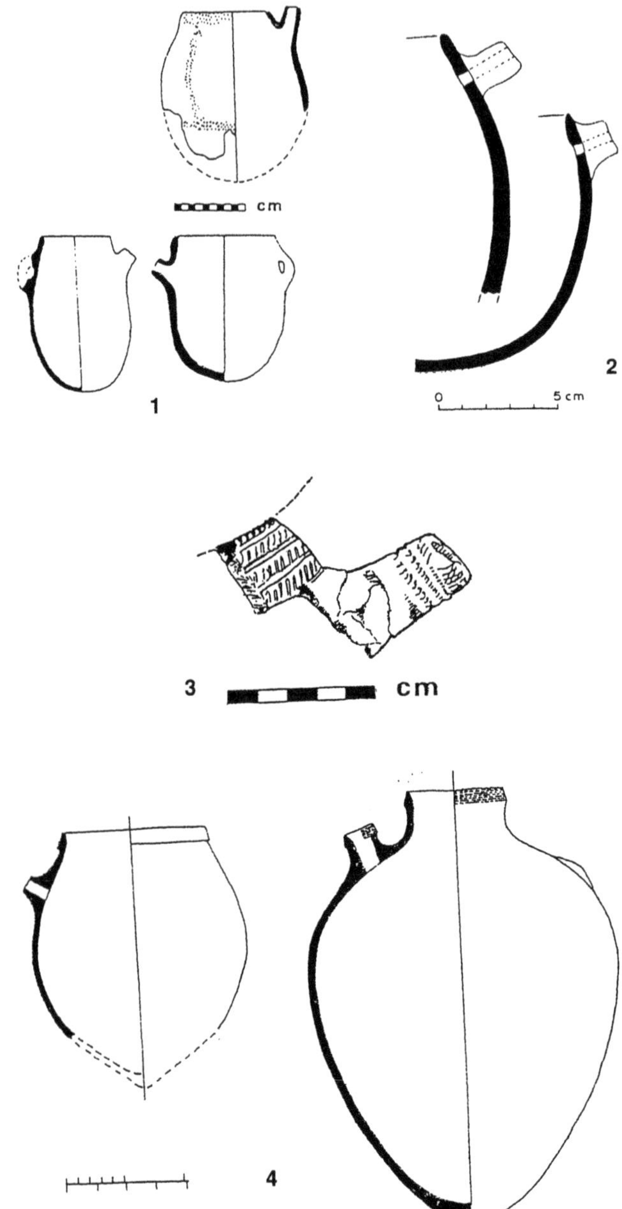

Figure 6.13. Spouted pottery from East and southern Africa: (1) Hyrax Hill, Kenya; (2) Ngamuriak, Kenya (after Robertshaw 1990); (3) Bambata Cave Zimbabwe (after Schofield 1940); (4) Western Cape, South Africa (after Rudner 1968).

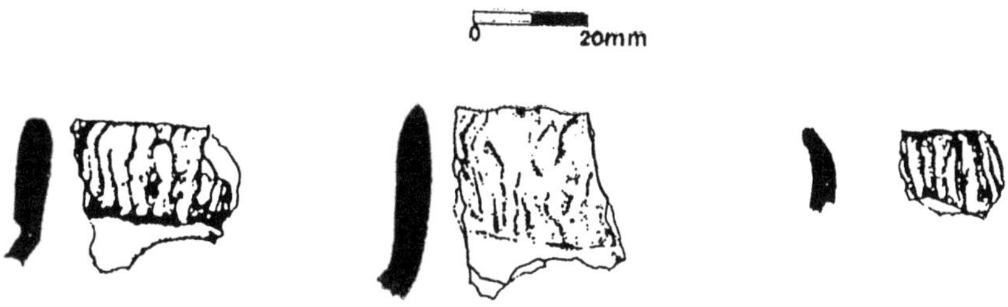

Figure 6.14. Ripple-rim ware from Geduld, northern Namibia.

we found sufficiently large pieces to be able to know what form these pots took. The closest analogy would appear to be those from the lower Later Stone Age level at Die Kelders (Schweitzer 1979: figs. 25–28). A close inspection of the top of the rim of at least four of these small vessels suggests burnishing and smoothing after incisions were made.

Although spouted wares (fig. 6.13) are possibly later than the dark, burnished pottery from Die Kelders described above, they are still some of the earliest forms that appeared in the Cape (Sadr and Sampson 1999). We might use this attribute as a clue to origins. Robertshaw (1990: figs. 9.2–9.5) excavated small spouted pots at Ngamuriak on the border between Kenya and Tanzania. These were pastoral people with large herds of cattle and sheep (Marshall 1990a). Some of the small (80–160 mm high), thin-walled pots of Ngamuriak have what appear to be casual incisions around the rim. This ware is absent from Huffman's compendium of pottery decorations (1989; 1994) from the Iron Age. Hall (1998) has stressed the importance of Iron Age pottery decoration in symbolic terms, which is widespread among African agricultural societies (David et al. 1988). While symbolism is probably just as important in decorating pots in pastoralist societies, the decoration may play a different role.

Small pots are appropriate milking vessels for sheep. Small wooden beakers were the only item of material culture (except for a ragged shirt) noted among child shepherds in the Sahel of Mali by the author in 1972. These little boys, probably no more than 10 years of age, lived off sheep's milk and *Acacia* gum for weeks on end.

Milk and milking are central to women's lives among herders of East and southern Africa. This sets them apart from their mixed agriculturist neighbors, among whom men only are allowed to deal with the herd (Schapera 1930: 295, n. 1; Krige 1950: 185). Women identify with their milking vessels, from which their children are fed (Hodder 1991: 73). Among the Ilchamus herders of East Africa, milk calabashes are cleaned with embers from the domestic hearth, and only women are allowed to remove the ash from this hearth (ibid: 76). Hodder (1991: 93) makes a point about the importance of the inside (domestic) world associated with the hearth. This manifests itself as dark, like the inside of a milk calabash.

Among the Khoekhoen there are similar identity points between women and milk. Hoernlé (1918) discusses the importance of the first milking by a young woman after her seclusion. The milk, *!nau deip*, may only be drunk by her *aba taras* (ritual mentor), and is certainly to be avoided by men. The ash heap is a personal identity point (Archer 1994). This belongs to a woman, and no other would think of contravening it, even if the camp is temporarily unoccupied (Smith and Webley 2000).

Hodder (1991) asks why the Ilchamus herders of East Africa decorate some calabashes and not others. Hodder (1991: 90) suggests that among the Ilchamus the calabash decorations create a discourse as a form of resistance between fertile women and young warriors, both of whom are under the thumb of elders.

The Ngamuriak pots, which are both decorated and undecorated, may have performed similar functions; in practical terms their size would be useful for milking sheep, and decoration could have been for personal identification, as well as having wider symbolic significance within the society.

Ngamuriak as a pastoralist site is archaeologically visible because of the environment of East Africa that allows herders to stay in one place for prolonged periods (Marshall 1990b). Whether the occupants of Ngamuriak during the Elmenteitan period were the donors of the domestic sheep and pottery to southern Africa is yet to be established. The dates from this site for the Elmenteitan are 2,135 years ago and 1,940 years ago (Robertshaw 1990: 303), but other dates would push the Elmenteitan back to around 2,300 years ago. These dates would at least be chronologically in line for the sequence of borrowing in southern Africa. It is also known that sheep were the first domestic animals to appear in southern Africa. Why cattle did not arrive at the same time has been the study of Gifford-Gonzalez (2000), described above, who presents a strong argument that epizootic diseases fatal to cattle would have required significant adjustment on the part of the cattle keepers and herds to overcome this barrier to southward movement.

The movement of pottery and sheep as far as the Cape would appear to have been very rapid, as these commodities were already at the sites of Blombos (Henshilwood 1996), Spoegrivier (Webley 2001), and Die Kelders (Schweitzer 1979) by 1,900 years ago. The quality of the pottery is such that there seems to be little reason to doubt that it was a technology that was introduced from the outside.

On the basis of two distinct archaeological signatures for hunters (Swartkop) and herders (Doornfontein) in Bushmanland and along the middle Orange River (Beaumont et al. 1995), the route of movement (fig. 6.4) is best postulated as across the northern Cape to the Vaal/Orange drainage, whence the animals and pottery were dispersed southward to the Cape coastal forelands. This separation of economies is what we further suggest continued at the Cape (Smith et al. 1991). There appears to be no archaeological evidence to support the previous hypotheses of Stow (1905) and Cooke (1965) that the movement was down the west coast, as the only sheep occurrence that might fill the gap between Geduld and the Orange River at Mirabib is from a somewhat later date (see Bousman 1998). The suggested trans-Kalahari route proposed by Elphick (1977) also has no archaeological support. It would have made more sense for herders to follow river systems as avenues of movement, particularly if they were entering new and unknown territory.

Linguistic Argument

Ehret (1998) has attempted to show linguistic connections through loan words between food producers in East and southern Africa. In his view, makers of the Elmenteitan archaeological tradition, such as those found at Ngamuriak (Robertshaw 1990), may trace their heritage to more distant Eastern Sahelian ancestry (Ehret 1998: 178–79). Ehret (1998: 216) goes on to say that eastern Sahelian language influences were to be found in northeastern Botswana and western Zimbabwe during the last millennium BC (2,800–2,000 years ago). In his estimation, Khwe speakers (people in that area who speak a Khoe language) in the second half of the millennium (2,400–2,000 years ago) borrowed a set of words from Eastern Sahelian, such as words meaning "ram," "milk ewe," "young ram," "grain," and "porridge." The southern extent of the Sahelian languages is estimated to have been south of the middle reaches of the Zambezi some 2,400–2,300 years ago, and Ehret relates this to what is known as "Bambata." The best fit, he says, is with the Sog (Eastern Sahelian) languages of the Great Lakes, whose speakers may have moved through tsetse-free corridors (fig. 6.4), such as the Batoka Plateau of southern Zambia, but have not been identified archaeologically (ibid: 217). This grassland area would have been an obvious route of entry southwestward toward the Caprivi and northern Namibia.

Even if only the rough outlines of this analysis are correct, Khwe (Khoe) speakers were in direct contact with food producers for a long time (Barnard 1992), perhaps over 400 years, before any spread to southern Africa, and certainly long enough to adopt the language and practice of herding small stock. Khoisan speakers, however, may not have extended as far north as Ehret suggests. Morris (2003) reiterates that there is no biological evidence for Khoesan north of the Zambezi, and the linguistic connection with Hadza and Sandawe remains weak. "Even if the clicks in the East African 'KhoiSan' languages can be shown to be related to southern African KhoiSan click consonants, then this can only indicate distant shared linguistic traits, not necessarily ancestor dependent relationships" (ibid.: 89). Assuming Ehret is still correct, that the transfer of words dealing with sheep came from northern Eastern Sahelian speakers, then we must assume from the above that it was the southward movement of the Eastern Sahelians, rather than the northward extension of Khoe speakers, that brought the two together.

The most recent research on Khoisan languages suggests that the Khoe (central), !Kung (northern), and !Ui-Taa (southern, which includes /Xam and !Xoo) Bushman languages are mutually unintelligible. All the words for cattle and goats in !Ui-Taa languages come from Khoe, and in !Xoo (the Taa branch of !Ui-Taa) so does the word for sheep. The words for sheep and shepherding activities in other !Ui languages seem to be more closely related to eastern Khoe, but are not found in Nama (Nigel Crawhall, pers. comm.). This may indicate that there was more than one connection between Khoe and most !Ui-Taa language speakers at the time that sheep appeared in southern Africa, before the appearance of cattle and goats.

If the hunters of Kasteelberg were the indigenous people of the Cape (having existed before and after the appearance of domestic stock), they were probably !Ui speakers. If this indeed is the case, does the lack of root words for sheep and shepherding indicate complete separation from a Khoe economic system? Whether this can be used to argue that the earliest exposure of the Cape people to domestic animals was not within a dominant Khoe ambit, or that they came into contact with the animals before Khoe moved into the area, as yet we are unable to say.

Social Anthropological Argument

Taking on food production is not a simple matter for southern African hunter-gatherers, due to their need for sharing and reciprocity, particularly of meat. As a matter of principle, food is not recognized as appropriate for *hxaro* internal exchange, or gift-giving between partners, among the Ju/' hoansi Bushmen (Wiessner 1994: 104), as affines and neighbors all come to demand their share. This would inhibit private ownership of domestic animals and make it very difficult for a person to accumulate large enough numbers that off take for food is possible, while nurturing the breeding part of the herd.

While Sadr (1998) is correct that there is a great deal of variability among southern African hunter-gatherers today, much of this may be predicated on modern pressures, such as loss of land and resources, sedentarization, and concomitant social anomie resulting from being placed in the lowest social rung (Suzman 2000). Those hunters who have retained a semblance of their traditional values still use sharing primarily as a mechanism to avoid risk (Widlock 1999). The need for this is fundamental to societies that live in environments that are highly seasonal and subject to drought years. The Ju/' hoansi (Lee 1979) have been used as a model for southern African foragers. They recognize the need for risk management, even though they have had resources that caused them to be seen as the "original affluent society" (Sahlins 1972). Lee's initial work among the Ju/' hoansi in 1963–64 was during a drought, yet the Bushmen managed to get sufficient food without major effort, probably due to the availability of mongongo nuts (Lee 1969). But such abundance may be highly seasonal, thus sharing and reciprocity, basic to Bushman social and economic needs, may be a survival mechanism.

The transition to herding may require a combination of a long-standing relationship with food producers and perhaps a degree of incorporation into neighboring agropastoral communities, by marriage or by trade networks. It may also require an environment where delayed return hunting/foraging strategies are practiced through control of resources and investment of labor, such as building dams for fishing, and thus a concept of individual "ownership" is accepted. It is exactly in these kinds of conditions that the Khoe-speaking Bushmen have participated in the local economy of the Okavango, Boteti, and Nata Rivers (Barnard 1992: 123–24), with some becoming food producers in their own right.

The differences between hunter-gatherers and herders was not just a figment of the colonial imagination. Gordon (Smith and Pheiffer 1994: 34–35), in his detailed letter to his mentor in Holland, Greffier Hendrik Fagel, in 1779, described the differences he had observed between the herders and Bushmen: "Their [herder's] government . . . is patriarchal, under a sort of chief, and uncomplicated; the elders and those who own the most cattle have influence on the rest. . . . The Bushmen and inlanders live by hunting, dig for roots, eat gum from the mimosa tree . . . also ants, ostrich eggs, locusts, a kind of grass seed. . . . These [people] mostly have the bravest and most dexterous as a sort of chief. . . . Otherwise they live as equals. . . . The inlanders' knives are split reeds, and sharpened stones."

Thus we see a pattern that suggests that hunters in the Cape were really not much different in social terms from those in the Kalahari described by Lee (1979) and Marshall (1976). Whether or not the prehistoric or historic hunters practiced an internal exchange system as coherent as the Ju/'hoansi *hxaro* (Wiessner 1994) will probably never be known. Risk and reciprocity seem to have been ubiquitous among southern African hunters, and this is more than just sharing of goods: "The regulated nature of sharing behavior is . . . embedded in a symbolic awareness of what the relationship entails, and the obligations and responsibilities undertaken. The compact to continue exchanges passes from generation to generation, dissipating anxiety or conflict, regulating behavior, and ameliorating antagonistic confrontations" (Kusimba 2003: 87).

Smith (1990) describes a model where hunters would become herders only if they were in some way incorporated into a structured, hierarchical society. At the time of writing, it was suggested that Early Iron Age farmers brought in the earliest domestic animals in southern Africa. The archaeological evidence now suggests that stock and pottery predate an Iron Age appearance, but this does not negate the original principle: that hunters, this time early Khoe speakers in Zambia, were in long-term contact with food producers, possibly even pastoralists who spoke an Eastern Sahelian language. It is from this group that the words relating to sheep were transferred to an early Khoe dialect (Ehret 1998: table 40), possibly along with the animals themselves.

To sum up these ideas, the model of aboriginal hunters of the Cape becoming herders fails to demonstrate that important social and environmental conditions were in place for this to have happened. We are discussing here, not just a change in food availability or knowledge of herding skills, but far-reaching changes in mode of production as well. This implies major social and economic shifts to encompass private or corporate ownership of resources and leadership roles that became evident with larger groups (cf. Ehret 1998: 219–20). It may have been this social dominance that resulted in Khoe languages being absorbed wholesale by other groups, for example, Damara in Namibia and Hietshware in Botswana.

Assuming contact between pastoral groups from Zambia with early Khoe speakers, it is perhaps significant that one of the loan words found in Khoe that comes from an Eastern Sahelian language is the word for *milk ewe*. This suggests milking of sheep was an important part of Khoe economy.

In a rapid expansion of pastoral people southward with sheep, the degree of archaeological visibility would drop off exponentially as they spread thinly across the area from northern Namibia to Limpopo Province (fig. 6.4). With Iron Age sites and their decorated pottery becoming dominant in the landscape, a few undecorated or relatively poorly decorated sherds from pastoralist sites may either have been unrecognized as different or ignored. An argument for the relationship between pastoral mobility and archaeological visibility can be supported by the later cattle economies of the Khoekhoen. After 900 years ago, Kasteelberg was no longer occupied by herders, an event possibly coincident with a rise in cattle numbers at the Cape to the levels that were described historically 300 years later, starting with the first Portuguese visitors to South Africa (Raven-Hart 1967). No traditional pastoralist sites with large numbers of cattle bones have been located in the Cape. Unlike with earlier sheep flocks, perhaps Khoekhoe cattle (bulk grazers) had to be constantly on the move to keep the herds healthy. This would have meant that their camps were not only ephemeral, but also not repeatedly occupied.

If we accept that the initial entry by shepherds to the Cape was made by Khoe speakers, and that these groups were small in number, this may explain the low archaeological visibility. That most of the aboriginal hunters in South Africa did not take up the Khoe words for sheep and shepherding, but did use the words for cattle and goats, suggests that there was a time separation between the two linguistic events and that, in the early contact when sheep arrived in South Africa, (a) there was no dominance (as may have been the case later when cattle arrived) and (b) there may have been limited interaction between the two groups. The incidence of pottery and sheep bones on hunter sites in the Cape may well have been a reflection of the differential contact between hunters and shepherds on the southwest coast at Kasteelberg and of what happened inland. The samples of words for sheep in non-Khoe languages come from the interior: from /Nu speakers on the southern edge of the Kalahari and from /Xam-speakers in Bushmanland (both part of the !Ui-Taa language family).

Kasteelberg remains the only direct window we have on traditional pastoralist societies in the southwestern Cape. Other sites occupied by hunters after 2,000 years ago have sheep bones and pottery, but these are a shadow of a probably more mobile pastoralist culture. Pottery and sheep found at KBG (about 2,000 years ago) predate the occupation of KBA (1,800–1,600 years ago). This may well be a reflection of initially low numbers of donor pastoralists in the early period, as a bow wave of entry into the Cape.

Kasteelberg later became an important focal point for herder activities. The hunter sites at Kasteelberg (e.g., KBG) were not nearly as intensively occupied as the later herder sites (KBA, KBB, KBC Upper, KBD, KBE, and KBE open). This is apparent, not only in the sheer amounts of occupational debris from the herder sites, but also in the soil color: gray ashy soil on the herder sites and red parent color on the hunter sites, thus the name of the farm Rooiheuwel (Red Hill) on which Kasteelberg stands.

Later Pastoral Development in the Eastern Cape, South Africa

The Eastern Cape probably had a somewhat different prehistoric trajectory of domestic animal development than the Western Cape, as it had the addition of a third economic group: Iron Age agropastoralists. Thus hunters (Soaqua), herders (Khoekhoen), and farmers (Iron Age Bantu speakers) all vied for the grazing resources or the animals that lived off them. The result was that ever-increasing demand for pasturage for domestic stock meant that hunters were pushed more and more onto the periphery, if they wished to maintain their foraging subsistence (Smith 1998b), and into areas that were considered marginal by herders, mainly the mountains or the dry interior. Relations between hunters and Iron Age farmers were often peaceful, and the genetic imprint of Khoesan in modern Nguni speakers, such as Xhosa, shows that Bushmen were incorporated into agropastoral society (Tobias 1974: fig. 1.7), probably through hypergyny (one-way marriage by women from hunting groups).

The restriction in the westward movement by agropastoralists was the distribution of summer rains that fed their African crops of sorghum and millet. The ecotone between summer and winter rainfall was occupied in the early historic period by people of mixed Khoekhoe/Xhosa ancestry, called Gonaqua.

Using historical data, Hall (1986) created a model of seasonal transhumance in the Winterberg area of the Eastern Cape. He has shown a move between the sourveld grasses of the interior, which are excellent grazing for a short period after the rains but whose protein content drops off markedly later in the year, to the coastal sweetveld, where pasture quality is lower, but pastures can be grazed year round. This pattern was later elaborated by early colonists who would have two farms, one in each area, to which their cattle would be seasonally driven.

The prehistory of herding in the Eastern Cape is poorly understood, but glimpses into the archaeological record suggest a trend similar to that of the Western Cape. Binneman (1996) reports on an Early Iron Age site at Kulubele, dated to the eighth and ninth centuries AD, from which mostly small stock bones were found. A dung layer in the site was seen (Simon Hall, pers. comm.) that may have come from mixed herds, but cattle probably did not arrive in any great numbers until the second wave of Iron Age farmers showed up in the eleventh century. It was these later Nguni immigrants who brought their wealth in cattle with them.

The impact on the region and the various economic groups already in residence must have been very strongly felt, as cattle herders began pushing the territorial edges to find pasture for their animals. This may have been the time that pressure was brought to bear on hunters, who were gradually pushed aside, and competition for space between Khoekhoen and Xhosa would have varied as the boundary between winter and summer rainfall fluctuated with changes in climatic conditions. Even a small increase in either direction for a few years would have had an effect on how the summer rainfall crops of the farmers would fare. By the time of the first colonists in the area, Xhosa were pushing the edges of their territory at the expense of the Khoekhoen, and the European presence just added more pressure on the local farmers who resisted with the four Xhosa wars.

Pastoral Rock Art in East and Southern Africa

Compared with the Sahara, depictions of domestic animals in East and southern Africa are comparatively few, which is surprising, considering the extent of pastoralism in this part of the subcontinent over the past 4,000 years. Even where there are rock walls that are painted, as in the Kondoa area of Tanzania, very few domestic animals are drawn.

Cattle

In East Africa, the best series has come from the Horn. Cervicek (1979) goes as far as suggesting that some of the art has affinities with the Arabian Peninsula. Le Quellec (2002–2003: 65) is more cautious, saying the similarities are based on poorly defined characteristics and that one could select paintings from as far afield as Angola, or even India, that could fit the definition. Paintings and engravings are found in the Republic of Somaliland (Clark 1954), Somalia (Brandt and Crader 1987), and Ethiopia (Breuil 1934; Graziosi 1964; Joussaume 1981), and new sites are still being reported (Siyakha Mguni, pers. comm.), suggesting more work could be done there. From many of these sites, there are elaborate depictions of coat colors. In Kenya, the best site for cattle paintings seems to be Tweedie's Cave on Mt. Elgon (Wright 1961). At this site, horn shapes are strongly emphasized. In almost all of the reported drawings from East Africa, only one or two of the cattle depictions show any indications of humps (e.g., Joussaume 1981: fig. 2: 22; Leakey 1983: 124). Thus most of the paintings may predate the introduction of zebu cattle into the Horn of Africa. A final period of rock art may be the crude line drawings in red or white representing cattle brands of people similar to the Maasai today (Sutton 1973: 36; Leakey 1983: 125). There are also depictions of milking cattle from Eritrea (Joussaume 1981, fig. 3: 16) and Ethiopia (Graziosi 1964, fig. 5).

In southern Africa, paintings of domestic animals are found in Zimbabwe and South Africa, with a few from the Brandberg in Namibia. The spatial distributional differences between sheep

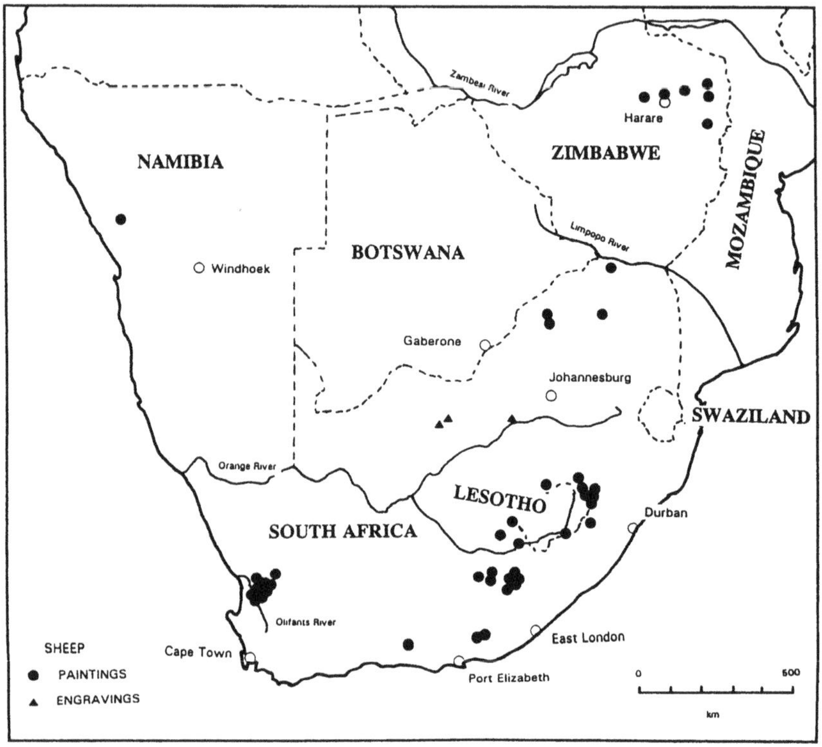

Figure 6.15. Distribution of sheep paintings in southern Africa (adapted from Manhire et al. 1986).

and cattle paintings are given in figures 6.15 and 6.16. Cattle depictions are apparently missing from the Southwestern Cape. Considering the historical reports of thousands of head of cattle from the seventeenth century, this is indeed surprising. It is possible that there is an implicit chronological sequence in rock art production by local Bushman (Soaqua) painters. Cattle were late arrivals in the Western Cape, probably after 1,000 years ago, so the sheep paintings may well predate this period. The detail in the cattle paintings from the Eastern Cape is remarkable (fig. 6.17), especially as it is apparent in some cases the cattle are painted over eland, the traditional rain animal of the Bushmen. This kind of detail we would normally expect from cattle herders involved with coat colors. It is possible that

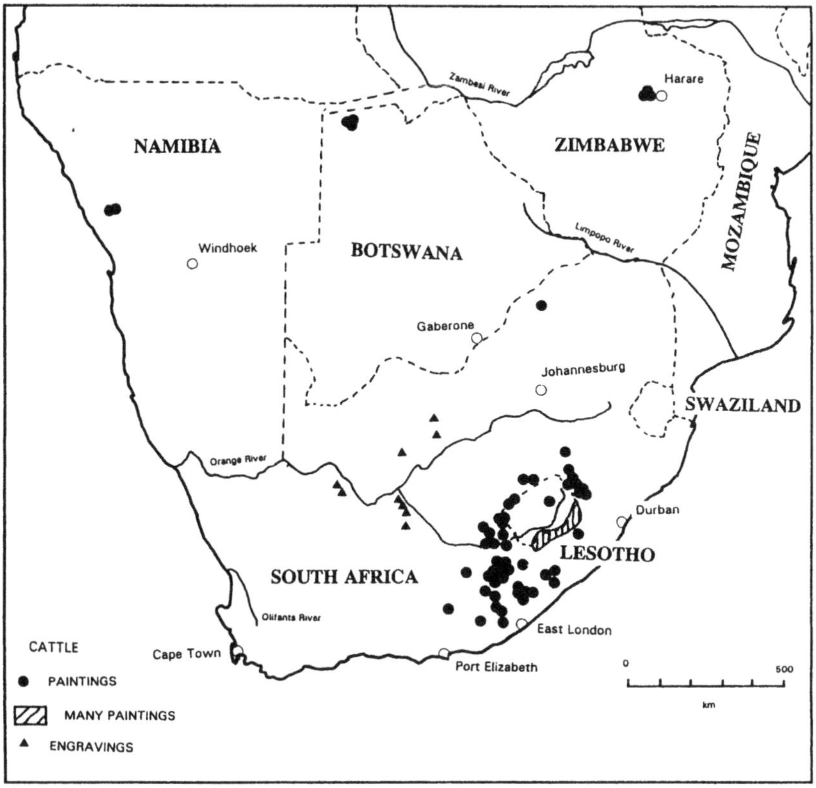

Figure 6.16. Distribution of cattle paintings in southern Africa (adapted from Manhire et al. 1986).

during the period of cattle painting the cultural intricacies of coat color had already been absorbed by the painters, who were being drawn into agropastoral life but still retained their ritual value as rainmakers (cf. Jolly 1995).

Sheep

There are fewer representations of sheep in sub-Saharan Africa. Black-headed sheep with thin tails are found in paintings from Eritrea (Joussaume 1981: fig. 3: 9). Much further south, in Zimbabwe, there are several sites showing fat-tailed sheep (Goodall 1946).

Figure 6.17. Cattle paintings from Brakfontein, western Winterberg, South Africa (Hall 1986; reprinted by permission).

Figure 6.18. Fat-tailed sheep from Grootfontein Agricultural College, Karoo, South Africa.

Fat-tailed sheep (fig. 6.18) are also found in the paintings of the Cape (Hollman 1993) (fig. 6.19). The ritual value of sheep to the Khoekhoen (Wilson 1969: 56) may be one reason why only sheep paintings were to be found in the Western Cape.

Camels

Depictions of camels are to be found in the rock art of Somalia (Clark 1954: plate 28: 1 and 4; Brandt and Crader 1987: fig. 3). According to Clark's description, these are weathered engravings, which might suggest they are of some antiquity and give additional support to

Figure 6.19. Fat-tailed sheep painting from Boskloof, Cederberg, South Africa (Smith).

the idea of contact between the Arabian Peninsula and the Horn of Africa.

Horses

Horses with riders have been recorded from Eritrea (Joussaume 1981, fig. 4: 30, 35, 36). These are also found in South Africa, where they are assumed to be of colonial date, as they often include firearms or are associated with wagons.

7

Cattle in Ritual

Thus from Egypt as far as Lake Tritonis Libya is inhabited by wandering tribes, whose drink is milk and their food the flesh of animals. Cow's flesh however none of these tribes ever taste.

—Herodotus IV: 186

Taçon and Chippindale (1998: 1) remarked that "human beings have increasingly marked landscapes in symbolic ways. A characteristically human trait, this is one of the ways we socialise landscapes." Symbols have a variety of purposes, a major one of which is ritual. The archaeology of ritual manifests itself in all art forms people have made, and rock art is possibly the most obvious in any landscape. Although rock art may be narrative at one level, there are probably many reasons why it was created. "The production and consumption of rock art was imbedded, as indeed all arts are, in the social, economic, and intellectual circumstances of the community in which the images were made" (Lewis-Williams 2002: 249). The images constitute important referents in the society of the artists and are seldom casual depictions. There is usually a much deeper meaning attached to the art, which means that traditional rock art genres are embedded in, and represent aspects of, belief. In fact, so powerful might these images be, only initiated people would think of drawing them. In some societies, even seeing the images could cause serious harm for the uninitiated.

Already we have noted the congruence between the large proportion of Barbary sheep bones from Uan Afuda (di Lernia 1999a) and depictions of these animals on the rock walls of the cave. These were wild animals, and there is no morphological evidence to suggest that they were domesticated, nor have these animals contributed to the genetic makeup of the modern domestic sheep of Africa. The dung layer in the cave indicates that they were being penned up in significant numbers. Thus a wild animal was being controlled. We can suggest this would have been a convenient way of keeping a meat source, but the rock art paintings are hints that the animals meant more than just food. The rock art drawings of the sheep were representations, raising the animals to a level of symbolic value possibly for use as sacrifice in propitiation ceremonies. The rock art may have been powerfully evocative of the spirit world and taken on attributes as links between humans and the spirits.

If we can generalize from the Nuer example and accept Evans-Pritchard's analysis (1956: 263), there would seem to be little question that they have a clear separation in their minds about the sacrificial role of all their animals. In fact, an animal should not be slaughtered for food, but only for sacrifice. Oxen and cows play different roles, and it is usually oxen, not cows, that are sacrificed. At the same time, an ox is often a symbol of personal identity (but see Gourlay 1972 for detailed discussion of this), and its sacrifice is for individuals. As Evans-Pritchard (1956: 260) says, "the lives of oxen are substituted for the lives of men." By contrast, cows are the ancestral, therefore the clan, animals. Descent in the herd is through the cows (matrilineal), because they are the stable thread on which the clan is based. "The unity of clans and lineages is symbolized in the names of the ancestral spears . . . and in honorific titles, chiefly derived from the names of cows. . . . [T]he cow stand(s) for the herd and hence also for the lineage of its masters" (258–59). Cattle are the center of Nuer life, so their most valued possession (278). Nuer piacular sacrifice is done "to establish communication with God" (275). They are a gift to God to get rid of danger or misfortune (276). Laying hands or rubbing ashes on the back of the sacrificial victim is done so that the "evil" will be transferred to the ox and flow out with its blood into the ground (280–81).

The Bodi example (chapter 1) gives us a clue that domestic animals equally have emotional and symbolic value in how pastoralists view their world, and we should be able to see this in the archaeological record. The importance of cattle to prehistoric Saharan pastoralists is obvious from the range of rock paintings from both bovidian periods. The coat colors of the cattle are so detailed that we can immediately place them within the cognitive and descriptive systems of modern African pastoralists. In addition, as has been shown here, rock paintings of decorated cattle from the later Bovidian II period are widespread across the Sahara, and these body markings may indicate ritual activity.

Lajoux (1963: 116–17) has already observed that, in the Bovidian I period drawings in the Tassili, men are often depicted standing close to their cattle with their hands outstretched toward them. In one case from Sefar (119), the herder seems to be actually touching the animal. Are these the chosen sacrificial victims? Does the rock art substitute for actual sacrifice? Of course, these details are lost to us, and we can only surmise from the ethnographic record what the relationship between men and cattle was.

Whole animals, under tumuli sealed with clay found in the Western Desert of Egypt, strongly suggest intentional burial for ritual purposes (Applegate et al. 2001). Other burials from Niger showing cut marks on the fifth cervical vertebra suggest that the animals were ritually sacrificed by slitting the throat (Paris 2000) and are indicators that the value of cattle went far beyond the purely economic. Herodotus (IV: 188), writing at the beginning of the fourth century BC (c. 2,430 years ago) notes: "the rites which the wandering Libyans use in sacrificing are the following. They begin with the ear of the victim, which they cut off and throw over their house: this done, they kill the animal by twisting the neck."

The Bull Cult of the Eastern Mediterranean

What might be the origins of such a belief system? There is a set of beliefs around cattle that became very widespread throughout the eastern Mediterranean and the Nile Valley: the bull cult. The historical trajectory of this belief system is not easy to recreate, nor can we be sure that every manifestation of it had a common origin.

As far back as 1896, Eduard Hahn had suggested that one of the reasons for the domestication of animals was that they were used in ritual (Sauer 1969: 88). Rituals among agriculturalists invariably revolve around fertility of the land (first fruits harvests, rainmaking, etc.) and, by extension, human fertility, with sexual symbolism often overt. Domestication of animals in the Near East occurred among agriculturalists, and it is interesting that although goat, ram, and ibex figurines were to be found in Neolithic Beidha (Singh 1974: 28–29), it was the bull, and not the ram, that became the major symbol of ritual activities. "The sacredness of the bull is expressed in particular through the emphasis on horns. They are sometimes as large as the whole animal figurine." As far back as the Upper Palaeolithic Aurignacian in Europe, the horn symbol is suggested as representing the waxing aspect of the moon (Gimbutas 1982: 91–93), and so had regenerative powers.

However, there appears to have been more to the bull symbolism than just regeneration. The bull seems to have been used to represent maleness. In the Near East, the bull symbol was already evident at Mureybet around 10,000 years ago and in the southern Levant in Pre-Pottery Neolithic B times some 9,000 years ago. Cauvin (2000: 123–25) refers to Pre-Pottery Neolithic B as "people of the bull," where the animal symbolized the brute force of the storm: "in man brute violence [that], once mastered ('humanised') could be converted into an organised power of confrontation. . . . [B]y bravery the wild bull–animal man could learn to seek the opportunity to prove his mastery over it. . . . [T]he confrontation between man and bull should be unfolded as a solemn ritual act." Cauvin goes even further and suggests that the wild bull symbolized an awakening "self-confidence" of Neolithic people in the Levant.

By 7,200 to 6,000 years ago, at Çatal Hüyük and Haçilar in Anatolia (Mellaart 1975: 109), the bull symbol manifested itself in bucrania (cattle horns) used in shrine walls and embedded into low platforms. There are also human female figures depicted as giving birth to bulls' heads (Mellaart 1975: 108). Like the horn symbol, stylized female figurines had been found much earlier in the Upper Palaeolithic of Europe. They have also been found in the Late Natufian of the Levant (Cauvin 2000: 25–29), are suggested as continuing down to Minoan Crete, and possibly even classical Greece, and are considered to be "mother goddesses" (Gimbutas 1982). The appearance of the bull as her male counterpart (son or consort) may have been a merging of two separate ideological systems in the Near East: one of fertility, the other of mastery over nature. The most recent excavations at Çatal Hüyük have produced the bones of both wild and domestic cattle.

Terra cotta figurines of both cattle and female humans, as well as depictions of horns on pottery, although not necessarily common, nonetheless became widespread and continued to appear in later Neolithic sites throughout the Near East (Gimbutas 1982; Singh 1974). Unlike the more public Çatal Hüyük shrines, these are usually small pieces that may have been for personal votive or household use.

In North Africa, cattle cults were also to be found in Dynastic Egypt. The remarkable central chamber from First Dynasty at Saqqara (c. 5,000 years ago) had 300 bulls' heads modeled in clay and real horns set above them on a low platform (Rice 1991: 124), similar to what had previously been found in Anatolia. The origins were initially thought to go back to the pre-Dynastic Badarian culture. It now appears from the intentional burial in the Late Neolithic of Nabta Playa that the desert dates are earlier, around 6,200 to 5,500 years ago (Applegate et al. 2001: 484–86) and that the Badarians (from 5,500 to 5,000 years ago) may have taken up their belief system from the Sahara.

The earliest rock paintings of the central Sahara may well even predate the cattle burials, and although most of the Bovidian I paintings probably belong to the Middle Pastoral Period (between 6,080 and 5,000 years ago), the dates for Uan Telocat in the Acacus Mountains may make some of them even older. Level III from this site was dated to 6,745 years ago, but after the deposit was removed from this level, some paintings were found on the cave wall (Mori 1965; Garcea 2003).

Fertility and sexuality have been associated with Saharan bovidian rock engravings. Focusing on the petroglyphs depicting cattle from Djebel Serkout in the eastern Hoggar Mountains of Algeria, Aïn-Séba (2002) has suggested that the horns of the cattle represented more than just the animals themselves. Human figures exhibiting overt male sexual characteristics are often seen with horns, so they may have had sexual significance. There is also the suggestion that horns, the lunar crescent, and females shown in open sexual position may have been equivalents.

If, as has been suggested here, the spread of domestic animals to Africa was from the Near East, then we can equally suggest that ritual beliefs came with them. Ritual use of wild animals had already been intimated by the penning of Barbary sheep in the cave at Uan Afuda and their depictions on the rock walls of the cave (di Lernia 1999b). The wild cattle of North Africa may have been incorporated into this system, resulting in the DNA admixture found in modern African cattle (Hanotte et al. 2002).

East African Cattle: Ritual and Sacrifice

The early Saharan prehistoric pastoral environment was not one of agriculture, but of herding and use of wild grains. The Saharan pastoralists thus took up the ritual concept and adapted it to their own needs. The cattle had their own social value, more in tune with the cattle beliefs of pastoral people of sub-Saharan Africa today. The detail of coat color of the Bovidian I art is so evocative of the identity of individual animals given to them by modern African pastoralists that it is possible that the peoples who produced the art were the ancestors of modern pastoralists and the first wave of herders moving southward into the southern Sudan and then on to East Africa 4,000 years ago. Cattle burials are recorded among modern pastoralists of sub-Saharan Africa. Herskovits (1926: 257), in his long survey of the "cattle complex" of East and southern Africa, has one anecdotal reference to a large mound of buried oxen bones dedicated to a "big man" among the Nuer. Shrines to Nuer prophets were built over the carcasses of sacrificial oxen (Johnson 1990: 50). Similarly, Evans-Pritchard (1956: 220) suggests that an individual might bury a few bones of an ox in a household *riek* (pole) shrine after sacrifice to a spirit, and Johnson (1990: 53) says that this could be a whole carcass. Equally, "mobile shrines," dedicated to various divinities are recorded in the form of cattle (ibid.: 53), and clay figurines of cattle are usually suspended from the roofs of byres covering the shrines of dead spear masters (ibid.: 54).

These shrines are at one level dedicated to spiritual needs: "The sacrifices involved in the building of shrines, whether of a person or an animal, are part of the process of the containment of spiritual power, fixing its transmission and making it approachable." At another level, however, they represent political power "and can be interpreted as identifying the centres of political focus within the region" (Johnson 1990: 54).

Many other aspects of Nuer herding society would appear to be very similar to that of the prehistoric Saharan pastoralists, even though by now grain agriculture has been adopted. Most pastoralists of East Africa look upon agriculture as a necessary evil and, given a choice, would rather spend time with their animals. The Nuer grow significant amounts of millet and maize, but "all alike regard horticulture as toil forced on them by poverty of stock" (Evans-Pritchard 1940: 16). Milk products are much more highly regarded. This is typified by the statement of Evans-Pritchard (1940: 21): "Even when millet is plentiful it is seldom eaten alone, for without milk, whey, or liquid cheese, Nuer find it stodgy, unpalatable, and, especially for children, indigestible."

Cattle are central to the life of the pastoralist. Among the Nuer, the ox given to a young man by his father is sung to, lovingly rubbed down with ash from the fire, and decorated with horn tassels. "(E)very man takes one of his names from the term by which one of his oxen is described, and these ox-names are the preferred salutations among age-mates" (Evans-Pritchard 1940: 45). If a young unmarried man dies, his favorite ox should be sacrificed (Evans-Pritchard 1956: 147). Unlike practice among many of the Bantu-speaking herd owners of southern Africa, where women are virtually banned from the herd, Nuer and Maasai women and young uninitiated boys milk the cattle.

Southern African Cattle in Ritual

Two quite different groups have traditionally carried out herding in southern Africa: the Bantu-speaking Sotho/Tswana and Nguni and the Khoekhoen.

Bantu-Speaking Agropastoralists

The ancestors of modern Bantu-speaking people were Iron Age farmers whose heartland was the Cross River area of Cameroon in West Africa. These were agricultural people whose ritual life revolved around ancestor worship, with shrines dedicated to their forebears. The ancestors are "deceased members of the clan who continue to watch over their descendants and take intense interest in their affairs" (Poland et al. 2003: 26). Since they are agriculturalists, they are concerned about the fertility of themselves and their fields, so propitiation and first harvest ceremonies are important events in their lives. If they sacrifice, usually a goat or a chicken is used.

The expansion out of the Cross River area, known as "Bantu origins" (Huffman 1970; 1979), occurred some 3,000 years ago. Farming people moved around the northern end of the tropical forest to the Great Lakes Region of East Africa, where they came into contact with African pastoral people. The farmers continued their agricultural way of life, but they combined it with wealth storage in cattle. In doing so, they took on many of the trappings of traditional herding societies, among which are detailed animal identification systems. They retain their belief in ancestral intervention to deal with misfortune or propitiation, and sacrifices of cattle are performed to appease the dead, "for the wrath of the ancestors is thought to be expressed through hunger for meat and, especially, gall," which by its bitterness is the opposite of the food of men and is licked by the shades, or spirits of the ancestors (Poland et al. 2003: 26–27).

Even the Himba of northern Namibia, who are semi-nomadic pastoralists and, at first glance, almost indistinguishable from East African herders, are nonetheless Bantu-speakers and have "holy fires" where the clan leader will say prayers to the ancestors; and on the death of an elder his sacred herd will be sacrificed and their horns stacked up above his grave. Thus the agricultural history of these southern African people shows through, even though their wealth/status and interest in cattle are almost as intense as that in other African pastoralists.

Khoekhoen

Very different from Bantu-speaking herders, the Khoekhoen (formerly known as "Hottentots") did not practice any agriculture. They are descended from one of the three aboriginal hunting populations of southern Africa. They are much closer to other African pastoralists in that their belief involves a supreme being who has a good side and an evil side (or in whom these two sides can be rivals), as well as spirits, and not ancestors, although the spirits of the dead may be invoked in curing rituals (Barnard 1992: 252). Today their traditional ritual life has been heavily overlain with Christianity, but although few of their pre-Christian ceremonies still exist, a number were still being practiced when Winifred Hoernlé did her fieldwork just before the First World War. In the past, their rituals mostly revolved around a concept of !nau, or transition. These *rites de passages* meant that an individual was in a liminal situation (Hoernlé 1918) and thus dangerous to him/herself and to the community at large. This required appropriate ceremonial purification, often in the form of sacrifice.

Although, by the time of the first European observers at the end of the fifteenth century, the Khoekhoen had large herds of cattle, it is primarily sheep that are slaughtered in ceremonies, a reflection of a time, over 1,000 years ago, before cattle arrived at the Cape in any significant numbers. Other animals, for example, a steenbok (*Raphicerus campestris*), might be used at certain times, and Robert Gordon noted in 1779 that a cow or an ox might be slaughtered on the last day of a ceremony that lasted two weeks (Smith and Pheiffer 1992: 10). Gordon also drew a picture of the grave of a newly dead Khoe chief on which the head of an ox was placed along with the hunting equipment of the deceased (Raper and Boucher 1988: plate 66). Men were usually the slaughterers, but in at least one ceremony women officiated. This Gordon referred to as a "mongoose slaughter," since the woman killing the animal needed to wear a piece of mongoose skin on her head (Smith and Pheiffer 1992: 12).

The ritual life of Khoekhoen has close ties to that of Khoisan hunters (Barnard 1992), but as the Khoekhoen were herders, their domestic stock played an important role. As with Bantu-speaking people, the introduction of domestic animals into southern Africa meant that those who took on the herding of animals adopted some aspects of the lifestyle of the people from whom the stock was obtained. The basic, deep meaning in ritual life was retained, but overlain with aspects of the pastoral interest in domestic animals and their involvement in the economy and ceremonies. In fact, the Nguni, who may have been later Bantu-speaking arrivals on the southern African scene, seem to have obtained the clicks, and possibly the words for sheep, in their language from the Khoekoen.

Domestic Animal Overlays on Pastoral Ritual Life

While cattle are central to the economic life of most African pastoralists, and in turn have deep-meaning ritual value, there are some societies where the economic value does not translate into ritual.

The Tuareg have a high regard for their camels, and status is accrued through the number of camels an individual owns, although a person's birth is by far the most significant factor in where the individual fits within the society. Camels are not central to ritual life, and Tuareg are averse to sacrifice their camels. They say it is "unseemly to eat a domestic camel who carries a name, and participates in the life of the group, in wars, migrations, and who is sometimes sung to in the evening during festivals" (Gast 1968: 128). Only sick or stolen animals and young camels are eaten, the latter at large political gatherings and marriages. They use ovicaprids in their family rituals, such as naming ceremonies.

Similarly, among the Khoekhoen in the historic period, cattle numbers defined a person's status, but in ritual life it is predominantly sheep that are used as sacrifice for various *rites de passage* (Wilson 1969; Smith and Pheiffer 1992). In the Khoe case, cattle were introduced as overlays upon a sheep-based husbandry system, so we can see, perhaps, why sheep still retained their ritual value.

Among the Tuareg, it is less obvious why camels would not be used ritually. One explanation might be that camels are an overlay on a previous system where small stock were the main economic resource, particularly after cattle rearing became difficult as a result of the aridification of the Sahara after 4,500 years ago.

Ex Africa Semper Aliquid Novi

After 5,000 years ago, when the Sahara started to dry up, new groups of herders of Mediterranean stock moved into the desert, either displacing the cattle herders who had been there before or filling the vacuum left by their departure. These new immigrants brought with them their ideas of mortuary architecture and probably the

Bovidian II paintings. It is these herders who started to experiment with grain domestication, so that shortly after 4,000 years ago conditions were right for a more sedentary lifestyle around semi-permanent villages with their gardens and cemeteries. These people also had rituals around cattle, although these were probably becoming more and more difficult to sustain in the dry environment. We know from the archaeology of the central Sahara (di Lernia 1999b) that cattle bones were decreasing in number in the Late Pastoral Period (from 5,000 to 3,500 years ago), being replaced by small stock bones. The rituals with cattle involved marking them and relating them to other aspects of ritual life, namely fire and fire spirits.

Contact with the Near East was, of course, not a one-way affair. There are suggestions that the Afro-Asiatic language family, of which Semitic and Berber are a part, may have originated in Africa and was spread by nomadic pastoralists (Brandt and Zarins 2004). Ene Metspalu of Tartu University, Estonia, claims, on the basis of genetic markers, to have evidence that these languages came out of Africa 10,000 years ago, although dating based on genetics is always difficult. The appearance of domesticated cattle in the Arabian Peninsula is relatively late, probably after 6,000 years ago, and contact with East Africa is also considered in the possible movement of obsidian from East Africa (Edens and Wilkinson 1998: 69–70). As mentioned before, some rock art styles are similar in the Horn and Arabia, but are not dated (but see Le Quellec 2002–2003 for discussion). While the data are equivocal at this point, considering how little attention has been given to contacts across the Red Sea and in the Gulf of Aden, we must accept the possibility of Africa having greater influence than previously assumed.

The origins of camel domestication in Arabia is still debated, but it would appear that these animals did not make a great impression on Arabian life until the development of urban mercantile centers between 2,900 and 2,400 years ago (Edens and Wilkinson 1998: 107), although they were probably domesticated prior to this. There is evidence that South Arabians settled in Ethiopia around 2,500 years ago, bringing a sophisticated urban culture (de Contenson 1981). Was this when the camel came to the Horn? Later, the Romans understood the value of camels as beasts of burden and used them heavily in North Africa.

The increasing aridity in the Sahara was also being felt in the Levant 4,500 years ago (Hassan 2000). Small stock herders seem to have been in place in the Negev by this time, prior to the introduction of the camel. That drought conditions unsettled pastoral nomads in this area is suggested by the movement of the Patriarch Abraham from Ur of the Chaldees, in the Tigris-Euphrates basin, to the Levant (Genesis 11:31; 12:5). With subsequent famine in the Levant, he later moved with his family to Egypt (Genesis 12:10). Is it purely coincidence that when Saharan pastoralists were developing new religious ideas during a period of environmental pressure, Abraham was communing with his God in the Levant?

> But at last Dahoum drew me: "Come and smell the very sweetest scent of all", and we went into the main lodging, to the gaping window sockets of its eastern face, and there drank with open mouths of the effortless, empty, eddyless wind of the desert, throbbing past.... "This," they told me, "is the best: it has no taste."... The Beduin of the desert, born and grown up in it, had embraced with all his soul this nakedness... felt but inarticulate, that there he found himself indubitably free. He lost material ties, comforts, all superfluities and other complications to achieve a personal liberty which haunted starvation and death.... In his life he had air and winds, sun and light, open spaces and a great emptiness. There was no human effort, no fecundity in Nature: just heaven above and the unspotted earth beneath. There unconsciously he came near God. (Lawrence 1962: 38)

8

The Future for African Pastoralists?

We left our herds tethered in the cattle camps
And followed Deng Nhial
When we reached the land of Congo
The Congo said: "Dinkas are matata"
I asked what does matata mean?
Ngor Makor answered: 'He says we are bad'

—Dinka exile poem (F. M. Deng, *The Dinka of the Sudan*)

The situation in Africa is economically, socially, and medically bleak at the beginning of the twenty-first century. HIV/AIDS is ripping through African populations, including traditional pastoralists. The war in Angola may be over, but the head of state, Eduardo dos Santos, is reputedly siphoning off US$5 billion of her oil revenues for his own use each year. Everywhere, African "big men" continue to show how corrupt they are, from Robert Mugabe, president of Zimbabwe, building a new residence while his countrymen either starve or flee gross human rights abuses, to Jacob Zuma, deputy president of South Africa, allegedly selling himself to foreign companies for arms tenders. In addition are all the "vultures," who have been tearing away at the carcass of the Democratic Republic of the Congo for their own greedy ends by supplying arms, radios, and cell phones to the rebels for diamonds, coltan, gold, tin, and tantalite . . . the list is endless (Brümmer 2004).

President Thabo Mbeki of South Africa wants an "African solution" to Africa's various social, economic, and medical problems through his New Economic Partnership for African Development (NEPAD). However, he denies there is any connection between HIV and AIDS and has stated publicly that he personally knows no one who has died of AIDS. In a country with over 20 percent of the population probably HIV positive, and his own spokesperson dying very young, this is surprising in the very least. Such beliefs have resulted in poor government engagement with the problem, to the extent that many of those most vulnerable have conflicting information thrown at them. Where do pastoralists fit into all this? In a recent article in *Newsweek*, Sayagues (2003) wrote that in order to educate herders about AIDS, nongovernmental organizations (NGOs) in Botswana say that HIV is like ticks, and they relate condoms to cattle kraals.

In Africa, the threat of growing human numbers (in spite of AIDS) means that many of the continent's resources are under threat for space. Logging is decimating the nonhuman primate populations by removal of habitat, and there is less and less space for elephants. And these are the high profile animals. Land mines in Angola and southern Sudan will take many years to remove, and with a generation of AIDS orphans it looks as if there will be major social problems ahead, since little education and few jobs are likely to come the way of these children.

Pastoralists in East Africa have been massively disrupted by conflict in the Democratic Republic of the Congo, southern Sudan, Rwanda, Burundi, and Somalia. Refugees have spilled over into Uganda and northern Kenya, and pastoralists have had to arm themselves from the huge numbers of automatic weapons that have become available from the war-torn areas (Gray et al. 2003). It is no exaggeration that availability of AK-47s and ammunition for them poses a major threat to peace in the continent. Young children are recruited as soldiers, and many know nothing but war.

> Ugandan Soldiers Kill 16 "Cattle Thieves"
>
> The Ugandan army says it killed at least 16 Karamojong tribesmen who had stolen hundreds of cattle from rival tribesmen in the Moroto district. "The warriors died in exchange of fire with the army. They put up stiff resistance," a spokesman said. (*Cape Times*, Tuesday, January 13, 2004: 2)
>
> Scores of Sudanese Wounded in Army Air Raids
>
> Tine, Chad: Cradling the bandaged stump that is left of his leg, Bakhit Abdallah, 24, says he was tending his cows with friends when a Sudanese aircraft bombed

> them. . . . Medical workers manning the field hospital here, the only one on the northern stretch of Chad's border with Sudan, say the number of people wounded in attacks by government bombers has increased sharply. . . . [M]ore than 35,000 refugees have poured across the border since December. . . . [M]any of the injured trek for days on camels and donkeys to reach the hospital, run by Doctors Without Borders. Their wounds are often infected. (*Cape Times*, Tuesday January 27, 2004: 2)

In Botswana, it is the herders who have charge of the central government. Tswana hegemony over the Basarwa (Bushmen) has meant sinking boreholes to open up the area for cattle in the western Sandveld, which has been the traditional hunting/foraging ground of the hunters for thousands of years. Landownership has been given to the herd owners at the expense of the Basarwa, who have been forcibly removed from the Central Kalahari Game Reserve to make way for diamond concessions. President Mogae of Botswana told protestors at Oxford University that the Bushmen will not be allowed to go home, saying "The CKGR is for animals not people," when it is really obvious that the policy is designed to make sure that aboriginal people cannot make claims against mineral wealth in the future, as has been successfully done in South Africa with platinum mines.

In twenty-first-century Africa, the one commodity that is probably going to make the most difference whether people adjust to present conditions or not is water. Countries are already negotiating with each other for access to river water and who has water rights. If global warming continues, rainfall patterns will change, and the marginal grasslands may be the worst hit. Pastoralists and farmers are in direct competition for groundwater. Irrigation schemes take water out of the system and lower the water table. Any area close to standing water is immediately snapped up by agriculturalists, leaving little for the pastoralist and his herd.

One of Namibia's remote beauty spots is Epupa Falls on the Kunene River (the northern border with Angola). This prime attraction is under threat by a proposal to build a dam. Local Himba herders have protested vigorously, even visiting Stockholm (the source of funds of the initial environmental impact assessment) to plead their case (Matthew and Chesselet 2001). The Himba claim their grazing lands and 100 ancestral grave sites will be inundated under the 250 sq km lake formed by the dam (Gubic 2004). All told, probably about 1,000 Himba will be affected. The Namibian government ministry seems to be oblivious to the plight of the herders, saying jobs will be created from the dam construction. Only a lack of funding has so far stopped the work.

Fine-grained rainfall records are rare in Africa, but one study by Verschuren et al. (2000) done on sediments from Lake Naivasha in the Kenyan Rift Valley indicates that natural fluctuations in rainfall are dramatic in East Africa. They show that over the past 1,000 years good rains are interspersed with periods of severe drought, to the extent that the lake level is estimated to have dropped from a high of over 35 m to a low of around 5 m (fluctuation within the past hundred years was 12 to 27 m). If these data are extrapolated into the future of this century, then a major drought can be expected. The conclusions of the authors are that: "the magnitude of natural decade-scale rainfall variability in sub-humid east Africa implies that sustainable development and protection of food security will require agricultural management strategies adjusted to long-term variation in water-resource availability, irrespective of any future effects of anthropogenic climate change on the hydrological cycle" (ibid.: 413).

If Bourn and Wint (1994) are correct that there is "a highly significant relationship between livestock biomass and the intensity of land use, and . . . that cultivation and human habitation are the best predictors of livestock distribution" in the Sahel of West Africa, then it follows that since the Sahelian drought of the early 1970s there has been a greater collaboration between farmers and pastoralists, and/or more pastoralists moving onto agricultural production. They conclude that the tsetse threat has vastly diminished, and that zebu cattle are being found further and further to the south, suggesting an increase in trypano tolerance among these animals. Certain areas of the Sahel may be becoming more depopulated of herds and herders, and as rural and urban populations to the south are increasing, it suggests some people are moving south (Hiernaux 1996).

In southern Africa, debate rages on whether land degradation has taken place due to overstocking (de Queiroz 1993; Abel 1993; Dahlberg 1993; White 1993). In the Kalahari, there seems to be a need for greater research into bush encroachment and whether it has had a negative effect on grazing and pastoral production on communal lands (Dougill and Cox 1995; Adams 1996; Cox and Dougill 1996). Government policy in Botswana has been to privatize the rangelands and to open new areas up by allowing additional borehole drilling in the western Sandveld. As mentioned above, this political decision occurs at the expense of the Basarwa, who seem to be intentionally kept out of the loop.

Is there a positive side to all of this? Not much of one, but small-scale initiatives in Internet access, and the growing cellular phone connections in areas far removed from land lines, mean there are new and exciting communications networks being set up that give rural people information about markets for their products in the outside world. This, of course, is a double-edged sword that means the world shrinks more rapidly, but the degree of isolation by people (including their political isolation) is becoming less as ideas spread. So potent is this as a political tool that places such as Zimbabwe are trying to control access.

The European colonial model of agrarian growth through agricultural extraction still permeates the development philosophies of Africa. This, like the traditional enmity between herder and farmer, with the latter in firm control of the state apparatus, means that less attention is paid to the drier grassland areas, which are not amenable to agriculture. Thus the poorer herdsman or hunter has little political pull in the corridors of power in the state capital. Political leaders are more concerned about feeding burgeoning urban growth (if they consider anything other than themselves).

There is a need for pastoralists to have rights, and in Kenya there are attempts to introduce these into the constitution. Driving this are NGOs who recognize that water and soil conservation strategies are critical in the equation, and this has to be integrated into indigenous knowledge systems for future growth. New technologies, such as geographical information systems (GIS), might help (Tegene 2003), but unless central governments give greater security to land tenure, or help with marketing strategies, little benefit will trickle down to the poorer sectors of the population.

A glimmer of hope for the descendants of the Khoekhoen in the Richtersveld, at the mouth of the Orange River in South Africa, was offered by the courts when the Khoekhoen won their appeal against the government-owned diamond mine. They laid claim to the coastal strip in which the diamond operations have taken place since the 1920s and were able to show that they were racially excluded from their former grazing lands by colonial policies that decreed that they were incompetent to administer their own traditional lands. The result of this case is that the Khoekhoen can now negotiate with the government for royalties or other infrastructure benefits, such as schools, clinics, and possibly job preference, since they will have representation on the mine board. They will also have a say on reconstituting the land that has been devastated by stripping the topsoil to get to the diamond-rich levels.

Livestock marketing policies developed during the colonial era have affected traditional pastoralists, and these continue down to the present (Kerven 1992). The analysis of Barrett et al. (2003) indicates that poor pastoralists of northern Kenya depend on their livestock, but variability in herd numbers due to health and climatic fluctuation is enormous. Ceremonial needs, cash to pay school fees, and quarantines all affect the market. Price volatility due to quarantine weakens marketing infrastructures and limits integration into the main terminal market in Nairobi. Pastoralists continue to have large herds despite the vagaries in the system, so herd sizes are regulated by mortality rather than marketing decisions. The authors suggest that there is a need for a better system to reduce losses from livestock mortality, although they recognize that this would directly affect the large ranch producers negatively: "Kenya's approach to animal disease control favors wealthy highlands ranches and consumers at the expense of poorer dryland herders" (ibid.: 127).

These notes on the current situation affecting pastoralists in Africa do not do justice to the detailed development work that continues throughout the continent. Many dedicated people work closely with herdsmen and are advocates for political intervention on their part. The Overseas Development Institute (ODI) in London has maintained a Pastoral Development Network since the 1980s, and the reader is directed toward the many position papers and discussions around pastoral issues that have appeared over the years. In particular, Blench (2001) has attempted an encyclopedic review of pastoralist societies today and their adaptation in the modern world, and this paper can be downloaded from the ODI website. The comprehensive bibliography offers the reader a good introduction to the literature on the subject.

The philosophy of African rangelands exploitation has changed radically over the past twenty years. A comprehensive study of Sahelian rangeland ecology that assumes that the traditional system of pastoral exploitation is both rational and efficient is provided by Penning de Vries and Djitèye (1982). There was an assumption that human impact resulted in pasture degradation, and that traditional herders were using the land ineffectively, so rangeland needed to be conserved, and the ranch model was assumed to be the most effective way of doing this. Traditional pastoralists have thus tended to be marginalized (Spencer 1998) and seen as more of a nuisance to the modern state, rather than important contributors. That almost two-thirds of the African continent is semiarid, and thirty million people with livestock live on these rangelands, can hardly be considered peripheral to modern state economies. Since many of these pastoral systems are thousands of years old and have adjusted to the ecological vagaries of dry lands, the effectiveness of traditional practices need to be recognized and supported in order to sustain rangeland production. Behnke and Kerven (1994) suggest this can be done by adding to pastoralist knowledge in improving veterinary programs, water harvesting techniques, and early warning systems to anticipate drought and famine. In addition, the pastoralists need to be supported by improved land tenure, market accessibility, and possibly training in fodder production. Discussion by leading pastoral researchers is offered in Behnke et al. (1993) and Scoones (1994).

African Pastoralist Archaeology in the Twenty-First Century

There is a great deal we do not know about the archaeology of pastoralism in Africa. The lacunae are to be found in all parts of the continent where herders have lived in the past, and filling these will depend in large part on concentrated efforts in various remote areas, such as the work that has been done in the Sahara by the University of Rome "La Sapienza" under Savino di Lernia and Barbara Barich, and by Southern Methodist University under Fred Wendorf. At the beginning of the twenty-first century, finding pastoralist sites will require dedication and fine-tuning of the cultural sequences already known. It will require greater sensitivity to the different economies in a specific area to be able to separate out herders from hunters from agropastoralists, as has been achieved in the Kenyan Rift Valley by Stanley Ambrose and Fiona Marshall.

The reader is directed to the fine introduction by Augustin Holl (1998) to the issue of the *Journal of Anthropological Archaeology* dedicated to African pastoralists. He raises a number of issues regarding gaps in the evidence and the need to relate what is known in wider regional terms to fully understand how pastoralism expanded throughout the continent.

North Africa

Since I believe much of what we need to know about the earliest pastoralist societies in Africa will have to come from the Sahara, new methods of exploration will need to be devised that will cut down on the expensive time needed in the field. These may be recognition techniques using pottery and frequency of artifact type, as well as having the zooarchaeologist working in the field. All this will be enhanced by new and better technology to extract ancient DNA from animal bones for comparison with modern breeds and AMS dating of very small samples.

A greater awareness of the contribution North Africa has made to the Levant, and vice versa, is long overdue. Perhaps better excavation techniques, which will allow deep sounding in the Nile Delta to extract early Neolithic material from the sediments, will allow a more coherent idea of the connections across the Sinai land bridge.

There is a need to build upon what Sadr (1991) has already shown to be a strong relationship between the desert and the Nile Valley. This relationship between the valley and hinterland on both sides has recently been given a fillip by the work of Toby Wilkinson (2003) in the Eastern Desert of Egypt. It is becoming increasingly apparent that people previously seen as living on the margins of Nile Valley society may well have had a very pronounced effect on the history of the valley. The "megaliths" described by Wendorf and Malville (2001) from Nabta Playa hint that an elaborate belief system was in operation on the Western Desert during the Late Neolithic at about the time of the early Dynastic development in the valley. Is there any connection between these megaliths and the megalithic stone pillars found in the Lake Turkana area of northern Kenya associated with the early Nderit pottery (Gifford-Gonzalez 2000: 101)?

The Italian researchers at the University of Rome "La Sapienza" have already begun a research project into understanding the relationships between the early Saharan states and the formation of trade networks. They are keen to see if they can find evidence for the early trade described in Herodotus, as well as for the spread of iron working in the Sahara (Liverani 2000). This should elucidate the role the Saharan pastoralists played in the trade and, hopefully, how interregional connections may have molded their more recent history. Equally, their valiant attempts to set up the new "Archaeological Park" in the Acacus Mountains of southwestern Libya will hopefully give jobs to local people and prevent damage to the sites and rock art of the region (Liverani et al. 2000; see also their website for photographs of damage already done, at www.acacus.it).

In Saharan pastoral rock art studies, there will have to be some serious revisiting of the work by Lhote (1959; 1976) and his colleagues. Not only has the critique by Keenan (2002) raised serious issues of forgery, but also the detailed paintings by Pierre Colombel, some of which were published in Kuper (1978), need to be shown in photographic form for authentication. With new digital cameras, false imagery can be used to enhance faded paintings.

West Africa

Programs are being devised by Rod McIntosh of Rice University to follow up on work he started with Susan McIntosh and Kevin MacDonald in Mali. Thus connections and spread of pastoralism from the Sahara to the Sahel will be further elaborated. The later archaeology of the relations between herders and farmers in the central Niger Delta and the origins of the Harratin are outstanding questions that need serious study. The Azaouad, connecting the Sahara to the Sahel, is poorly known, and my own work in the Tilemsi Valley needs much greater elaboration. The archaeology of the Gaussens' facies K and facies B in the lower Tilemsi (1988), as well as connections further north need far greater work. In one of my surveys in the Tin Aoukert area, I found forging areas exposed on the surface. When was metalworking introduced into the area?

East Africa

While a great deal of work has been done on pastoralism in East Africa and the relations between various economic groups, it has mostly been confined to the Kenyan Rift Valley. Ethiopia needs greater exploration, and there are vast areas of Uganda and Tanzania that are archaeologically terra incognita. There is some debate over the earliest domestic animals in northern Kenya, and links to the Sudan will have to await a long-term solution to the unsettling strife in that region so more work can be done. The international boundary between Kenya and Tanzania is an artificial one in prehistoric pastoralist terms. Most work has been done on the Kenyan side, in Maasai Mara (Robertshaw 1990) and Tsavo (Wright 2003). How does this information expand across the border into Tanzania? Like in the Sahara, the archaeology of modern herders (not just ethnoarchaeology) is long overdue, and is needed to give time depth to herders' tenure. Information in this area no doubt will grow as DNA studies of living people untangle the complex diversity of culture history in the subcontinent and support, reject, or fine-tune Christopher Ehret's linguistic modeling (1998).

Contact between Arabia and East Africa needs to be more fully elaborated, particularly when dealing with the potential introduction of domestic animals, such as the zebu cattle and camels. Recent analysis of sheep genetic material has indicated that the extant breeds of Africa may well have come from two sources. The thin-tailed West African and fat-tailed North African sheep have genetic similarities to Middle Eastern types, so might have come via Suez/Sinai. The fat-tailed sheep of East and southern Africa are closer to Arabian breeds, suggesting entry to Africa via the Horn (Muigai et al. 2004). The latter may have been related to the broader Red Sea and Indian Ocean trade, perhaps during the Aksum period. Were zebu cattle, sheep, and camels all introduced at the same time?

Nuer and Dinka are archetypal African pastoralists in the traditional sense, and would be logical descendants of the expansion of herding societies out of the Eastern Sahelian region 4,000 years ago. Yet they both exhibit low levels of lactase preference (table 5.1). Even the Nama, a Khoe group, have higher levels, and we estimate their ancestral contact with milk to only be about 2,500 years. Is it possible that, as with the Bantu-speaking Herero herders, Nuer pastoral history is not as deep as that of other East African groups, such as the Tutsi? Souring or fermenting milk can help avoid lactose intolerance, but if the Nuer have been pastoralists as long as the Nama, we would still expect higher levels, so perhaps anthropology has given us only a narrow window on their history.

Southern Africa

Connections between East and southern Africa are well established in Iron Age studies, but the same cannot be said for pastoralist archaeology. As in the Sahara, being able to recognize cultural variables from small, discrete scatters will be important to make sense of the expansion of mobile herding societies. The movement of shepherds ahead of Iron Age farmers was rapid, which will equally compound the visibility problem. Work done in the Western Cape suggests there are separate archaeological signatures for hunters and herders (Smith et al. 1991). Although this is more easily seen in large, repeatedly occupied sites, small scatters can offer similar results if enough sites can be built into the research (Beaumont et al. 1995). The frequency of different animal types may be a good way to separate the economies of hunters from herders, just as are the types of tools and frequency of potsherds (Sadr 1997). The routes of expansion of sheep through South Africa to the Cape are poorly known. Who brought the sheep and what role the aboriginal hunters played need to be worked out. The archaeology of the Khoekhoen is almost nonexistent. Were their ancestors the first herders at the Cape? Determining this will be a real challenge for the future.

It is extraordinary that ethnographic work among farm workers in the drier parts of South Africa has recently tapped untouched reserves. Because of apartheid, these people were shunted aside as inconsequential, low-class laborers. As a result of their exclusion, and often isolation, many of the older people retain both linguistic and cultural skills that need to be collected before they die with them, as the younger generation is becoming separate from their past, due to globalization and migrant labor.

Nigel Crawhall has already started looking at the linguistic evidence for historical connections among Khoesan languages in southern Africa. This needs to be expanded and cross-correlated with the archaeology and genetics. Modern people of the north, for example, in Zimbabwe, Angola, and Zambia, need to be included in any linguistic reconstruction. The genetic relationships are an independent variable that could also lead to new interpretations of the archaeological data. Alec Knight and colleagues at Stanford have already started looking at the questions involved in the challenge raised by Alan Morris (2003) suggesting there were no Khoisan people north of the Zambezi in the Holocene.

General

The future of all of this must include researchers who were born as pastoralists and can give the academic world new insights into pastoralist adaptations, particularly in the ceremonial and ritual realm. Hodder's insightful work (1991) on herding containers offers a major breakthrough in how material culture mediates between the daily lives of herders and the world of belief. It is only through such work that exciting reinterpretation of rock art will come.

It must be obvious to the reader how closely interlinked an archaeological study of African herdsmen is with ethnography. Since pastoral nomadism is 8,000 years old in North Africa, 4,000 years old in East Africa, and 2,000 years old in southern Africa, the closer to the present the more applicable will be our modeling based on modern people. It is really unfortunate that colonial society obliterated so much of the Khoekhoe traditional life at the Cape in the seventeenth and eighteenth centuries, before any trained ethnographer was on the scene. Also, while we have records by the colonists of their contact with these herders, these are 300 years old. Only in West Africa, with the Arab geographers, do we have an older written record. Thus, archaeology becomes crucial to giving a past to herding people for most of the continent. The trick will be in recognizing their imprint on the landscape, particularly in areas where farmers have expanded their territory. The greater amount of non-perishable cultural material produced by agriculturalists potentially may obscure more ephemeral sites, making it difficult to recognize their significance.

References

Abel, N. 1993. "Carrying capacity, rangeland degradation and livestock development for the communal rangelands of Botswana." *ODI Pastoral Development Network Paper* 35c: 1–9.

Abell, P., Hoelzmann, P., and Pachur, H.-J. 1996. "Stable isotope ratios of gastropod shells and carbonate sediments of NW Sudan as palaeoclimatic indicators." *Palaeoecology of Africa* 24: 33–52.

Abu-Lughod, L. 1986. *Veiled Sentiments: Honor and Poetry in a Bedouin Society.* Berkeley: University of California Press.

Adams, M. 1996. "When is ecosystem change land degradation?" *ODI Pastoral Development Network Paper* 39e: 1–9.

Aïn-Séba, N. 2002. "La symbolique du cornage dans l'art grave saharien." In *Ithyphalliques, traditions orales, monuments lithiques et art rupestre au Sahara: Hommages à Henri Lhote,* ed. J.-L. Le Quellec, 19–28. Saint-Lizier, France: AARS.

Allard-Huard, L., and Huard, P. 1983. " Les gravures rupestres du Sahara et du Nil: II. L'ère pastorale." *Études scientifiques* (March–June).

Amblard, S. 1996. "Agricultural evidence and its interpretation on the Dhars Tichitt and Oualata, south-eastern Mauritania." In *Aspects of African Archaeology: Papers from the 10th Congress of the Pan-African Association for Prehistory and Related Studies,* ed. G. Pwiti and R. Soper, 421–27. Harare: University of Zambia Publications.

Amblard, S., and Pernès, J. 1989. "The identification of cultivated pearl millet (*Pennisetum*) amongst plant impressions on pottery from Oued Chebbi (Dhar Oualata, Mauritania)." *African Archaeological Review* 7: 117–26.

Ambrose, S. H. 1982. "Archaeology and linguistic reconstructions of history in East Africa." In *The Archaeological and Linguistic Reconstruction of*

African History, ed. C. Ehret and M. Posnansky, 104–57. Berkeley: University of California Press.

Ambrose, S. H. 1998. "Chronology of the Later Stone Age and food production in East Africa." *Journal of Archaeological Science* 25: 377–92.

Amin, M., Willetts, D., and Eames, J. 1987. *The Last of the Maasai*. Cape Town: Struik.

Applegate, A., Gauthier, A., and Duncan, S. 2001. "The north tumuli of the Nabta Late Neolithic ceremonial complex." In *Holocene Settlement of the Egyptian Sahara, Vol. 1: The Archaeology of Nabta Playa*, ed. F. Wendorf and R. Schild et al., 468–88. New York: Kluwer Academic/Plenum.

Archer, F. 1994. Ethnobotany of Namaqualand: The Richtersveld. M.A. thesis, University of Cape Town.

Arkell, A. J. 1949. *Early Khartoum*. Oxford: Oxford University Press.

Arkell, A. J. 1953. *Es Shaheinab*. Oxford: Oxford University Press.

Aumassip, G. 1980–1981. "Tin-Hanakaten, Tassili-n-ajjer, Algérie." *Libyca* 28–29: 115–27.

Badi, D. 2002. "L'archéologie du peuplement de Tadmekka d'après les traditions orales des Kel Essuk de l'Adragh des Iforas." In *Ithyphalliques, traditions orales, monuments lithiques et art rupestre au Sahara*, ed. J.-L. Le Quellec, 53–64. Saint-Lizier, France: AARS.

Bailey, C., and Danin, A. 1981. "Bedouin plant utilization in Sinai and the Negev." *Economic Botany* 35 (2): 145–62.

Bailloud, G. 1997. *Art Rupestre en Ennedi*. Saint-Maur, France: Sépia.

Balasse, M. 1999. De l'exploitation du lait au Néolithique moyen, en Europe temperée. Examen des modalités de sevrage des bovines, par l'analyse isotopique des ossements archéologiques. Doctoral diss., University of Paris.

Balasse, M., Ambrose, S., Smith, A. B., and Price, T. D. 2002. "The seasonality mobility model for prehistoric herders in the south-western Cape of South Africa assessed by isotopic analysis of sheep tooth enamel." *Journal of Archaeological Science* 29: 917–32.

Balasse, M., Smith, A. B., Ambrose, S., and Leigh, S. 2003. "Determining birth seasonality by analysis of tooth enamel oxygen isotope rations: The Late Stone Age site of Kasteelberg (South Africa). *Journal of Archaeological Science* 30: 205–15.

Balikci, A. 1970. *The Netsilik Eskimo*. New York: Natural History Press.

Barnard, A. 1992. *Hunters and Herders of Southern Africa: A Comparative Ethnography of the Khoisan Peoples*. Cambridge: Cambridge University Press.

Baroin, C. 1985. *Anarchie et cohésion sociale chez les Toubou: Les Daza Kéšerda (Niger)*. Cambridge: Cambridge University Press.

Baroin, C. 1987. "The position of Tubu women in pastoral production: Daza Kesherda, Republic of Niger." *Ethnos* 52 (1–2): 137–55.

Barrett, C. B., Chabori, F., Bailey, D., Little, P. D., and Coppock, D. L. 2003. "Livestock pricing in the northern Kenyan rangelands." *Journal of African Economies* 12 (2): 127–55.

Barth, F. 1959–1960. "The land use pattern of migratory tribes of South Persia." *Norsk Geografisk Tidsskrift* 17: 1–11.

Barth, H. 1859. *Travels and Discoveries in North and Central Africa.* 3 vols. New York: Harper Brothers.

Barthelme, J. W. 1985. *Fisher-Hunters and Neolithic Pastoralists in East Turkana, Kenya.* BAR International Series, no. 254. Oxford: British Archaeological Reports.

Bar-Matthews, M., Ayalon, A., Kaufman, A. and Wasserburg, G. J. 1999. "The Eastern Mediterranean paleoclimate as a reflection of regional events: Soreq Cave, Israel." *Earth and Planetary Science Letters* 166 (1–2): 85–95.

Bar-Yosef, O. 1981. "Neolithic sites in Sinai." In *Beiträge zur Umweltgesichte des Vorderen Orients,* ed. W. Frey and H.-P. Uerpmann, 217–35. Wiesbaden, Germany: Ludwig Reichert.

Bar-Yosef, O., and Phillips, J. L. 1977. *Prehistoric Investigations in Gebel Maghara, Northern Sinai.* Jerusalem: Hebrew University Institute of Archaeology.

Beaumont, P. B., Smith, A. B., and Vogel, J. 1995. "Before the Einiqua: Archaeology of the frontier zone." In *Einiqualand: Studies of the Orange River Frontier,* ed. A. B. Smith, 236–64. Cape Town: University of Cape Town Press.

Beckwith, C., and Van Offelen, M. 1983. *Nomads of Niger.* New York: Abrams.

Behnke, R., and Kerven, C. 1994. "Redesigning for risk: Tracking and buffering environmental variability in Africa's rangelands." *ODI Natural Resource Perspectives* 1.

Behnke, R., Scoones, I., and Kerven, C. 1993. *Range Ecology at Disequilibrium: New Models of Natural Variability and Pastoral Adaptation in African Savannas.* London: ODI.

Beja-Pereira, A., Ferrand, N., Mashkour, M., Taberlet, P., and Luikart, G. 2004. "Two African origins of the domestic puzzle: The last piece of the livestock domestication puzzle." Paper presented at the Human Genome Conference, Cairo, March 2004.

Beltrami, V. 2002. "Igiene e medecina fra nomadi sahariani: il caso dei tubu." In *Ithyphalliques, traditions orales, monuments lithiques at art rupestre au Sahara: Hommages à Henri Lhote,* ed. J.-L. Le Quellec, 65–74. Saint Lizier, France: AARS.

Bernus, E. 1981. Touaregs nigeriens: Unité culturelle et diversité régionale d'un peuple pasteur. Paris: Mémoire ORSTOM94.

Bernus, E. 1996. "Marques de propriété touarègues et pierres tombales (Plaines au sud-ouest de l'Aïr)." *Sahara* 8: 7–18.

Bernus, F. 1979. "Le contrôle du milieu naturel et du troupeau par les éleveurs touaregs sahélien." In *Pastoral Production and Society, L'Equipe écologie et anthropologie des sociétés pastorals*, 67–74. Cambridge: Cambridge University Press.

Biesele, M. 1993. *Women Like Meat*. Bloomington: Indiana University Press.

Binford, L. R. 1968. "Post-Pleistocene adaptations." In *New Perspectives in Archaeology*, S. R. Binford and L. R. Binford, 313–41. Chicago: Aldine.

Binneman, J. 1996. "Preliminary report on the investigations at Kulubele, an Early Iron Age farming settlement in the Greater Kei River Valley, Eastern Cape." *Southern African Field Archaeology* 5: 28–35.

Blench, R. 2001. "'You can't go home again': Pastoralism in the new millennium." At www.odi.org.uk/staff/r.blench.

Bökönyi, S. 1969. "Archaeological problems and methods of recognizing animal domestication." In *The Domestication and Exploitation of Plants and Animals*, ed. P. J. Ucko and G. W. Dimbleby, 219–29. London: Duckworth.

Bonnet, C. 1992. "Excavations at the Nubian royal town of Kerma: 1975–91." *Antiquity* 66: 611–25.

Booyens, J. C. A. 2000. "In search of Kaditshwene." *South African Archaeological Bulletin* 55: 3–17.

Boule, M., and Vallois, H. 1932. *L'homme fossile d'Asselar.* Paris: Archives de l'IPH.

Bourdieu, P. 1973. "The Berber House." In *Rules and Meanings*, ed. M. Douglas, 98–110. Harmondsworth, U.K.: Penguin Books.

Bourdieu, P. 1977. *Outline of a Theory of Practice*. Cambridge: Cambridge University Press.

Bourn, D., and Wint, W. 1994. "Livestock, land use and agricultural intensification in sub-Saharan Africa." *ODI Pastoral Development Network Paper* 37a: 1–22.

Bousman, C. B. 1998. "The chronological evidence for the introduction of domestic stock into southern Africa." *African Archaeological Review* 15 (2): 133–50.

Bower, J. R. F., Nelson, C. M., Waibel, A. F., and Wandibba, S. 1977. "The University of Massachusetts' Later Stone Age/Pastoral 'Neolithic' comparative study in central Kenya: An overview." *Azania* 12: 119–46.

Braidwood, R. J. 1971. "The earliest village communities of southwestern Asia reconsidered." In *Prehistoric Agriculture*, ed. S. Struever, 236–51. New York: Natural History.

Braidwood, R. J., Howe, B., et al. 1960. *Prehistoric Investigations in Iraqi Kurdistan*. Chicago: University of Chicago Press.

Brandt, S. A. 1984. "New perspectives on the origins of food production in Ethiopia." In *From Hunters to Farmers: The Causes and Consequences of Food Production in Africa*, ed. J. D. Clark and S. A. Brandt, 173–90. Berkeley: University of California Press.

Brandt, S. A., and Crader, N. 1987. "Pastoral rock art in the Horn of Africa: Making sense of udder chaos." *World Archaeology* 19 (2): 194–213.

Brandt, S. A., and Zarins, J. 2004. *Origins of Semitic Languages in Northeastern Africa*. Paper presented at Society for American Archaeology Meetings, Montreal, March 2004.

Breasted, J. H. 1916. *Ancient Times: A History of the Early World*. Boston: Ginn.

Brett, M., and Fentress, E. 1996. *The Berbers*. Oxford: Blackwell.

Breuil, H. 1934. "Peintures rupestres préhistorique du Harar (Abyssinie)." *L'Anthropologie* 14: 473–83.

Brewer, D. J. 1989. "A model for resource exploitation in the prehistoric Fayum." In *Late Prehistory of the Nile Basin and the Sahara*, ed. L. Krzyzaniak and M. Kobusiewicz, 127–37. Poznan, Poland: Poznan Archaeological Museum.

Briggs, L. C. 1957. "Living tribes of the Sahara and the problem of their prehistoric origins." In *Proceedings of the 3rd Pan-African Congress on Prehistory. Livingstone 1955*, ed. J. D. Clark, 195–99. London: Chatto and Windus.

Brümmer, S. 2004. "SA's war vultures." *Mail & Guardian*, Johannesburg, January 16–22, 4–6.

Bruun, D. 1898. *The Cave Dwellers of Southern Tunisia*. London: Thacker.

Bulliet, R. W. 1975. *The Camel and the Wheel*. Cambridge, Mass.: Harvard University Press.

Burchell, W. J. 1822. *Travels in the Interior of Africa*. 2 vols. London: Longmans Green.

Camps, G. 1961. *Aux origins de la Berbérie. Monuments et rites funeraires protohistoriques*. Paris: A.M.G.

Camps, G. 1974. *Les civilisations préhistoriques de l'Afrique du Nord et du Sahara*. Paris: Plon.

Caneva, I. 1989. "Typological notes: The Sudanese case." In *Late Prehistory of the Nile Basin and the Sahara*, ed. L. Krzyzaniak and M. Kobusiewicz, 375–79. Poznan, Poland: Poznan Archaeological Museum.

Carter, P., and Clark, J. D. 1976. "Adrar Bous and African cattle." In *Proceedings of the 7th Panafrican Congress of Prehistory and Quaternary Studies*, ed. B. Abebe, J. Chavaillon, and J. E. G. Sutton, 487–93. Addis Ababa: Ministry of Culture.

Casajus, D. 1987. *La tent dans la solitude: La société et morts chez les Kel Ferwan.* Cambridge: Cambridge University Press.
Cauvin, J. 2000. *The Birth of the Gods and the Origins of Agriculture.* Cambridge: Cambridge University Press.
Cavalli-Sforza, L. L., Menozzi, P., and Piazza, A. 1994. *The History and Geography of Human Genes.* New Jersey: Princeton University Press.
Cervicek, P. 1979. "Some African affinities of Arabian rock art." *Rassegna di Studi Etiopici* 27: 5–12.
Chapelle, J. 1955. "Les populations sahariennes: Les Toubous." In *Le Sahara français,* ed. J. Charbonneau, 101–8. Paris: Cahiers Charles de Foucauld.
Chapelle, J. 1957. *Nomades noirs du Sahara.* Paris: Plon.
Childe, V. G. 1936. *Man Makes Himself.* London: Watts.
Childe, V. G. 1954. *New Light on the Most Ancient East.* London: Routledge & Kegan Paul.
Churcher, C. S. 1972. *Late Pleistocene Vertebrates from Archaeological Sites in the Plain of Kom Ombo, Upper Egypt.* Toronto: Royal Ontario Museum, Life Sciences Contribution 82.
Clark, J. D. 1954. *Prehistoric Cultures of the Horn of Africa.* Cambridge: Cambridge University Press.
Clark, J. D. 1976. "Epi-palaeolithic aggregates from Greboun Wadi, Aïr, and Adrar Bous, North-western Tenere, Republic of Niger." *Proceedings of the 7th Pan-African Congress of Prehistory and Quaternary Studies,* ed. B. Abebe, J. Chavaillon, and J. E. G. Sutton, 67–78. Addis Ababa: Ministry of Culture.
Clark, J. D., and Williams, M. A. J. 1978. "Recent archaeological research in southeastern Ethiopia (1974–1975)." *Annales d'Ethiopie* 11: 19–44.
Clark, J. D., Williams, M. A. J., and Smith, A. B. 1973. "The geomorphology and archaeology of Adrar Bous, central Sahara: A preliminary report." *Quaternaria* 17: 245–97.
Clark, J. D., et al. 2004. "Adrar Bous: Archaeology of a central Saharan granite ring complex in Niger." *Annales de Musée Royale de l'Afrique Centrale.*
Clark, W. T. 1938. "Manners, customs and beliefs of the northern Beja." *Sudan Notes and Records* 25: 1–30.
Collett, D., and Robertshaw, P. T. 1983. "Pottery traditions of early pastoral communities in Kenya." *Azania* 18: 107–25.
Cooke, C. K. 1965. "Evidence of human migrations from the rock art of Southern Rhodesia." *Africa* 35 (3): 263–85.
Coombes, A. E. 1994. *Reinventing Africa: Museums, Material Culture and Popular Imagination.* New Haven, Conn.: Yale University Press.
Cordell, D. D. 1977. "Eastern Libya, Wadai and the Sanusiya: A Tariqa and a trade route." *Journal of African History* 18: 21–36.

Courtney-Clarke, M. 1996. *Imazighen: The Vanishing Traditions of Berber Women*. London: Thames and Hudson.
Cox, J., and Dougill, A. 1996. "Ecosystem dynamics and degradation in the Kalahari —A reply." *ODI Pastoral Development Network Paper* 39e: 10–15.
Cranstone, B. A. L. 1969. "Animal husbandry: The evidence from ethnography." In *The Domestication and Exploitation of Plants and Animals*, ed. P. J. Ucko and G. W. Dimbleby, 247–63. London: Duckworth.
Cribb, R. 1991. *Nomads in Archaeology*. Cambridge: Cambridge University Press.
Cronk, L. 1989. "From hunters to herders: Subsistence change as a reproductive strategy among the Mukogodo." *Current Anthropology* 30 (2): 224–34.
Cruciani, F., Santolamazza, P., Shen, P., Macaulay, V., Moral, P., Olkers, A., Modiano, D., Holmes, S., Destrol-Bisol, G., Coia, V., Wallace, D. C., Oefner, P. J., Torroni, A., Cavali-Sforza, L. L., Scozzari, R., and Underhill, P. A. 2002. "A back migration from Asia to sub-Saharan Africa is supported by high-resolution analysis of human Y-chromosome haplotypes." *American Journal of Human genetics* 70 (5): 1197–1214.
Dahlberg, A. 1993. "The degradation debate: Is clarification possible?" *ODI Pastoral Development Network Paper* 35c: 10–14.
Daniel, S. 1804–1805. *African Scenery and Animals*. London: The Artist.
Danin, A. 1983. *Desert Vegetation of Israel and Sinai*. Jerusalem: Cana.
David, N., and Kramer, C. 2001. *Ethnoarchaeology in Action*. Cambridge: Cambridge University Press.
David, N., Sterner, J. and Gavua, K. 1988. "Why pots are decorated." *Current Anthropology* 29 (3): 365–89.
Davis, S. J. M. 1982. "Climatic change and the advent of domestication: The succession of ruminant artiodactyls in the Late Pleistocene–Holocene in the Israel region." *Paléorient* 8: 5–15.
Davis, S. J. M. 1987. *The Archaeology of Animals*. London: Batsford.
De Contenson, H. 1981. "Pre-Aksumite culture." In *UNESCO General History of Africa II*, ed. G. Mokhtar, chapter 13. London: Heinemann.
Deng, F. M. 1972. *The Dinka of the Sudan*. Prospect Heights, Ill.: Waveland.
De Queiroz, J. S. 1993. "Range degradation in Botswana: Myth or reality?" *ODI Pastoral Development Network Paper* 35b: 1–17.
Desanges, J. 1981. "The proto-Arabs." In *UNESCO General History of Africa II*, ed. G. Mokhtar, chapter 17. London: Heinemann.
Dickson, H. 1951. *The Arab of the Desert*. London: Jonathan Cape.
Di Lernia, S. 1998. "Cultural control over wild animals during the early Holocene: The case of Barbary sheep in central Sahara." In *Before Food Production in North Africa*, ed. S. di Lernia and G. Manzi, 113–26. Forli: A.B.A.C.O. Edizioni.

Di Lernia, S. 1999a. *The Uan Afuda Cave: Hunter-Gatherer Societies of Central Sahara*. Rome: Arid Zone Archaeology.
Di Lernia, S. 1999b. "Discussing pastoralism: The case of the Acacus and surroundings (Libyan Sahara)." *Sahara* 11: 7–20.
Dougill, A., and Cox, J. 1995. "Land degradation and grazing in the Kalahari: New analysis and alternative perspective." *ODI Pastoral Development Network Paper* 38c: 1–22.
Dupuy, C., 1998. "Reflexion sur l'identité des guerriers représentés dans les gravures rupestres de l'Adrar des Iforas et de l'Aïr." *Sahara* 10: 31–54.
Dyson-Hudson, N. 1966. *Karimojong Politics*. Oxford: Oxford University Press.
Edens, C., and Wilkinson, T. J. 1998. "Southwest Arabia during the Holocene: Recent archaeological developments." *Journal of World Prehistory* 12 (1): 55–119.
Ehret, C. 1976. "Cushitic prehistory." In *The Non-Semitic Languages of Ethiopia*, ed. M. L. Bender, 85–96. East Lansing: Michigan State University.
Ehret, C. 1998. *An African Classical Age: Eastern and Southern Africa in World History, 1000 BC to AD 400*. Oxford: James Currey.
Elphick, R. 1977. *Kraal and Castle*. New Haven: Yale University Press.
Epstein, C. 1984. "A Pottery Neolithic site near Tel Qatif." *Israel Exploration Journal* 34 (4): 209–19.
Evans-Pritchard, E. E. 1940. *The Nuer*. Oxford: Oxford University Press.
Evans-Pritchard, E. E. 1951. *Kinship and Marriage among the Nuer*. Oxford: Oxford University Press.
Evans-Pritchard, E. E. 1956. *Nuer Religion*. Oxford: Oxford University Press.
Ferhat, N., Striedter, K. H., and Tauveron, M. 1996. "Un cimetière de boeufs dans le Sahara central: La nécropole de Mankhor." In *La Préhistoire de l'Afrique de l'Ouest*, 103–7. St. Maur, France: Sépia.
Flannery, K. V. 1969. "Origins and ecological effects of early domestication in Iran and the Near East." In *The Domestication and Exploitation of Plants and Animals*, ed. P. J. Ucko and G. W. Dimbleby, 73–100. London: Duckworth.
Fratkin, E., Roth, E. A., and Galvin, K. A. 1994. "Introduction." In *African Pastoralist Systems: An Integrated Approach*, ed. E. Fratkin, K. A. Galvin, and E. A. Roth, 1–15. Boulder: Lynne Rienner.
Froment, A. 1999. "Les Bella d'Oursi: Une anthropobiologie des populations dites captives de l'aire saharo-sahélienne." In *Les temps du Sahel: Hommage à Edmond Bernus*, ed. Y. Poncet. Paris: Institut de Recherches pour le Développement.
Fukui, K. 1979. "Cattle colour symbolism and inter-tribal homicide among the Bodi." *Senri Ethnological Studies* 3: 147–77.

Fukui, K., and Turton, D. 1979. "Introduction." *Senri Ethnological Studies* 3: 1–13.

Galaty, J. 1979. "Pollution and pastoral antipraxis: The issue of Maasai inequality." *American Ethnologist* 6: 803–16.

Galaty, J. 1989. "Cattle and cognition: Aspects of Maasai practical reasoning." In *The Walking Larder: Patterns of Domestication, Pastoralism and Predation*, ed. J. Clutton-Brock, 215–30. London: Unwin Hyman.

Gallay, A. 1966. "Quelques gisements néolithiques du Sahara malien." *Journal de la Société des Africanistes* 36 (2): 167–208.

Garcea, E. A. A. 2003. "Animal exploitation and pottery technology during pastoral times: The evidence from Uan Telocat, Libyan Sahara." *Journal of African Archaeology* 1: 111–26.

Garrod, D. A. E. 1932. "A new Mesolithic industry: The Natufian of Palestine." *Journal of the Royal Anthropological Institute* 62: 257–69.

Gast, M. 1968. *Alimentation des populations de l'Ahaggar*. Algiers: Centre de Recherches Anthropologiques, Préhistoriques et Ethnographiques, Memoire 8. Paris: AMG

Gaussen, J., and Gaussen, M. 1988. *Le Tilemsi préhistorique et ses abords*. Cahiers du Quaternaire, no. 11. Paris: C.N.R.S.

Gautier, A. 1984. "The fauna of the Neolithic site of Kadero (Central Sudan)." In *Origin and Early Development of Food-Producing Cultures in North-eastern Africa*, ed. L. Krzyzaniak and M. Kobusiewicz, 317–19. Poznan, Poland: Poznan Archaeological Museum.

Gautier, A. 2001. "The Early to Late Neolithic Archeofaunas from Nabta and Bir Kiseiba." In *Holocene Settlement of the Egyptian Sahara, Volume 1: The Archaeology of Nabta Playa*, ed. F. Wendorf and R. Schild et al., 609–35. New York: Kluwer/Plenum.

Gauthier, Y., Gauthier, C., Morel, A., and Tillet, T. 1996. *L'Art du Sahara*. Paris: Seuil.

George, U. 2000. "Der Stein des Tutanchamun." *Geo* 10: 18–46.

Gifford, D. P., Isaac, G. L., and Nelson, C. M. 1980. "Evidence for predation and pastoralism at Prolonged Drift: A Pastoral Neolithic site in Kenya." *Azania* 15: 57–108.

Gifford-Gonzalez, D. 1998. "Early pastoralists in East Africa: Ecological and social dimensions." *Journal of Anthropological Archaeology* 17: 166–200.

Gifford-Gonzalez, D. 2000. "Animal disease challenges to the emergence of pastoralism in sub-Saharan Africa." *African Archaeological Review* 17 (3): 95–139.

Gifford-Gonzalez, D. P., and Kimengich, J. 1984. "Faunal evidence for early stock-keeping in the Central Rift of Kenya: Preliminary findings." In *Origin and Early Development of Food-Producing Cultures in North-Eastern*

Africa, ed. L. Krzyzaniak and M. Kobusiewicz, 457–71. Poznan, Poland: Poznan Archaeological Museum.

Gimbutas, M. 1982. *The Goddesses and Gods of Old Europe: Myths and Cult Images*. Berkeley: University of California Press.

Gkiasta, M., Russell, T., Shennan, S., and Steele, J. 2003. "Neolithic transition in Europe: The radiocarbon record revisited." *Antiquity* 77 (295): 45–62.

Goodall, E. 1946. "Domestic animals in rock art." *Transactions of the Rhodesia Scientific Association* 41: 57–62.

Goodfriend, G. A. 1991. "Holocene trends in ^{18}O in land snail shells from the Negev Desert and their implications for changes in rainfall source areas." *Quaternary Research* 35: 417–26.

Gordimer, N. 2003. "Genius who sought to reconcile the Other: Obituary for Edward W. Said." *Sunday Independent*, October 12, 11.

Goring-Morris, N. 1991. "The Harifian of the Southern Levant." In *The Natufian Culture in the Levant*, ed. O. Bar-Yosef and F. R. Valla, 173–216. Archaeological Series, no. 1. Ann Arbor, Mich.: International Monographs in Prehistory.

Gourlay, K. A. 1972. "The ox and identification." *Man* (ns) 7: 244–54.

Gray, S., Sundal, M., Wiebusch, B., Little, M. A., Leslie, P. W., and Pike, I. L. 2003. "Cattle raiding, cultural survival, and adaptability of East African pastoralists." *Current Anthropology* 44 (supplement): S3–S30.

Graziosi, P. 1964. "New discoveries of rock paintings in Ethiopia." *Antiquity* 38: 91–98, 187–94.

Grigson, C. 1989. "Size and sex: Evidence for the domestication of cattle in the Near East." In *The Beginnings of Agriculture*, ed. A. Milles, D. Williams, and N. Gardner, 77–109. Oxford: BAR International Series 496.

Gubic, K. 2004. "Tapping its own source." *Mail & Guardian*, Johannesburg, February 6–12, 40.

Guerin, C., and Faure, M. 1996. "Chasse au chacal et domestication du boeuf dans le site néolithique d'Asa Koma (République de Djibouti)." *Journal des Africanistes* 66: 299–311.

Guild, P. W. 1972. "Metallurgy and the New Global Tectonics." *Proceedings of the 24th International Geological Congress* 4: 17–24.

Gulliver, P. H. 1955. *The Family Herds*. London: Routledge & Kegan Paul.

Hall, S. L. 1986. "Pastoral adaptations and forager reactions in the Eastern Cape." In *Prehistoric Pastoralism in Southern Africa*, ed. M. Hall and A. B. Smith, 42–49. Goodwin Series, no. 5. Cape Town: South African Archaeological Society.

Hall, S. L. 1998. "A consideration of gender relations in the Late Iron Age 'Sotho' sequence of the Western Highveld, South Africa." In *Gender in African Prehistory*, ed. S. Kent, 235–58. Walnut Creek, Calif.: AltaMira.

Hampaté Ba, A., and Dieterlen, G. 1961. *Koumen: Texte initiatique des pasteurs Peuls*. Paris: Mouton.

Hampaté Ba, A., and Dieterlen, G. 1966. "Les fresques d'époque bovidienne du Tassili n'Ajjer et les traditions des Peuls: Hypothèse d'interpretation." *Journal de la Société des Africanistes* 36 (1): 141–57.

Hanotte, O., Bradley, D. G., Ochieng, J. W., Verjee, Y., Hill, E. W., and Rege, J. E. O. 2002. "African pastoralism: Genetic imprints of origins and migrations." *Science* 296 (12 April): 336–39.

Harlan, J. R. 1971. "Agricultural origins: Centers and noncenters." *Science* 174: 468–74.

Hassan, F. A. 2000. "Holocene environmental change and the origins and spread of food production in the Middle East." *Adumatu* 1: 7–28.

Hecker, H. M. 1989. "Beidha Natufian: Faunal report." In *The Natufian Encampment at Beidha*, ed. B. F. Byrd, 97–101. Jutland Archaeological Society Publications, Aarhus, Denmark no. 23.

Helmer, D. 1991. "Etude de la faune de la phase 1a (Natoufien final) de Tell Mureybet (Syrie), fouilles Cauvin." In *The Natufian Culture in the Levant*, ed. O. Bar-Yosef and F. R. Valla, 359–70. Archaeological Series, no. 1 Ann Arbor, Mich.: International Monographs in Prehistory.

Henshilwood, C. 1996. "A revised chronology for pastoralism in southernmost Africa: New evidence of sheep at c. 2000 b.p. from Blombos Cave, South Africa." *Antiquity* 70: 945–9.

Herodotus. 1910. *The History of Herodotus (Translated by George Rawlinson)*. 2 vols. London: J. M. Dent.

Herre, W. 1969. "The science and history of domestic animals." In *Science in Archaeology*, ed. D. Brothwell and E. Higgs, 257–72. London: Thames and Hudson.

Herskovits, M. J. 1926. "The cattle complex in East Africa." *American Anthropologist* 28: 230–72, 361–88, 494–528, 633–64.

Hiernaux, P. 1996. "The crisis of Sahelian pastoralism: Ecological or economic? *ODI Pastoral Development Network Paper* 39a: 1–20.

Higham, C., and Message, M. 1969. "An assessment of a prehistoric technique of bovine husbandry." In *Science in Archaeology*, 2nd ed., ed. D. Brothwell and E. Higgs, 315–30. London: Thames and Hudson.

Hjort, A., and Dahl, G. 1991. *Responsible Man: The Atmann Beja of Northeastern Sudan*. Stockholm: Stockholm Studies in Social Anthropology.

Hodder, I. 1982. *Symbols in Action*. Cambridge: Cambridge University Press.

Hodder, I. 1991. "The decoration of containers: An ethnographic and historical study." In *Ceramic Archaeology*, ed. W. A. Longacre, 71–94. Tucson: University of Arizona Press.

Hodgson, D. L. 2000. "Pastoralism, patriarchy and history among Maasai in Tanganyika, 1890–1940." In *Rethinking Pastoralism in Africa*, ed. D. L. Hodgson, 97–120. London: James Currey.

Hoernlé, A. W. 1918. "Certain rites of transition and the conception of !nau among the Hottentots." *Harvard African Studies* 2: 65–82.

Hoffman, M. A. 1980. *Egypt before the Pharaohs*. London: Routledge & Kegan Paul.

Holden, C., and Mace, R. 2002. "Pastoralism and the evolution of lactase persistence." In *Human Biology of Pastoral Populations*, ed. W. R. Leonard and M. H. Crawford, 280–307. Cambridge: Cambridge University Press.

Hole, F., Flannery, K. V., and Neely, J. A. 1969. *Prehistory and Human Ecology of the Deh Luran Plain*. Ann Arbor: University of Michigan Museum of Anthropology.

Holl, A. 1985. "Background to the Ghana Empire: Archaeological investigations on the transition to statehood in the Dhar Tichitt region (Mauritania)." *Journal of Anthropological Archaeology* 4: 73–115.

Holl, A. 1993. "Late Neolithic cultural landscape in southeastern Mauritania: An essay in spatiometrics." In *Spatial Boundaries and Social Dynamics*, ed. A. Holl and T. E. Levy, 95–133. Ethnoarchaeological Series, no. 2. Ann Arbor: International Monographs in Prehistory.

Holl, A. 1994. "Pathways to elderhood. Research on past pastoral iconography: The paintings from Tikadiouine (Tassili n'Ajjer)." *Origini* 18: 69–113.

Holl, A. 1998. "The dawn of African pastoralisms: An introductory note." *Journal of Anthropological Archaeology* 17 (2): 81–96.

Holl, A., and Dueppen, S. A. 1999. "Iheren I: Research on Tassili pastoral iconography." *Sahara* 11: 21–34.

Hollman, J. 1993. "Preliminary report on the Koebee rock paintings, western Cape Province, South Africa." *South African Archaeological Bulletin* 48: 16–25.

Holt, P. M. 1961. *A Modern History of the Sudan*. London: Weidenfeld & Nicolson.

Horwitz, L. K. 1996. "The impact of animal domestication on species richness: A pilot study from the Neolithic of the southern Levant." *Archaeozoologia* 8 (1–2): 53–70.

Huffman, T. N. 1970. "The Early Iron Age and the spread of the Bantu." *South African Archaeological Bulletin* 25: 3–21.

Huffman, T. N. 1979. "African origins." *South African Journal of Science* 75: 233–37.

Huffman, T. N. 1986. "Archaeological evidence and conventional explanations of southern Bantu settlement patterns." *Africa* 56 (3): 280–98.

Huffman, T. N. 1989. *Iron Age Migrations*. Johannesburg: Witwatersrand University Press.
Huffman, T. N. 1994. "Toteng pottery and the origins of Bambata." *Southern African Field Archaeology* 3: 3–9.
Ingold, T. 1980. *Hunters, Pastoralists and Ranchers*. Cambridge: Cambridge University Press.
Ingold, T. 2000. *The Perception of the Environment: Essays in Livelihood, Dwelling and Skill*. London: Routledge.
Issawi, B., and El Hinnawi, M. 1984. "Contributions to the study of the playas in the southeastern part of the Western Desert of Egypt." In *Cattle Keepers of the Eastern Sahara*, ed. F. Wendorf et al., 41–48. Dallas: Southern Methodist University, Department of Anthropology.
Jabbur, J. S. 1995. *Bedouin of North Arabia*. Albany: State University of New York Press.
Jacobson, L. 1984. "Comment on Bambata pottery." *South African Archaeological Bulletin* 39: 142.
Jacobsohn, M. 1995. Negotiating meaning and change in space and material culture: An ethno-archaeological study among semi-nomadic Himba and Herero herders in North-western Namibia. Ph.D. diss., University of Cape Town.
Jerardino, A., and Parkington, J. 1993. "New evidence for whales on archaeological sites in the south-western Cape." *South African Journal of Science* 98: 6–7.
Johnson, D. H. 1990. "Fixed shrines and spiritual centres in the Upper Nile." *Azania* 25: 41–56.
Jolly, P. 1995. "Melikane and upper Mangolong revisited: The possible effects on San art of symbiotic contact between southeastern San and southern Sotho and Nguni communities." *South African Archaeological Bulletin* 50: 68–80.
Jordan, A. M. 1986. *Trypanosomiasis Control and African Rural Development*. London: Longman.
Joubert, S. C. J. 1989. "Animal behaviour." In *Game Ranch Management*, ed. J. du Bothma, 148–58. Pretoria: van Schaik.
Joussaume, R. 1981. "L'Art rupestre de l'Éthiopie." In *Préhistoire africaine: Mélanges offerts au doyen Lionel Balout*, ed. C. Roubet, H.-J. Hugot, and G. Souville, 159–75. Paris: Editions A.D.P.F.
Kajale, M. D. 1988. "Ancient plant economy at Chacolithic Tuljapur Garhi, District Amraoti, Maharashtra." *Current Science* 57 (7): 377–79.
Keenan, J. H. 2002. "The lesser gods of the Sahara." *Public Archaeology* 2: 131–50.

Kelley, H. 1934. "Collections africains du département de préhistoire exotique: Harpoons, etc. de Taferjit et Tamaya Mellet." *Journal de la Société des Africanistes* 4 (1): 135–43.
Kerven, C. 1992. *Customary Commerce: A Historical Reassessment of Pastoral Livestock Marketing in Africa*. London: ODI.
Kinahan, J. 1991. *Pastoral Nomads of the Central Namib Desert*. Windhoek: New Namibia Books.
Klein, R. G. 1973. *Ice-Age Hunters of the Ukraine*. Chicago: University of Chicago Press.
Klein, R. G. 1978. A preliminary report on the larger mammals from the Boomplaas Stone Age Cave site, Cango Valley, Oudtshoorn District, South Africa. *South African Archaeological Bulletin* 33: 66–75.
Klein, R. G., and Cruz-Uribe, K. 1989. Faunal evidence for prehistoric herder-forager activities at Kasteelberg, Western Cape Province, South Africa. *South African Archaeological Bulletin* 44: 82–97.
Klein, R. G., and Scott, K. 1986. "Re-analysis of faunal assemblages from the Haua Fteah and other Late Quaternary archaeological sites in Cyrenaican Libya." *Journal of Archaeological Science* 13: 515–42.
Kleppe, E. J. 1984. "Village life in the upper White Nile Region over a period of 3500 years." Paper presented at 2nd Dymaczewo Conference on the Nile basin and the Sahara, Poznan, Poland.
Knight, A., Underhill, P. A., Mortenson, H. M., Zhivotovsky, L. A., Lin, A. A., Henn, B. M., Louis, D., Ruhlen, M., and Mountain, J. 2003. "African Y chromosome and mtDNA divergence provides insight into history of click languages." *Current Biology* 13: 464–73.
Kolb, P. 1731. *The Present State of the Cape of Good-Hope*. 2 vols. London: Innys.
Krige, E. J. 1950. *The Social System of the Zulus*. 2nd ed. London: Longmans Green.
Krige, E. J. 1977. *The Social System of the Zulus*. 2nd ed. Pietermaritzburg: Shuter and Shooter.
Kruijt, I., and Goring-Morris, N. 2002. Foraging, farming, and social complexity in the Pre-Pottery Neolithic of the southern Levant: A review and synthesis. *Journal of World Prehistory* 16: 362–440.
Krzyzaniak, L. 1984. "The Neolithic habitation at Kadero (Central Sudan)." In *Origin and Early Development of Food-Producing Cultures in North-eastern Africa*, ed. L. Krzyzaniak and M. Kobusiewicz, 309–15. Poznan, Poland: Poznan Archaeological Museum.
Kuper, R. 1978. *10.000 Jahre zwischen Weide und Wüste*. Cologne: Museen der Stadt.
Kusimba, S. B. 2003. *African Foragers: Environment, Technology, Interactions*. Walnut Creek, Calif.: Altamira.

Lajoux, J.-D. 1963. *The Rock Paintings of Tassili*. London: Thames and Hudson.
Lawrence, T. E. 1962. *Seven Pillars of Wisdom*. Harmondsworth, U.K.: Penguin Books.
Leakey, L. S. B. 1931. *The Stone Age Cultures of Kenya Colony*. Cambridge: Cambridge University Press.
Leakey, M. D. 1983. *Africa's Vanishing Art: The Rock Paintings of Tanzania*. London: Hamish Hamilton.
Lebeuf, A. M. D. 1959. *Les Populations du Tchad*. Paris: Presses Universitaires de France.
Lee, R. B. 1969. "!Kung Bushman subsistence: An input-output analysis." In *Environment and Cultural Behavior*, ed. P. Vayda, 47–79. New York: Natural History Press.
Lee, R. B. 1979. *The !Kung San*. Cambridge: Cambridge University Press.
Legge, A. J. 1975. "The fauna of Tell Abu Hureyra: Preliminary analysis." *Proceedings of the Prehistoric Society* 41: 74–76.
Legge, A. J., and Rowley-Conwy, P. A. 1987. "Gazelle killing in stone age Syria." *Scientific American* 257 (Aug.): 76–83.
Le Quellec, J.-L. 2002. "Henri Lhote et le lootoori." In *Ithyphalliques, traditions orales, monuments lithiques et art rupestre au Sahara: Hommages à Henri Lhote*, ed. J.-L. Le Quellec, 141–56. Saint-Lizier, France: AARS.
Le Quellec, J.-L. 2002–2003. "L'Art rupestre de style dit 'arabo-éthiopien' et l'école de Chabbè-Galma." *Afrique: Archéologie & Arts* 2: 47–68.
Levtzion, N. 1973. *Ancient Ghana and Mali*. London: Methuen.
Lewis-Williams, J. D. 1981. *Believing and Seeing: Symbolic Meanings in Southern San Rock Paintings*. New York: Academic.
Lewis-Williams, J. D. 2002. *A Cosmos in Stone: Interpreting Religion and Society Through Rock Art*. Walnut Creek, Calif.: AltaMira.
Lewis-Williams, J. D., and Dowson, T. 1989. *Images of Power: Understanding Bushman Rock Art*. Johannesburg: Southern Books.
Lhote, H. 1944 (1955). *Les Touaregs du Hoggar*. Paris: Payot.
Lhote, H. 1947. "La poterie dans l'Ahaggar." *Travaux de l'Institut de Recherches sahariennes* 4: 145–54.
Lhote, H. 1959. *The Search for the Tassili Frescoes*. New York: Dutton.
Lhote, H. 1976. *Vers d'Autres Tassilis*. Paris: Arthaud.
Little, P. D. 1987. "Woman as Ol Payian (Elder): The status of widows among the Il Chamus (Njemps) of Kenya." *Ethnos* 52 (1–2): 81–102.
Liverani, M. 2000. "Looking for the southern frontier of the Garamantes." *Sahara* 12: 31–44.
Liverani, M., Cremaschi, M., and di Lernia, S. 2000. "The 'Archaeological Park' of the Tadart Acacus and Messak Settafet (southwestern Fezzan, Libya). *Sahara* 12: 121–40.

MacDonald, K. C. 1996. "Tichitt-Walata and the Middle Niger: Evidence for cultural contact in the second millennium BC." In *Aspects of African Archaeology*, ed. G. Pwiti and R. Soper, 429–40. Harare: University of Zimbabwe Publications.

MacDonald, K. C. 1998. "Before the Empire of Ghana: Pastoralism and the origins of cultural complexity in the Sahel." In *Transformations in Africa: Essays on Africa's Later Past*, ed. G. Gonnah, 71–103. Leicester: Leicester University Press.

MacEachern, S. 2000. "Genes, tribes, and African history." *Current Anthropology* 41 (3): 357–84.

Maingard, L. F. 1934. "The linguistic approach to South African prehistory and ethnology." *South African Journal of Science* 31: 122–29.

Maisels, C. K. 1990. *The Emergence of Civilization*. London: Routledge.

Manhire, A. H., Parkington, J. E., Mazel, A. D., and Maggs, T. M. O'C. 1986. "Cattle, sheep and horses: A review of domestic animals in the rock art of southern Africa." In *Prehistoric Pastoralism in Southern Africa*, ed. M. Hall and A. B. Smith, 22–30. Goodwin Series, no. 5. Cape Town: South African Archaeological Society.

Marshall, F. 1990a. "Origins of specialized pastoral production in East Africa." *American Anthropologist* 92 (4): 873–94.

Marshall, F. 1990b. "Cattle herds and caprine flocks." In *Early Pastoralists of South-western Kenya*, ed. P. T. Robertshaw, 205–60. Nairobi: British Institute in Eastern Africa.

Marshall, F. 1991. "Mammalian fauna from Gogo Falls." *Azania* 26: 175–79.

Marshall, F. 2000. "The origins and spread of domestic animals in East Africa." In *The Origins and Development of African Livestock: Archaeology, Genetics, Linguistics and Ethnography*, ed. R. M. Blench and K. C. MacDonald, 191–221. London: UCL.

Marshall, F., and Hildebrand, E. 2002. "Cattle before crops: The beginnings of food production in Africa." *Journal of World Prehistory* 16 (2): 99–143.

Marshall, F., Stewart, K., and Barthelme, J. 1984. "Early domestic stock at Dongodien in northern Kenya." *Azania* 19: 120–27.

Marshall, L. 1976. *The !Kung of Nyae Nyae*. Cambridge, MA: Harvard University Press.

Matthew, C., and Chesselet, J. 2001. *Ochre and Water: Himba Chronicles from the Land of Kaoko*. VHS. Cape Town: Doxa Productions.

Meinhof, C. 1912. *Die Sprachen der Hamiten*. Hamburg: Friederichen.

Mellaart, J. 1975. *The Neolithic of the Near East*. London: Thames and Hudson.

Mentzel, O. F. 1944. *A Geographical and Topographical Description of the Cape of Good Hope*. Cape Town: Van Riebeeck Society no. 25.

Mercuri, A. M. 1999. "Palynological analysis of the early Holocene sequence." In *The Uan Afuda Cave*, ed. S. di Lernia, 149–81. Rome: Arid Zone Archaeology.
Mintz, E., and Ben-Ami, D. 1977. "Neolithic occurrences." In *Prehistoric Investigations in Gebel Maghara, Northern Sinai*, ed. O. Bar-Yosef and J. L. Phillips, 219–44. Jerusalem: Hebrew University Institute of Archaeology.
Mitchell, P. 2002. *The Archaeology of Southern Africa*. Cambridge: Cambridge University Press.
Mloszewski, M. J. 1983. *The Behavior and Ecology of the African Buffalo*. Cambridge: Cambridge University Press.
Mohammed-Ali, A. S., and Khabir, A.-R. M. 2003. "The wavy line and dotted wavy line pottery in the prehistory of the central Nile and the Sahara–Sahel belt." *African Archaeological Review* 20 (1): 25–58.
Monès, H. 1988. "The conquest of North Africa and Berber resistance." In *UNESCO General History of Africa III*, ed. M. El Fasi and I. Hrbek, 224–45. London: Heinemann.
Moore, A. M. T., Hillman, G. C., and Legge, A. J. 2000. *Village on the Euphrates: From Foraging to Farming at Abu Hureyra*. Oxford: Oxford University Press.
Mori, F. 1965. *Tadrart Acacus*. Torino: Einaudi.
Morris, A. G. 2002. "Isolation and the origin of the Khoisan: Late Pleistocene and Early Holocene human evolution at the southern end of Africa." *Human Evolution* 17 (3–4): 231–40.
Morris, A. G. 2003. "The myth of the East African 'Bushmen.'" *South African Archaeological Bulletin* 58: 85–90.
Muigai, A. W. T., Hirbo, J., Rege, J. E. O., and Hanotte, O. 2004. " Origin and migration of sheep in Africa." Paper presented at the Human Genome Conference, Cairo, March 2004.
Munson, P. J. 1976. "Archaeological data on the origins of cultivation in the southwestern Sahara and their implications for West Africa." In *Origins of African Plant Domestication*, ed. J. R. Harlan, J. M. J. de Wet, and A. B. L. Stemler, 187–210. The Hague: Mouton.
Munson, P. J. 1980. "Archaeology and the prehistoric origins of the Ghana Empire." *Journal of African History* 21: 457–66.
Murdock, G. P. 1959. *Africa: Its Peoples and Their Culture History*. New York: McGraw-Hill.
Murphy, R. F. 1964. "Social distance and the veil." *American Anthropologist* 66: 1257–74.
Murphy, R. F. 1967. "Tuareg kinship." *American Anthropologist* 69: 163–70.
Mütti, B. J. Use of domestic space in formative pastoral society at Kasteelberg, Southwestern Cape. Unpublished Hons Thesis, Department of Archaeology, University of Cape Town.

Mütti, B. J. Forthcoming. Excavations at Die Krans, Vredenburg Peninsula, Western Cape. Unpublished M.A. thesis, University of Cape Town.

Nachtigal, G. 1974. *Sahara and Sudan*. 4 vols. London: Hurst.

Neumann, K. 1989. "Vegetationsgeschichte der Ostsahara im Holozän Holzkohlen aus prähistorischen Fundstellen." In *Forschungen zur Umweltgeschichte der Ostsahara*, ed. R. Kuper, 13–181. Köln: Heinrich Barth Institut.

Neumann, K., Ballouche, A., and Klee, M. 1996. "The evidence of plant food production in the West African Sahel: New evidence from northeast Nigeria and northern Burkina Faso." In *Aspects of African Archaeology*, ed. G. Pwiti and R. Soper, 441–48. Harare: University of Zimbabwe Publications.

Nicolaisen, J. 1963. *Ecology and Culture of the Pastoral Tuareg*. Nationalmuseets Skrifter, Etnografisk Raekke, no. 9. Copenhagen: National Museum of Copenhagen.

Nicoll, K. 2004. Recent environmental change and prehistoric human activity in Egypt and Northern Sudan. *Quaternary Science Reviews* 23: 561–80.

Oren, E. D., and Gilead, I. 1981. "Chalcolithic sites in northeastern Sinai." *Tel Aviv* 8: 25–44.

Paris, F. 1984. "La région d'In Gall-Teggida n-Tesemt (Niger): Programme archéologique d'urgence III. Les sépultures du néolithique final à l'Islam." *Études nigériennes* 50.

Paris, F. 1990. "Les sepultures monumentales d'Iwelen (Niger)." *Journal des Africanistes* 60 (1): 47–74.

Paris, F. 1992. "Chin Tafidet village néolithique." *Journal des Africanistes* 62: 33–53.

Paris, F. 1996. *Les Sépultures du Sahara nigérien du néolithique à l'Islamisation*. 2 vols. Paris: ORSTOM.

Paris, F. 2000. "African livestock remains from Saharan mortuary contexts." In *The Origins and Development of African Livestock: Archaeology, Genetics, Linguistics and Ethnography*, R. M. Blench and K. C. MacDonald, 111–26. London: UCL Press.

Parker, R. B. 1984. *Inscrutable Earth: Explorations into the Science of Earth*. New York: Charles Scribner's Sons.

Parkington, J. E., and Fisher, J. 2004. *Small Mammal Remains from the Later Stone Age Campsite(s) of Dunefield Midden, Western Cape, South Africa: Culinary or Ritual Events?* Paper presented at Society for American Archaeology Meetings, Montreal, March 2004.

Parkington, J. E., and Mills, G. 1991. "From space to place: The architecture and social organisation of Southern African mobile communities." In *The use of Space among Mobile Peoples*, ed. C. Gamble and W. Boismier, 355–70. Ann Arbor, Mich.: International Monographs in Prehistory.

Penning de Vries, F. W. T., and Djitèye, M. A. 1982. *La productivité des pâturages sahèliens: Une étude des sols, des végétations et de l'exploitation de cette ressource naturelle*. Wageningen, Holland: Centre for Agricultural Publishing and Documentation.

Perlès, C., and Phillips, J. L. 1991. "The Natufian conference: Discussion." In *The Natufian Culture in the Levant*, ed. O. Bar-Yosef and F. R. Valla, 637–44. Archaeological Series, no. 1. Ann Arbor, Mich.: International Monographs in Prehistory.

Petit-Maire, N., and Dutour, O. 1987. "Holocene populations of the Western and Southern Sahara: Mechtoids and paleoclimates." In *Prehistory of Arid North Africa*, ed. A. E. Close, 259–85. Dallas: Southern Methodist University Press.

Phillipson, D. W. 1993. *African Archaeology*, 2nd ed. Cambridge: Cambridge University Press.

Poland, M., Hammond-Tooke, D., and Voigt, L. 2003. *The Abundant Herds: A Celebration of the Nguni Cattle of the Zulu People*. Cape Town: Fernwood.

Raper, P. E., and Boucher, M. 1988. *Robert Jacob Gordon: Cape Travels, 1777–1786*. Johannesburg: Brenthurst.

Rasmussen, S. J. 1992. "Ritual specialists, ambiguity and power in Tuareg society." *Man* 27: 105–28.

Rasmussen, S. J. 1995. *Spirit Possession and Personhood among the Kel Ewey Tuareg*. Cambridge: Cambridge University Press.

Rasmussen, S. J. 2000. "Exalted mothers: Gender, aging and postchildbearing experience in a Tuareg community." In *Rethinking Pastoralism in Africa*, ed. D. L. Hodgson, 186–205. London: James Currey.

Raven-Hart, R. 1967. *Before van Riebeeck*. Cape Town: Struik.

Reygasse, M. 1934. "Le Ténéréen. Observations sur un faciès nouveau du néolithique des confines algero-soudanais." *XIe Session Congrès Préhistorique de France*: 577–84.

Ribot, I., and Morris, A. G. 2003. "Identity of prehistoric South-Central Africans: Attempting a craniometrical approach in the light of sub-Saharan African diversity." Poster presented at the 33rd Annual Conference of the Anatomical Society of Southern Africa, Golden Gate.

Rice, M. 1991. *Egypt's Making: The Origins of Ancient Egypt 5000–2000 BC*. London: Routledge.

Riesman, P. 1977. *Freedom in Fulani Social Life*. Chicago: University of Chicago Press.

Rindsberger, M., Magaritz, M., Carmi, I., and Gilad, D. 1983. "The relation between air mass trajectories and the water isotope composition of rain in the Mediterranean Sea area." *Geophysical Research Letters* 10 (1): 43–46.

Robertshaw, P. T. 1978. "The archaeology of an abandoned pastoralist campsite." *South African Journal of Science* 74: 29–31.

Robertshaw, P. T. 1979. "Excavations at Duiker Eiland, Vredenburg District, Cape Province." *Annals of Cape Provincial Museum (Human Sciences)* 1 (1): 1–26.

Robertshaw, P. T. 1989. "The development of pastoralism in East Africa." In *The Walking Larder: Patterns of Domestication, Pastoralism and Predation*, ed. J. Clutton-Brock, 207–14. London: Unwin Hyman.

Robertshaw, P. T. 1990. *Early Pastoralists of South-western Kenya.* Nairobi: British Institute in Eastern Africa.

Robertshaw, P. T. 1991. "Gogo Falls: A complex site east of Lake Victoria." *Azania* 26: 63–195.

Rosen, S. A. 1988. "Notes on the origins of pastoral nomadism: A case study from the Negev and Sinai." *Current Anthropology* 29 (3): 498–506.

Rosenberg, M. 1994. "Hallan Çemi Tepesi: Some further observations concerning stratigraphy and material culture." *Anatolica* 20: 11–140.

Roset, J.-P. 1978. "Poteries néolithiques du Ténéré." *Cahiers O.R.S.T.O.M.*, sér. Sci. Hum. 15 (4): 379–406.

Roset, J.-P. 1983. "Nouvelles données sur le problème de la néolithisation du Sahara méridional: Aïr et Ténéré, au Niger." *Cahiers O.R.S.T.O.M.*, sér. Géol. 13: 119–42.

Roset, J.-P. 1987. "Paleoclimatic and cultural condition of Neolithic development in the Early Holocene of northern Niger (Aïr and Ténéré)." In *Prehistory of Arid North Africa*, ed. A. E. Close, 211–34. Dallas: Southern Methodist University Press.

Roset, J.-P., de Broin, F., Faure, M., Gayet, M., Guerin, C., and Mouchet, F. 1990. "La faune de Tin Ouaffadene et d'Adrar Bous 10, deux gisements archéologiques de l'Holocène ancien au Niger nord-oriental." *Géodynamique* 5 (1): 67–89.

Rossi, L. 2000. "Siti d'arte rupestre lungo il Mourdi e il versante orientale del'Ennedi (Ciad)." *Sahara* 12: 150–53.

Roubet, C. 1978. "Une économie pastorale pré-agricole en Algerie orientale: Le néolithique de tradition capsienne." *L'Anthropologie* 82 (4): 583–86.

Rudner, J. 1968. "Strandloper pottery from South and South West Africa." *Annals of the South African Museum* 49 (2): 441–663.

Sadr, K. 1991. *The Development of Nomadism in Ancient Northeast Africa.* Philadelphia: University of Pennsylvania Press.

Sadr, K. 1997. "Kalahari archaeology and the Bushman debate." *Current Anthropology* 38 (1): 104–12.

Sadr, K. 1998. "The first herders at the Cape of Good Hope." *African Archaeological Review* 15 (2): 101–32.

Sadr, K. 2003. "The Neolithic of southern Africa." *Journal of African History* 44: 195–209.
Sadr, K., Castiglioni, A., Castiglioni, A., and Negro, G. 1994. "Archaeology of the Nubian Desert." *Sahara* 6: 69–75.
Sadr, K., and Sampson, C. G. 1999. "Khoekhoe ceramics of the upper Seacow River Valley." *South African Archaeological Bulletin* 54: 3–15.
Sadr, K., Smith, A. B., Plug, I., Orton, J., and Mütti, B. 2003. "Herders and foragers on Kasteelberg." *South African Archaeological Bulletin* 58.
Sahlins, M. 1972. *Stone Age Economics*. London: Tavistock.
Said, E. W. 1995. *Orientalism*. Harmondsworth: Penguin Books.
Salama, P. 1981. "The Sahara in classical antiquity." In *UNESCO General History of Africa II*, ed. G. Mokhtar, 513–32. London: Heinemann.
Sauer, C. O. 1969. *Agricultural Origins and Dispersals*, 2nd ed. Cambridge, Mass.: MIT Press.
Saxon, E. C., Close, A. E., Cluzel, C., Morse, V., and Shackleton, N. J. 1974. "Results of recent investigations at Tamar Hat." *Libyca* 22: 49–91.
Sayagues, M. 2003. "Witchcraft, vengeful spirits and the plague." *Newsweek*, December 15, 41.
Schapera, I. 1930. *The Khoisan Peoples of South Africa*. London: Routledge & Kegan Paul.
Schild, R., and Wendorf, F. 1984. "Lithostratigraphy of Holocene lakes along the Kiseiba Scarp." In *Cattle Keepers of the Eastern Sahara*, ed. F. Wendorf, 9–40. Dallas: Southern Methodist University, Department of Anthropology.
Schild, R., and Wendorf, F. 2001. "Geomorphology, lithostratigraphy, geochronology and taphonomy of sites." In *Holocene Settlement of the Egyptian Sahara, Vol. 1: The Archaeology of Nabta Playa*, ed. F. Wendorf and R. Schild et al., 11–50. New York: Kluwer/Plenum.
Schleidt, W. M., and Shalter, M. D. 2003. "Co-evolution of humans and canids: An alternative view of dog domestication: *Homo homini lupus*?" *Evolution and Cognition* 9 (1): 57–72.
Schofield, J. F. 1940. "A report on the pottery from Bambata Cave." *South African Journal of Science* 37: 361–72.
Schweitzer, F. R. 1979. "Excavations at Die Kelders, Cape Province, South Africa: The Holocene deposits." *Annals of the South African Museum* 78: 101–233.
Scoones, I. 1994. *Living with Uncertainty: New Directions in Pastoral Development in Africa*. London: IT.
Sealy, J. C., and Yates, R. 1994. The chronology of the introduction of pastoralism to the Cape, South Africa. *Antiquity* 68: 58–67.
Servant, M., and Servant-Vildary, S. 1980. "L'environnement Quaternaire du basin du Tchad." In *The Sahara and the Nile*, ed. M. A. J. Williams and H. Faure, 133–62. Rotterdam: Balkema.

Sherwood, J. H. 1948. "Upper Nile Province." In *Agriculture in the Sudan*, ed. J. D. Tothill, 810–26. Oxford: Oxford University Press.
Simonis, R., Faleschini, G., and Negro, G. 1994. "Niola Doa, il luogo delle fanciulle (Ennedi, Ciad)." *Sahara* 51–62.
Singh, P. 1974. *Neolithic Cultures of Western Asia*. New York: Seminar.
Smith, A. B. 1974. Adrar Bous and Karkarichinkat: Examples of Post-Palaeolithic human adaptation in the Saharan and Sahel zones of West Africa. Ph.D. diss., University of California, Berkeley.
Smith, A. B. 1975. "A note on the flora and fauna from the post-palaeolithic sites of Karkarichinkat Nord and Sud." *West African Journal of Archaeology* 5: 201–4.
Smith, A. B. 1976. "A microlithic industry from Adrar Bous, Tenere Desert, Niger." *Proceedings of the 7th Pan-African Congress of Prehistory and Quaternary Studies*, ed. B. Abebe, J. Chavaillon, and J. E. G. Sutton, 181–96. Addis Ababa: Ministry of Culture.
Smith, A. B. 1978. "Terracottas from the Tilemsi Valley, Mali." *Bulletin de l'Institut fundamental d'Afrique noire* 40, sér. B (2): 223–28.
Smith, A. B. 1979. "Biogeographical consideration of colonization of the Lower Tilemsi Valley in the 2nd millennium BC." *Journal of Arid Environments* 2: 355–61.
Smith, A. B. 1980. "Neolithic tradition in the Sahara." In *The Sahara and the Nile*, ed. M. A. J. Williams and H. Faure, 451–65. Rotterdam: Balkema.
Smith, A. B. 1984. *Prehistoric Pastoralism in the South-western Cape*. Final Project Report to Human Sciences Research Council.
Smith, A. B. 1992. *Pastoralism in Africa: Origins and Ecological Development*. London: Hurst.
Smith, A. B. 1993a. "Exploitation of marine mammals by prehistoric Cape herders." *South African Journal of Science* 89: 162–65.
Smith, A. B. 1993b. "New approaches to Saharan Rock Art." In *L'Arte e l'Ambiente del Sahara Preistorico: Dati e Interpretazioni*, ed. G. Calegari, Memorie della Società Italiana di Scienze Naturale 26, fasc. II: 467–77.
Smith, A. B. 1998a. "Intensification and transformation processes towards food production in Africa." In *Before Food Production in North Africa*, ed. S. di Lernia and G. Manzi, 19–33. Forli: ABACO Edizioni.
Smith, A. B. 1998b. "Keeping people on the periphery: The ideology of social hierarchies between hunters and herders." *Journal of Anthropological Archaeology* 17 (2): 201–15.
Smith, A. B. 2000a. "The origins of pastoralism in Namibia." In *People, Cattle and Land: Transformations of a Pastoral Society in Southwestern Africa*, ed. M. Bollig and J.-B. Gewald, 55–76. Cologne: Rüdiger Köppe.

Smith, A. B. 2000b. "The origins of the domesticated animals of southern Africa." In *The Origins and Development of African Livestock: Archaeology, Genetics, Linguistics and Ethnography*, ed. R. M. Blench and K. C. MacDonald, 222–38. London: UCL Press.

Smith, A. B., Halkett, D., Hart, T., and Mütti, B. 2001. "Spatial patterning, cultural identity and site integrity on open sites: Evidence from Bloeddrift 23, a pre-colonial herder camp in the Richtersveld, Northern Cape Province, South Africa." *South African Archaeological Bulletin* 56: 1–7.

Smith, A. B., and Jacobson, L. 1995. "Excavations at Geduld and the appearance of early domestic stock in Namibia." *South African Archaeological Bulletin* 50: 3–14.

Smith, A. B., and Mütti, B. 1992. *Guide to Archaeological Sites in the Southwestern Cape*. Cape Town: South African Association of Archaeologists.

Smith, A. B., and Pheiffer, R. H. 1992. "Col. Robert Jacob Gordon's notes on the Khoikhoi 1779–80." *Annals of South African Cultural History Museum* 5 (1): 1–56.

Smith, A. B., and Pheiffer, R. H. 1994. "Letter from Robert Jacob Gordon to Hendrik Fagel, 1779." *Brenthurst Archives* 1 (2): 29–46.

Smith, A. B., Sadr, K., Gribble, J., and Yates, R. 1991. "Excavations in the south-western Cape, South Africa, and the archaeological identity of prehistoric hunter-gatherers within the last 2000 years." *South African Archaeological Bulletin* 46: 71–91.

Smith, A. B., and Webley, L. 2000. "Women and men of the Khoekhoen of southern Africa." In *Rethinking Pastoralism: Gender, Culture and the Myth of the Patriarchal Pastoralist*, ed. D. Hodgson, 72–96. London: James Currey.

Smith, H. S. 1969. "Animal domestication and animal cult in dynastic Egypt." In *The Domestication and Exploitation of Plants and Animals*, P. J. Ucko and G. W. Dimbleby, 307–14. London: Duckworth.

Smith, S. E. 1980. "The environmental adaptation of nomads in the West African Sahel: A key to understanding prehistoric pastoralists." In *The Sahara and the Nile*, ed. M. A. J. Williams and H. Faure, 467–87. Rotterdam: Balkema.

Spencer, P. 1965. *The Samburu: A Study of Gerontocracy in a Nomadic Tribe*. London: Routledge & Kegan Paul.

Spencer, P. 1988. *The Maasai of Matapato: A Study of Rituals of Rebellion*. Bloomington: Indiana University Press.

Spencer, P. 1998. *The Pastoral Continuum: The Marginalization of Tradition in East Africa*. Oxford: Oxford University Press.

Stenning, D. J. 1957. "Transhumance, migratory drift, migration: Patterns of pastoral Fulani nomadism." *Journal of the Royal Anthropological Institute* 87: 57–73.

Stenning, D. J. 1959. *Savannah Nomads*. Oxford: Oxford University Press.
Stiner, M. C., Munro, N., Surovell, T. A., Tchernov, E., and Bar-Yosef, O. 1999. "Paleolithic population growth pulses evidenced by small animal exploitation." *Science* 283: 190–94.
Stow, G. W. 1905. *The Natives Races of South Africa*. London: Swan Sonnenschein.
Striedter, K. H., and Tauveron, M. 2002–2003. "The most ancient rock engravings in the central Sahara?" *Afrique: Archéologie & Arts* 2: 31–38.
Sullivan, S. 2000. "Gender, ethnographic myths and community-based conservation in a former Namibian 'homeland.'" In *Rethinking Pastoralism in Africa*, ed. D. Hodgson, 142–64. Oxford: James Currey.
Sutton, J. E. G. 1973. *The Archaeology of the Western Highlands of Kenya*. Nairobi: British Institute in Eastern Africa.
Suzman, J. 2000. *"Things from the Bush": A Contemporary History of the Omaheke Bushmen*. Basel Namibia Studies Series, no. 5. Basel: Schlettwein.
Taçon, P. S. C., and Chippindale, C. 1998. "An archaeology of rock art through informed methods and formal methods." In *The Archaeology of Rock Art*, ed. C. Chippindale and P. S. C. Taçon, 1–10. Cambridge: Cambridge University Press.
Tegene, B. 2003. "Combining land capability evaluation, geographical information systems and indigenous technologies for soil conservation in northern Ethiopia." *Eastern African Social Science Research Review* 19 (2): 23–53.
Thesiger, W. 1987. *The Life of My Choice*. Glasgow: HarperCollins.
Thom, H. B. 1954. *Journal of Jan van Riebeeck*, vol. 2. Cape Town: Balkema.
Thomas, E. M. 1965. *Warrior Herdsmen*. London: Secker Swarburg.
Tilley, C. 1994. *A Phenomenology of Landscape: Places, Paths and Monuments*. Oxford: Berg.
Tobias, P. V. 1974. "The biology of the southern African Negro." In *The Bantu-Speaking Peoples of Southern Africa*, ed. W. D. Hammond-Tooke, 3–45. London: Routledge & Kegan Paul.
Tubiana, M.-J. 1964. *Survivances préislamiques en Pays Zaghawa*. Paris: Travaux et Mémoires de l'Institut d'Ethnologie 67.
Tubiana, M.-J., and Tubiana, J. 1977. *The Zaghawa from an Ecological Perspective*. Rotterdam: Balkema.
Uerpman, H-P. 1981. "The major faunal areas of the Middle East during the late Pleistocene and early Holocene." In *Prehistoire du Levant*, ed. J. Cauvin and P. Sanlaville, 99–106. Paris: CNRS.
Valla, F. R. 1981. "Les établissements natoufiens dans le nord d'Israel." In *Préhistoire du Levant*, ed. J. Cauvin and P. Sanlaville, 409–19. Paris: Éditions du C.N.R.S.

Vansina, J. 1984. *Art History in Africa*. London: Longman.

Vercoutter, J. 1988. "Le Sahara et l'Egypte pharaonique." *Sahara* 1: 9–19.

Vermeersch, P., Van Peer, J., and Van Neer, W. 1996. "Sodmein Cave site, Red Sea Mountains (Egypt)." *Sahara* 6: 31–40.

Vernet, R. 1998. *Le Sahara et le Sahel paléenvironnements et occupation humaine à la fine du Pléistocène et l'Holocène: Inventaire des datations*. Université de Nouakchott, Département d'Histoire.

Verschuren, D., Laird, K. R., and Cumming, B. F. 2000. "Rainfall and drought in equatorial East Africa during the past 1,100 years." *Nature* 403 (27 June): 410–14.

Vogelsang, R, Albert, K.-D., and Kahlheber, S. 1999. "Le sable savant: Les cordons dunaires sahéliens au Burkina Faso comme archive archéologique et paléoécologique du Holocène." *Sahara* 11: 51–68.

Voigt, E. A. 1983. *Mapungubwe: An Archaeozoological Interpretation of an Iron Age Community*. Pretoria: Transvaal Museum.

Von den Driesch, A., and Deacon, H. J. 1985. "Sheep remains from Boomplaas Cave, South Africa." *South African Archaeological Bulletin* 40: 39–44.

Walker, N. J. 1983. "The significance of an early date for pottery and sheep in Zimbabwe." *South African Archaeological Bulletin* 38: 88–92.

Walker, N. J. 1985. "Bambata pottery and the origins of Iron Age and Khoi pottery: Reply to Jacobson." *South African Archaeological Bulletin* 40: 55.

Walker, N. J. 1995. "The archaeology of the San: The Late Stone Age of Botswana." In *Speaking for the Bushmen*, ed. A. J. G. M. Sanders, 54–87. Gaborone: Botswana Society.

Webley, L. 2001. "The re-excavation of Spoegrivier Cave on the west coast of southern Africa." *Annals of Eastern Cape Museums* 2: 19–49.

Wendorf, F. 1968. *The Prehistory of Nubia*. 2 vols. Dallas: Southern Methodist University Press.

Wendorf, F., and Malville, J. M. 2001. "The megalithic alignments." In *Holocene Settlement of the Egyptian Sahara, Volume 1: The Archaeology of Nabta Playa*, ed. F. Wendorf and R. Schild et al., 489–502. New York: Kluwer Academic/Plenum.

Wendorf, F., and Schild, R. 1980. *Prehistory of the Eastern Sahara*. New York: Academic.

Wendorf, F., Schild, R., and Close, A. E. 1984. *Cattle Keepers of the Eastern Sahara: The Neolithic of Bir Kiseiba*. Dallas: Southern Methodist University, Department of Anthropology.

Wendorf, F., and Schild, R., et al. 2001. *Holocene Settlement of the Egyptian Sahara, Volume 1: The Archaeology of Nabta Playa*. New York: Kluwer Academic/Plenum.

Western, D., and Dunne, T. 1979. "Environmental aspects of settlement site decisions among pastoral Maasai." *Human Ecology* 7 (1): 75–98.

White, R. 1993. *Livestock Development and Pastoral Production on Communal Rangeland in Botswana*. Gaborone: Botswana Society.

Whitelaw, G. 1997. "Southern African Iron Age." In *Encyclopedia of Precolonial Africa*, ed. J. O. Vogel, 444–55. Walnut Creek: AltaMira.

Widlock, T. 1999. *Living on Mangetti*. Oxford: Oxford University Press.

Wiessner, P. 1994. "The pathways of the past: !KungSan hxaro exchange and history." In *Überlebens-strategien in Afrika*, ed. M. Bollig and F. Klees, 101–24. Cologne: Heinrich Barth Institute.

Wilkinson, T. 2003. *Genesis of the Pharaohs*. London: Thames and Hudson.

Williams, M. A. J., Abell, P. I., and Sparks, B. W. 1987. "Quaternary landforms, sediments, depositional environments and gastropod isotope ratios at Adrar Bous, Tenere Desert of Niger, south-central Sahara." In *Desert Sediments: Ancient and Modern*, ed. L. Frostick and I. Reid, 105–25. Geological Society Special Publications, no. 35. Boston: Blackwell for the Geological Society.

Wilson, M. 1969. "The hunters and herders." In *The Oxford History of South Africa*, ed. M. Wilson and L. Thompson, 40–74. Oxford: Oxford University Press.

Woodborne, S. 1996. A taphonomic study of seal remains from archaeological sites on the Western Cape coast. Ph.D. diss., University of Cape Town.

Wright, D. K. 2003. "Survey, excavation and preliminary analysis of Pastoral Neolithic sites, Tsavo, Kenya. *Nyame Akuma* 59: 54–61.

Wright, J. 1996. "Sonqua, Bosjesmans, Bushmen, abaThwa: Comments and queries on pre-modern identification." *South African Historical Journal* 35: 16–29.

Wright, R. 1961. "A painted rock shelter on Mt. Elgon, Kenya." *Proceedings of the Prehistoric Society* 27: 28–34.

Yeivin, E., and Olami, Y. 1979. "Nizzanim: A Neolithic site in Nahal Evtah. Excavations of 1968–1970." *Tel Aviv* 6: 99–135.

Index

About the Author

Andrew B. Smith is associate professor in the Archaeology Department, University of Cape Town, South Africa. He received his Ph.D. in 1974 from the University of California, Berkeley, and has taught and worked in the United States and many countries in North, West, and southern Africa.

www.ingramcontent.com/pod-product-compliance
Ingram Content Group UK Ltd.
Pitfield, Milton Keynes, MK11 3LW, UK
UKHW020905190926
475560UK00010B/258

9 780759 107472